*The Vietnamese Boat People,
1954 and 1975–1992*

Also by Nghia M. Vo

*The Bamboo Gulag:
Political Imprisonment in Communist Vietnam*
(McFarland, 2004)

The Vietnamese Boat People, 1954 and 1975–1992

NGHIA M. VO

McFarland & Company, Inc., Publishers
Jefferson, North Carolina, and London

LIBRARY OF CONGRESS CATALOGUING-IN-PUBLICATION DATA

Vo, Nghia M., 1947–
    The Vietnamese boat people, 1954 and 1975–1992 / Nghia M. Vo.
       p.   cm.
    Includes bibliographical references and index.

    ISBN 0-7864-2345-5 (softcover : 50# alkaline paper) ∞

    1. Refugees — Vietnam.   2. Political refugees — Vietnam.
I. Title
HV640.5.V5V6   2006
305.9'0691409597 — dc22   2005031117

British Library cataloguing data are available

©2006 Nghia M. Vo. All rights reserved

No part of this book may be reproduced or transmitted in any form or by any means, electronic or mechanical, including photocopying or recording, or by any information storage and retrieval system, without permission in writing from the publisher.

Cover photograph ©2005 Image Stock

Manufactured in the United States of America

McFarland & Company, Inc., Publishers
  Box 611, Jefferson, North Carolina 28640
    www.mcfarlandpub.com

To those who survived
the diaspora.
And in memory of those
who lost their lives
searching for freedom.

Table of Contents

Introduction   1

I. The 1954 Exodus

1. Vietnam 1939–1954   9
2. Operation Exodus 1954–1955   17
3. Resettlement   31
4. The Rumbles of War   42

II. The 1975–1992 Diaspora

5. Prelude to the 1975 Diaspora   55
6. The 1975 Wave   64
7. The Post–1975 Waves   83
8. The Planning   101
9. The Boat People   115
10. The Routes   130
11. The Pirates   142
12. The Camps   152
13. International Response   163
14. The Lands of Freedom   173
15. Struggles and Achievements   181

Epilogue	193
Chapter Notes	199
Bibliography	203
Index	207

Introduction

Wars always have consequences, both immediate and remote, and the consequences are often tragic. One tragic circumstance often caused by war is the forceful, disorganized and uncontrollable mass movement of both civilians and soldiers trying to escape the horrors of the wars or of an oppressive regime. At one time, populations fled from one region or state to another. As wars have become international however, such movements began to spread beyond their initial boundaries, sometimes to countries very far away.

The Vietnamese communists, by taking power in the North in 1954 and then in the South in 1975, caused two major upheavals in the land of the Small Dragon, as Vietnam was once called. The first Vietnam War led to the 1954 exodus during which one million people fled from the North to the South. The Second Vietnam War ended with the 1975–1992 diaspora that dispersed of two million Vietnamese all over the world.

These significant, unplanned and uncoordinated mass movements around the world not only dislocated millions of people, but also caused thousands and thousands of agonized deaths at sea. They forever changed the way foreigners perceived the Vietnam War: how could a war in a country so far away send wave after wave of staggering, hungry, and dispirited refugees landing on their peaceful shores and arriving at their own doorsteps? Wars finally had widespread international repercussions. No longer were the consequences limited to one country or a corner of the globe; they had spilled all over the world.

The diaspora was similar to the cap blowing off a dormant volcano, which then spewed fumes and lava to the four corners of the globe. Vietnamese, who were rarely seen in Western countries before 1975, suddenly became a fixture in these lands, as they were given refuge in more than

50 different countries worldwide. In the United States, within less than three decades, the Vietnamese were transformed from a ting minority of perhaps 1,000 persons to the second largest refugee group behind Cubans. The communists, whose actions became divisive and threatening in 1954 and again after 1975, were at the root of this diaspora. Not happy with forcing people to the seas after 1975, they sent all males connected to the Saigon government to detention camps. They also converted the whole southern society into a socialist country, frightening local people and causing them to run for freedom.

More than two million Indochinese were involved in the 1975–1992 diaspora. Most resettled in third countries: 1.4 million arrived in the United States, 260,000 in China, 200,000 in Canada, 185,000 in Australia, and 130,000 in France. More than 1.6 million refugees survived the post–1975 diaspora, the biggest sea escape in the twentieth century. There were 839,228 Vietnamese: 796,310 boat people and 42,918 who escaped overland.[1] The first 130,000 refugees picked up by the U.S. on the heels of the fall of Saigon were excluded from this group. Untold numbers of people also perished during this risky journey, their dreams forever lost in the depths of the ocean.

The forces leading ordinary people to take to the seas merit some discussion. Escape was not something people undertook lightly, for escaping abroad without any support mechanism is a dangerous venture. They simply felt they could not live under an oppressive regime that took over their country and jailed part of the population. Men were forced into detention camps to be converted into hard-core believers in communism. Women were pushed into selling their belongings for everyday survival. Children were sent to the dumpsters to forage for food. As a result, the post–1975 southern society changed deeply and almost over night: rich and middle-class individuals were stripped of their houses, jobs, and belongings, and the communists, previously poor, became the new rich in a poor and starving postwar country.

The sheer number of people willing to risk everything, including death, to try to escape points to the brutality of the communist regime. Those who had little money bought their way out unofficially and risked encountering pirates or sinking in the depths of the ocean, while rich people were allowed to leave officially after paying a hefty sum of gold. The fact that communist Vietnam officially sanctioned certain departures — the departures that brought money to the state coffers and to local officials — raised questions about the depth of the regime's corruption. Nowhere in the world had a government officially trafficked in its own citizens. Nowhere had a government cared so little about their wellbeing.

While the first refugees came as a group between 1954 and 1955, those from the second diaspora came in waves from 1975 to 1992. The first wave of people escaped in 1975 aboard anything that floated: marine or merchant ships, tugboats, fishing boats, trawlers, and landing crafts. These sea-unworthy vessels took them to ships of the U.S. Seventh Fleet that were anchored outside Vietnamese territorial waters on the orders of President Gerald Ford. The fleet was ready to pick up the refugees and give them help, although no one expected the enormous number of refugees willing to brave the seas in search of freedom. Had Saigon not been encircled, many more would have escaped to the ships. Besides the 60,000 picked up by the U.S. fleet, 60,000 more escaped on their own and landed in Malaysia or the Philippines. These first-wave refugees were rapidly brought to the U.S. and other countries for resettlement.

The second and third waves of refugees from 1976 onward went through a more difficult time. They had to buy their way out and to hide from the soldiers and the police who hunted them down. After catching them, the police either asked for bribes or threw the escapees into jails. Those who evaded the police, still had to face engine failures, sea storms, pirates, and push-backs by other Southeast Asian countries. They then had to survive in overcrowded boats for days or weeks, during which food and water could not be replenished and living conditions were terrible. There was no room to move or even stretch out. The sun was torrid and the storms violent. The sky was pitch black at night and the winds often terrible. The constant rocking of the boat and the continuous rumbling of the engine made the trip more unbearable. Many people died from exhaustion, dehydration, and hunger. Others suffered at the hands of terrifying pirates who stole from the passengers and beat, raped, and killed them. The horrors were unforgettable, and the sea, once associated with peace and beauty, became a symbol of darkness, violence, separation, and death.

After the sea ordeal came the overcrowded camps where living conditions were most often substandard and where security was painfully lacking. No two camps were alike; some were more tolerable than others. They were, however, considered to be temporary jails where refugees once again found they had lost their freedom. There were the long hours waiting for food and news of relocation or resettlement. There were also the depressing, desperate feelings of waiting and waiting sometimes for years in the camps, of putting their lives on hold for a long time and not being able to accomplish anything worthwhile. The confinement alone drove some insane. The lucky ones were resettled, while the unlucky ones were rejected and faced the nightmare of having to be repatriated against their will. The latter would be subjected to the scorn of their neighbors or families and the relentless monitoring of the government.

The perilous sea escapes turned out to be the largest diaspora in Vietnamese history and world history. It affected not only millions of Vietnamese but also hundreds of organizations, and countries, and millions of unselfish people who stepped forward to provide relief and relocation. Without their boundless compassion, unmatched energy, and unending goodwill, the refugees would have been left to die on the seas or in the camps.

This is the story of these refugees who had to leave their homeland to search for freedom. It is the story of a nation in turmoil that ruthlessly and savagely pounded on its weakest members. It is also the story of a heartless and senseless government, which decided to get rid of its citizens in order to assert its control over the whole country. It is the story of courageous individuals who braved all odds to look for the freedom they had lost in their own country. They were the modern-day heroes of Vietnam and the world.

The goal of this book is to review the 1954 exodus and the 1975–1992 diaspora, to compile stories of these sea and land voyages, and to retrace the dangerous paths these modern voyagers took to reach the lands of freedom. In 1954 and 1955, the northerners who were displaced out of North Vietnam landed in South Vietnam, where they happily settled for almost two decades. Then, along with the southerners, they again were forced to take to the seas and landed in many countries all around the world. The 1975–1992 diaspora was nothing more than a repeat of the 1954 exodus, except for its scope, the extent of travel and the relentless ardor with which the refugees tried to escape Vietnam and its new masters.

Many, unfortunately, did not survive the journey. May those who died at sea or on land during these perilous voyages live forever in peace. Their failed escape was only a testament to their courage and their will to live the way their hearts and minds led them. Their determination and yearning for freedom under adverse conditions will be the guiding light for future seekers of freedom elsewhere in the world. This book is dedicated to them.

I finally would like to offer my thanks to the refugees who courageously wrote and shared their painful experiences in books or journals all around the world. Many thanks to all those who are interested in and have researched this painful subject; they have made it a worthwhile theme to read and study. This book would not have been possible without their groundbreaking work, or without the unselfish support of my family and friends. Many thanks to Jim Freeman, who provided important information about the Asian camps.

Part I

The 1954 Exodus

1

VIETNAM 1939–1954

At the beginning of World War II, Vietnam was a powder keg ready to explode. All the frustration, resentment, and anger that had been built up for the last 81 years since the French set foot in Vietnam in 1858 just waited for that magic spark that would ignite it and blow away the French domination. That spark turned out to be World War II, which all of the sudden made France look like a very vulnerable country.

As the French sought to dismantle the authority of the Vietnamese Nguyen emperor and replace it with colonial rule, a new society began emerging with a middle class that was aware of its rights and asked for more freedom. On the political side, local leaders who for a long time had raised the question of independence to the French colonial authorities became more vocal and rebellious. Phan Boi Chau, after years of political struggle, was finally caught and sentenced to death in 1925; his sentence was later commuted to house arrest for life. Phan Chu Trinh rallied people to the cause of independence, suggesting collaboration instead of an armed struggle. Thirteen nationalists who promoted the uprising at a French fort in Yen Bai, North Vietnam, were executed in 1929. On the social side, education was widely promoted, causing an upsurge in the number of students, including girls, attending school. The number of students going abroad for study and training increased. Newly published newspapers dealt with various topics ranging from women's health to politics. The *quoc ngu* emerged as the national language and allowed rapid spread of information and news. The *ao dai* was suggested as the national women's dress. Women who for centuries had occupied a secondary role under Confucian rules were for the first time taught about health, hygiene, and rights issues.

Mistreatment and oppression by the colonial French became major issue as the exploitation of the Vietnamese for economical reasons worsened. All these social and political forces coalesced and came to a head before World War II. As the Vietnamese became economically successful and better educated, they demanded more freedom. As freedom could not be obtained through legal channels, violence would ensue: riots were followed by insurrections. Leaders were detained and executed. More violence ensued, followed by skirmishes and then wars. The Vietnamese conflict thus was an outgrowth of deep aspirations for freedom that had been tampered with and held prisoner for too long.

1858–1939

As the costs of conquering Vietnam became enormous, the French governor in Vietnam, Paul Doumer, decided to centralize authority, reorganize the finances, and make Vietnam self-sufficient in order to serve the needs of France. He set out to exploit Vietnam economically and to shift the burden of running the country to the Vietnamese people by saddling them with taxes and duties. Taxes were raised on three new items: alcohol, salt, and opium. There was not a big market for opium at that time, except for a few Chinese users in Cholon-Saigon. Doumer, by building a refinery to produce a brand of opium that burned quickly, encouraged local consumption. The British did the same thing in China. As addiction rose, opium revenues soon accounted for a third of the state's income. By creating a market which had been non-existent and by legalizing the sale of opium, Doumer essentially created a major health hazard that in time would destroy Vietnam's economy and increase its health care costs. He created a legion of drug addicts and an untold number of wrecked families.

He nationalized the production and sale of alcohol. Everyone had to buy alcohol from the state, which rapidly raised its revenues. A peasant who used to make moonshine for his own needs now had to buy his liquor at state stores. Doumer accelerated the transfer of land ownership to French colons, rendering many peasants landless. He used the landless peasants to work in the mines and on rubber plantations. These people worked in appalling conditions and died from malaria, dysentery, and malnutrition. Twelve thousand out of 45,000 rubber-plantation workers died between 1917 and 1954. The miners at the Hon Gay pits in North

Vietnam were forced to work 12- to 14-hour shifts under unsafe conditions and were frequently brutalized. This led miners and plantation workers to rebel against the authorities. Peasants also sided with them. The French who saw rice as an export commodity urged the peasants to produce it in large quantities: Vietnam soon became the third biggest rice exporter in the world at the expense of shortages at home, as the bulk of rice production was shipped abroad. In 1944–45, a shortage of rice due to natural disaster created a famine in North Vietnam that killed two million people. The amount of rice exported remained unchanged during this period.

The flagrant exploitation of the people and the economy was so successful it put Vietnam rapidly in the black. However, it drove the Vietnamese toward political violence. As the number of insurrections rose, the French suppressed them readily thanks to an excellent military system. By 1938 eighteen million Vietnamese were kept in check by a mere 27,000 colonial troops. Tax revolts occurred as early as 1908. Nationalists Phan Boi Chau and Phan Chu Trinh organized insurrections against the French. A Viet Nam Quoc Dan Dang (VNQDD) member, equivalent to the Chinese political party's Kuomingtan, assassinated Bazin, the hated recruiter of cheap labor. The French arrested the activists. VNQDD reacted by inciting colonial soldiers to mutiny against the French in a fort in Yen Bai. The French seized 13 VNQDD leaders and sent them to the guillotine in 1929.[1]

General Gallieni, the great French colonial officer and World War I hero, wrote the following mighty words after serving in Vietnam in the late 19th century: "A country is not conquered and pacified by crushing its people through terror. After overcoming their initial fear, the masses grow increasingly rebellious, their accumulated bitterness steadily rising in reaction to the brutal use of force."[2] It was unfortunate the French authorities did not heed his sound advice.

1939–1946

The defeat of the French by Germans on June 25, 1940, sent political shockwaves to Vietnam. The Japanese forced the defeated French to give them transit rights in North Vietnam in August 1940 and to allow them to establish bases and a military presence in Vietnam in July 1941.

From there, the Japanese would launch sea and air attacks on the rest of Southeast Asia. The French, however, continued to run the administrative functions in Vietnam.

The collapse of France sent the Vietnamese scrambling to enroll in one political party or another. There was a new fervor in the air. France was no longer perceived as an invincible giant who had held Vietnam captive for so long. It had been beaten by Germany in Europe and controlled by Japan in Indochina. As the Vietnamese nationalists for the first time saw France's Achilles tendon, they positioned themselves and their parties to take over control of Vietnam when the time proved to be right. The main parties were the Dai Viet, VNQDD and the Viet Minh (communist party). The Japanese were also trying to form a party that would remain under their control. The emperor, Bao Dai, the last member of the Nguyen dynasty, also had his supporters. Educated in France, he returned to Vietnam in 1930 to take control of his administration, although he remained a figurehead within the French colonial system.

Alarmed by the political instability in Vietnam, Japan decided in December 1944 to displace the French and grant independence to Vietnam. Encouraged by the Japanese, Bao Dai declared Vietnam independent in Hue in March 1945 and named it the State of Vietnam. The first prime minister was Tran Trong Kim.

Ho and his Viet Minh in the meantime developed bases in China's Yunan and had occasionally received help from the Office of Strategic Services, a precursor of the CIA. He adroitly "played Americans against French, French against Chinese, Chinese against Americans, and even Chinese against each other.[3] Realizing the Japanese were finished, he announced the formation of the Committee for the Liberation of Vietnam in an attempt to grab power. Assuming that Ho Chi Minh had allied support, which he did not have, Bao Dai abdicated in his favor. In Hanoi Ho proclaimed the country independent with the establishment of the Democratic Republic of Vietnam (DRV) on September 2, 1945. To appeal to Woodrow Wilson to support his cause, Ho even borrowed a passage from the American Declaration of Independence: "We hold the truth that all men are created equals, that they are endowed by their Creator with inalienable rights."

Saigon was in chaos in 1945. Various political parties attacked the French in an attempt to seize power. Massive demonstrations occurred. On September 22, French paratroopers went on a rampage shooting and killing civilians and demonstrators. In response, the Binh Xuyen and Viet Minh slipped into a French district and murdered one hundred French civilians, sparing neither women nor children.[4] France had to send additional troops to reestablish order in Saigon. This being done, the French then negotiated with the Chinese, who were sent to Vietnam to disarm the Japanese, the right to return to North Vietnam. After the Chinese acquiesced, Ho agreed to France's return in exchange for its recognition of the DRV as a "free state" within the French Union. Everyone in Hanoi was furious at Ho's betrayal. He responded: "I prefer to sniff French shit for five years than eat Chinese shit for the rest of my life.[5] He knew the immediate dangers that the close proximity of China presented to Vietnam. A few months later, Ho went to France to discuss the future of Vietnam. On September 19, 1946, after months of haggling, he signed a *modus vivendi*, an interim understanding deferring to the French on the Cochinchina (South Vietnam) issue. Part of North Vietnam belonged to the communists while the rest of the country, including the south, remained under French control. He walked out and said: "I've just signed my death warrant." This decision would obsess him the rest of his life and made his ambition to reunify Vietnam more compulsive.[6] On his return, hardcore militants accused him one more time of selling out to the French.

After the deal with the French was settled, Ho launched an all-out assault against nationalist bases in the Red River provinces with the help of the French. In Hanoi and Hai Phong, he ruthlessly had all nationalists from other parties tracked down and liquidated. They all went underground or fled to China.[7] Dai Viet's chief, Truong Tu Anh, was liquidated. The Viet Minh soon had established political control over North Vietnam. Having ruthlessly disposed of his rivals, he turned against the French. The dispute hinged on the collection of taxes.

1946–1954

On December 19, 1946, the Viet Minh began an eight-year war against the French (first Indochina war). The battle for Hanoi began with an attack on a power plant and on French homes in the city. It turned into a street-to-street fight with French troops. Overwhelmed by French military power, the Viet Minh withdrew to Viet Bac, a mountainous area 80 miles north of Hanoi.

In the fall of 1947, the French launched Operation Lea involving 20 battalions in an effort to destroy the Viet Minh forces. The latter lost 9,500 men, their main headquarters and many of their supply depots. In China, the communist Chinese, having routed the Chinese Nationalists, moved their troops into the Guangxi and Yunnan provinces across the borders from North Vietnam. From there, they provided the Viet Minh with automatic weapons, howitzers, mortars and trucks. With this new military assistance, Giap transformed his army into a conventional military organization. He then targeted French outposts along the Chinese border using massive firepower and overwhelming forces. One by one these outposts fell, leaving the countryside in the hands of the Viet Minh.[8]

Thrilled by these successes, Giap sent his troops down the Red River delta to confront the French. Giap, however, miscalculated his chance — the open delta could not provide enough cover and concealment for his troops. French firepower was also superior in the delta. Giap launched three separate attacks in 1951: at Vinh Yen, Mao Khe, and at Phat Diem. He was badly beaten and lost a total of 20,000 men. Other battles ensued and culminated into the Dien Bien Phu battle.

General Navarre made the fateful decision to accept a battle that he felt "must be held at all cost." Dien Bien Phu was a valley surrounded by hills, which made positioning of artillery guns difficult. Giap overcame these difficulties by using porters to haul guns and artillery up the hills one by one. He gathered 33 battalions against the French's 12 battalions. With the enemy occupying the high ground, outgunned in artillery and outnumbered five to one, the French could not hope to win. One outpost fell after another and on May 7, 1954, the French surrendered.

If the French lost Dien Bien Phu, they did not lose the war. They still had control of Hanoi and South Vietnam. Tired by the long war and demoralized by the loss of Dien Bien Phu, France realized that there was no way they could win without a massive effort and this was politically impossible. It had other important duties to attend to and could not afford to squander its scarce resources for a colony that was located a month away by ship and that could only bring headaches. It therefore decided to negotiate.

In Saigon, Bao Dai inaugurated the State of Vietnam that had control over South Vietnam and chose Ngo Dinh Diem as his prime minister.

Diem back in 1933 had declined to work for Bao Dai and stayed out of the political arena during all this time. He had exiled himself in the U.S. and remained in a New Jersey seminary for two years. He befriended Cardinal Spellman of New York, who later became one of his ardent promoters in the U.S.

Geneva Accords 1954

Fresh from its victory, the Viet Minh hoped to lay claim on all of Vietnam in Geneva. But China and the Soviet Union sought to restrain their ambition and pressured Ho to accept half of a victory. The Viet Minh also negotiated with the French in private and came up with the decision to partition Vietnam without the agreement of the State of Vietnam. Colonel Le Van Kim, Diem's representative at the convention, was left out of the secret meeting. This action flagrantly violated the condition on which Bao Dai agreed to have his delegation participate in the talks.

The 1954 Geneva treaty had the same saddening effect on the State of Vietnam as the 1973 Paris Accords had on the Republic of South Vietnam. The only difference had to do with the players: the French in 1954 and the Americans in 1973 secretly negotiated with the northern communists. The loser was the State of Vietnam, which not only lost the chance to obtain freedom from the French but also had to accept the partition deal without its express consent. The South Vietnamese accepted the treaty with sadness and stoic resignation: flags flew at half-staff throughout South Vietnam. Therefore in Saigon, July 20, the Armistice Day was observed as a day of shame.[9]

No party was happy with the accords. The French got their wish to get out of Vietnam; they were bruised and bleeding to death with a loss of 58,000 soldiers (the same number as the Americans three decades later), and looking for a way to heal. The Americans, fresh from their victory in Korea, thought about duplicating their success elsewhere in the world. The North Vietnamese were not happy with the partition at the 17th parallel: they wished to take some more land and aimed to go down to the 12th parallel. The South Vietnamese thought they had lost their control over the whole Vietnam, which they claimed to be the natural inheritor through Bao Dai. All these unfulfilled dreams set the stage for another confrontation down the road and kept the conflict alive. The Americans eventually replaced the French in this new venture.

The 1954 Geneva Accords actually just created a temporary truce to the Indochinese conflict, which would blaze fiercely again in the second part of the 20th century with a new cast of nations and more murderous weapons.

The accords ended the first Vietnam War between the French and the North Vietnamese. If they officially divided Vietnam into two halves, they also allowed the population to move freely between the two areas for a certain period of time. The clause, however, was not always widely respected. The northern part belonged to the communists led by Ho Chi Minh while the south remained under the democratic government of Bao Dai and Ngo Dinh Diem. France, England, the USSR, China, Cambodia, Laos, and North Vietnam signed the accords while South Vietnam and the U.S. abstained.

2

OPERATION EXODUS
1954–1955

The flight of people from the war between the French and the Viet Minh in North Vietnam took place long before the 1954 armistice. Between 1946 and 1948, about 55,000 Vietnamese escaped to Thailand and some of them were sympathetic to the Viet Minh. The Thai government had since tried to have them repatriated without success. This was the only large group that went abroad prior to the 1975 diaspora.[1]

The Operation Exodus started in August 1954 and ended in May 1955. Behind all the political multinational maneuverings about the fate of the Vietnamese people in Geneva, the State of Vietnam had become voiceless and almost meaningless as the French tried to negotiate their withdrawal.

In North Vietnam, General Ely, commander-in-chief of the French forces, on July 12 decided to pull back and abandon the southern Red River delta. That move exposed the Catholic communities of Bui Chu and Phat Diem to a takeover by the communists. This in turn created a mass hysteria of people trying to leave the area, for there was no love lost between Catholics and communists.[2] Ely knew very well that any announcement of the partition would create a mass exodus, especially if the French forces were no longer present to serve as a buffer between the advancing communists and the nationalist citizens.

As of July 20, 1954, a vast exodus got underway, especially in the areas not yet controlled by the communists. People moved around frantically, although they did not know where to go and how to escape. Most of them moved from inland to the shore where they hoped to get assistance to go south. As a result of the accords, French troops and northern civilians willing to relocate to the south were allowed three hundred days to complete their move. On the other hand, about 90,000 Viet Minh and 40,000 dependents were transported northward. Another 5,000 Viet Minh and 3,000 political cadres and their dependents remained behind in South Vietnam. The latter formed the seed of the future southern revolutionary army, the Viet Cong.

Causes

Multiple causes unleashed this massive exodus: a land reform campaign, brutality of the war, and famine. The biggest cause remained the fear of the communists. Living under these rulers for some time gave northerners a thorough understanding of their mentality.

Land Reform Campaign. In an attempt to socialize the north, the communists forced farmers to study the evils and errors of capitalism and democracy. Land reform was initiated in communist-controlled areas sometimes as early as 1951: anyone owning more than an acre could be labeled as counterrevolutionary and brought to a people's tribunal. As time went by, anyone who owned any small plot of land was also denunciated as bourgeois.

Case 1: Duong Thu Huong, a former communist youth brigade leader and party member, described how uncle Chinh, a communist official, wrecked the lives of his own sister, Que, and another woman, Tam, during this reform period. Everything started when Que married Ton, whose only error was to belong to a family of landlords, the "mortal enemies of the peasantry." Ton's sister (Tam) actually worked herself "ragged" in her two-acre paddy fields with the help of migrant workers. One day, Tam and her elderly mother were "forced to prostrate themselves, heads bowed, arms crossed behind their back" in the village courtyard before Chinh serving as judge. They were denounced for having exploited the workers before a jury composed of an alcoholic vagabond villager and a huge good-for-nothing woman. The villagers were encouraged to shout out slogans and slurs against the exploiters during the public trial. At the second session, the two women were forced to squat in a deep pit, a position that let them feel the full weight of their helplessness. Humiliated and ashamed of the treatment, Tam's mother fell ill and died.[3] Ton escaped from the village in an attempt to avoid a similar treatment. He roamed alone and hungry in a nearby forest where he was later found dead. Que was forced to sell her house and move to the city to become a street vendor. The roof of her shack was composed of "sheet metal patched together with tar paper." The roof leaked on rainy days and the odor of the tar was nauseating in the summer heat. As for Tam, she was dispossessed of her land and forced to work in the fields for a living. With unusual moral strength and determination, she gradually worked her way upwards. She toiled in the communal fields day in and day out and saved every single penny she earned. She slept with a knife under her neck for her own protection. Years later she became the owner of a noodle shop and bought back all her property.

Case 2: In another situation, a small landowner and his wife were brought to the people's tribunal during the land reform for trial. They were accused of not having contributed to the revolution, although they had given almost everything to the communists. After a full day of accusations and trial, they were thrown on the ground, their hands tied to a bamboo post. Guards were left to watch them. They were released after one week, but all their possessions were confiscated. The old man became distraught and dispirited; he went home and hanged himself. His wife fell ill and died three months later.[4]

Case 3: Le Minh Khue lost both her parents to land reform. They were just ordinary teachers who just liked to lead a middle class lifestyle. Their family background, however, pointed toward an upper class position, a red flag for those who fought for the proletariat: her grandfather was a former mandarin at the Hue court. The execution of her parents left her an orphan; her aunt and uncle, staunch communists, picked her up and raised her. She listened to them out of respect and later enrolled in the communist youth brigade, where she served her country during the Vietnam War.[5]

Initiated by Ho and his communists during the 1953–1956 years, land reform was a copy of the 1946–1952 Chinese Maoist Land Reform. Ho saw it as a class struggle, a form of a war, and even addressed the land reform cadres as follows:

"Land reform is a revolutionary task.... You are fighters too: fighters to the anti-feudal front.... Those among you who perform outstanding deeds will be awarded medals, just like soldiers fighting the enemy.[6]

Unlike in the Mekong delta in the south, the majority of farmers in the Red River delta did not own more than two acres of farmland each and they usually cultivated it themselves with the help of migrant workers. This did not prevent the communists from going ahead with land reform. People were classified as landlords, rich peasants, middle peasants, poor peasants, and landless workers. There were also criminal subcategories of landlords, rich peasants, traitors (collaborating with the French), despots, and reactionaries. The first two groups were harshly punished.

Villagers were coached by a group of cadres who "worked, lived, and ate with them" and forced them to falsely denounce farmers who in reality were no big time landowners. Some also used the program to settle personal vendettas by accusing others of being counter-revolutionary. Others wanted to demonstrate their support for the system in order to remain in good graces with the new leaders. Much of the violence was later found to be deliberately instigated by party officials responsible for carrying out the program. Ho Chi Minh, despite being appalled by the violence, was intimidated by Mao Zedong and was afraid to contradict Chinese officials stationed in North Vietnam.[7] Torture had also been inflicted on the prisoners. The communist cadres became self-serving and used the occasion to seize the property of the accused for themselves.

The real goal of the reform, however, was the total control of the population, which had not been completely receptive to the communist takeover. The presence of the cadres in any village cowed the inhabitants into following their strict instructions, lest they be placed on trial for disobeying the revolution. The most brutal effect of the reform was the isolation of the family members of the convicted landlords. They were shunned, insulted, not allowed to work for one year or to receive food. They moved from village to village begging for food, but were usually turned away at every place. No one would associate with or want to be seen with them or give them a hand for fear of being labeled as sympathizers. They became the undesirables in the communist strongholds. And without moral and material support, they usually died of starvation.

The campaign would move forward and every single landowner, big or small, was dragged to the tribunal. There was almost no way to escape justice because everyone would accuse his neighbor in order to play it safe. Over and over again, the theme of hatred was forced down on the population. Le Duc Tho, the future Nobel Prize winner with Kissinger, once said: "If one wishes to convince the peasants to take up arms, first of all you have to fill them with hatred of the enemy." People were not only encouraged, but also incited to accuse whomever they wanted. "It was better to have killed your father and mother and admitted it than to say nothing and to have done nothing wrong."[8] To survive, peasants would have to embrace this policy of terror. The degree of fear and violence rose to a high level. It reached a point where people were afraid to talk to each other; disobedience and hatred of the regime began to spread.

The reform not only brought destruction to the agricultural and social systems, but also death and suffering to tens of thousands of farmers and their families. Overall more than 100,000 "landlord" farmers were brought to "justice," summarily sentenced, and either killed, sent to labor camps, or disowned; their lands were parceled out to other people. The devastation caused by the reform was so tragic and profound that a campaign of "Rectification of Errors" was later promoted to relieve some of the damage. Those sent to labor camps were freed under strict orders "to forgive and forget." With untold numbers of executions and broken-up families, the campaign, however, left bitter feelings among villagers and anger toward the communists. Everyone knew that people could betray anyone or his own family just for the sake of pleasing the government. The trust that formed the foundation of the society and bonded all the individuals together was forever lost under the communist system. Truong Chinh, the promoter and executor of the campaign reform, was demoted, although he retained his position and role in the communist party.

The brutality of the reform caused the exodus, which in turn deprived Hanoi of many of its affluent, creative and industrious people. Twenty-nine of the 30 factories owned by the French in Hai Phong were closed. Gasoline was in short supply. Disastrous December floods raised the specter of another famine.[9]

A revolt occurred in November 2, 1956, in Quynh Luu district when a group of Catholic peasants presented petitions to the International Control Commission (ICC) to let them go south. Land reform had swept through that region in the summer of 1956 and had caused severe bitterness among the Catholics, who also complained of religious persecution. In 1955 communist officials had kept these people from moving south. Violence broke out when the local police tried to prevent Quynh Luu villagers from meeting with the ICC. An entire division was brought in to quell the revolt and 6,000 peasants were deported or executed.

As a result Ho Chi Minh abolished land reform tribunals as of November 8. A series of political upheavals like these would have toppled any government in the South, "but in the communist dictatorship of the north, which was prepared to use the most ruthless method of control, the people were gradually molded into instruments of production."[10]

Famine. If the Japanese and the French, by burning rice and maize in place of fuel in the factories, were responsible for causing famine in North Vietnam in 1944–45, the communists also had their hands in this problem. The French stored 500,000 tons of rice from 1943 to 1945 and shipped 1,000,000 tons in 1943 and 500,000 tons in 1944 to Japan, creating an unnecessary shortage.[11] The Viet Minh also exacted a portion of the production from the peasants. Some villagers used rice to buy the communists in order to remain in their good graces.[12] Natural disaster also played a role in this devastation. The shortage led to the biggest famine in Vietnamese history and the death toll rose to two million people. Many died like flies in the streets. A few greedy parents even saved the rice for themselves and let their children starve and die on their doorsteps.[13] A woman, Nga, who witnessed the situation wrote:

> Worse for us than the bombs
> was the famine.
> We had money,
> but there was no rice to buy.
> People ate grass.[14]

Servants, who were fired begged to stay, for if they left they would have nothing to eat. Hungry and weak people collapsed against the walls of the houses and laid there to die. They had no one to care for them and nowhere to go. Nga's father had to pay soldiers to remove the corpses. Sometimes soldiers removed bodies that still showed some signs of life. When the dying people realized they were being taken away for burial, they weakly argued from the cart: "Don't take me. Don't take me. I'm not dead yet." These soft and muffled voices seemed to have been uttered from the depth of a grave.

War. The brutal eight-year war between the French and the communists destroyed the fabric of the northern society. Infighting caused explosions to fill the air and severe destruction to houses, buildings, and fields. Atrocities were noted on both sides; maimed bodies were everywhere. People left the battle zones in a hurry and left behind those less able to escape: the elderly, the crippled, and the young — orphaned and abandoned. Three and four year old children, "rheumy-eyed and lost, their clothes tattered, their skins covered with scabs, waited for someone to claim them."[15]

The brutality of the communists and their total disregard for law and private property made people cringe. To support their cause, they exacted men and material support from all the villages under their control. Those who did not give enough were tried, sentenced, and sometimes killed. The Viet Minh displaced people from Hanoi and other cities and demolished their homes[16]: these actions foreshadowed future forced relocations designed to keep people under their control. People became homeless and could no longer afford to feed themselves or send their children to school. In some areas children were taught not only to disobey, but also to accuse their parents. A young girl who joined the revolutionary forces came back to challenge her father. She was taught it was wrong for him to have been rich; she learned that people only got rich because they took advantage of others working under them. She believed all rich people should be killed to make way for a new nation that would be more equal for all citizens.[17] Her father in the mean time also worked for the revolutionaries. As an engineer, he fixed blown up dams and bridges in one region and then another while his family trailed behind him. This was not a steady or well-paid job.

The brutality with which the Viet Minh treated people during the war and the land reform caused them to be afraid of its reprisals. Unable to tolerate oppression any longer, many elected to escape.

Refugee Population

The various groups participating in the exodus included: the landowners, the Catholics and Buddhists, the intellectuals, the government workers, and the Chinese. The intellectuals were never welcome in the land of proletarians. In purging these people to keep the revolution pure, the communists lost a large intellectual heritage, which they sorely missed during the rebuilding phase of the country.

Landowners. The well to do businessmen and landowners who had benefited from the French system had no choice but to leave with the French. They knew they could not work or cooperate with the communists, whose goal was to set up a proletarian revolution in North Vietnam.

Do's father came from a longstanding landowner family in Nam Dinh, North Vietnam. His great-grandfather, a mandarin at the Nguyen imperial court, owned a chunk of land which he left to his descendants after his death. Coming from a privileged upper class, the family was a visible target for the communists. In 1954, when the news of the partition broke out, Do's father thought he had seen enough of the communists' actions and deeds and decided to move south. He and his brothers walked several hundred kilometers from Nam Dinh to the port of Hai Phong to take a ship to the South. The inland trip was dangerous because of the presence of the Viet Minh at various checkpoints; it forced them to travel only at night. They hid behind the bushes and trees during the day to avoid being spotted by soldiers. Checkpoints were used to harass the common people and to prevent them from going south. Regarded as "exploitative landowners," Do's father and his uncles would likely be caught if they ventured freely on the roads during daytime. At best they would be sent back to their villages to be jailed and at worst they would be shot on the spot. They were lucky not to have to deal with any communists and took the boat to Saigon without incident.

Do's father arrived in Saigon empty handed at the young age of 17. He stayed with his uncle's family for schooling. They lived in Ban Co, a crowded Saigon neighborhood filled with refugees, and worked as nurses for a living. Life was difficult for these uprooted people. They had almost nothing materially. Do's father wore the same shirt and pants for weeks and weeks. He washed them at night, hung them to dry in the back yard, slept naked and the next morning put on the same washed outfit. He did not have much to eat and consumed plain rice with salt or soy sauce for days. Meat or fish was unheard of. In this wretched environment, he had to study hard and went to the Cao Thang technical school to study engineering. He was drafted into the South Vietnamese army in the midst of college to fight the communists during the height of the war.[18] He was later assigned to a post in Vung Tau, where he met his future wife. Not being a landowner himself, he was forced to endure the rigors of life because his family once owned a chunk of land.

Catholics. In 1954, there were 1,133,000 Catholics north of the 17th parallel, compared to only 461,000 in the south. These numbers alone denoted the deep faith, the cohesion, the *esprit de corps*, and the intransigence of northerners in general. Nowhere else in Vietnam could one see whole villages and cities led by priests like the Bui Chu, Phat Diem, Nam Dinh and Ninh Binh communities in the north. For a long time, the people in Phat Diem knew no war or conflict. Phat Diem was a town of 30,000 people with another 100,000 living around the area. They lived in peace under the leadership of Father Le Huu Tu, who acted as head of the church and as military chief. The Viet Minh treated him with kid gloves and avoided antagonizing him.[19] He organized the village into militia and kept the Viet Minh and the French out. The battles took place around these enclaves that remained untouched by wars. Eventually, the war came to them and they too had to escape. They could not stay neutral for a long time; the French accused them of negotiating with the Viet Minh and vice versa.

When the armistice was signed, Catholic bishops tested their will with the Viet Minh. They used their militia to oppose Viet Minh's occupation. The latter reacted violently by burning churches, killing villagers, confiscating church property, and torturing priests.[20] Catholics who feared reprisals escaped en masse later on. They formed the bulk of the refugees. They were mostly villagers, a group that included laborers, farmers, fishermen, and housewives. Lacking education, they faithfully followed their leaders, the priests. The latter in no uncertain terms advised them to shun the atheist communists. This attitude of dependency on higher authorities explained how whole villages were able to escape together with their priests.

It has been suggested that the CIA had promoted the exodus operation in hopes of providing a political base for the new southern Catholic president Diem. CIA operatives flooded northern villages with leaflets suggesting that Jesus and the Virgin Mary had moved south. Since most of these villagers were illiterate, it was unlikely they understood what the leaflets meant.[21] The most effect these leaflets could have had on these villagers was to drive them to reach a decision faster, before the red curtain forever dropped on them.

Buddhists. More than 100,000 Buddhists participated in the exodus. Buddhists, being in general conservative, benevolent, and cooperative, were less likely to run away because of political dissension. They mainly followed the bulk of refugees and simply fled with them. They could have worked for the French led government, but were tired of the war or afraid of the communists.

Intellectuals. The intellectuals and people who worked for the French fled the North for fear of reprisal. Others became disillusioned with the communists and came to the conclusion the Viet Minh's leaders were often ignorant and uneducated. The leaders also held grudges against anyone who came from the upper class society whether they fought for the same cause or not. The revolutionaries descended on villages and rounded up all the rich people. They made them kneel down and asked them all kinds of questions that were demeaning to them. Those who argued were simply killed.[22] Others, just left for ideological reasons.

Thu Lam's father, an engineer by education, had witnessed on many occasions the brutality of the communists' justice. It was swift and always went unchallenged. The Viet Minh once arrested 25 villagers they suspected of being traitors. They were about to put their prisoners on trial when the French arrived during one of their routine rounds. They fled into the jungle and left the prisoners to a new recruit, a third year law student. The villagers argued their case with the student-jailor: they told him they did not do anything wrong. They had lied about the size of their livestock to reduce the taxes owed to the Viet Minh. The new recruit, feeling compassion toward the poor peasants, released them. The revolutionaries became furious when they realized their prisoners had escaped. They put the young recruit on trial and did not allow him to defend himself. They found him guilty and sentenced him to death. They dug a hole in the ground, dumped him in, covered him with dirt up to his chin and left him to die in the hot sun.[23]

On another occasion in Bien Hoa, the Viet Minh stormed into the house where Lam's father was living and ransacked everything. All they found was a replica of a ship that was labeled "made in France." They accused him of being a traitor, bound his hands with rope, put a black cloth over his eyes, and led him away for trial. His error was to stay in his rich friend's house while waiting to make his way to the North to help the revolutionaries. He was accused of being a "wealthy owner" and regarded as a traitor. He was led to the jungle and forced to walk for hours around and around in circles, right, then left, and left, then right, in order to confuse him. He was dumped into a buffalo stable, matted with manure and thick with flies and mosquitoes. His jailors were ready to dump him into a river with a large rock tied to his neck execution style. Luckily for him, a heavy downpour delayed the execution. He was placed on trial the next day but was recognized by a revolutionary who turned out to be his friend. He was released after further questioning.[24]

Despite these encounters, he moved to the North to help the Viet Minh. He went to the fields for weeks and even months to repair bridges and dikes. The dikes were built to tame the Red River, which tended to overflow in rainy seasons and cause severe flooding. Bombing and shelling aggravated the damage caused by nature. Villagers were enrolled to work at night to repair the dams while others would build shelters for protection against warplanes.

Lam's father one day realized that commitment to the revolutionary cause led to nowhere. He had dragged his family from one village to another for years; this was not a life for his wife and children. His wife had to sell medications she bought on the black market or food on the side to make a living in whatever village they stayed. Good meals consisting of rice, fish sauce, a bit of egg, and vegetables were hard to come by. His young children were deprived of basic commodities and suffered from lack of nutrition and schooling. He finally decided he had enough of the revolution. On the other hand, having witnessed the errors of the land reform, he became mad at the ignorant peasants who terrorized those wealthier than they.[25] He moved to Hanoi where he began working for those who backed the French. Many North Vietnamese left the North because they could no longer bear the exactions in men and material support demanded by the Viet Minh.

Chinese. Chinese people came to Vietnam in the late 18th and early 19th centuries. Some settled in Hanoi but most went to Saigon and the southern regions that were fairly unpopulated. Known as the *Hoa*, they came in groups and therefore did not lose their ancestral heritage. They formed close-knit communities.

Dong was one of the refugees who escaped communism twice, the first time in 1954 and the second time in 1975. His forefathers came to Vietnam and settled in Hanoi where they did business with the French. They worked so well with the French oppressors and the oppressed Vietnamese that neither regarded them as enemies; they even served as buffers between the two groups. They therefore got the best deal possible and just focused on doing businesses.

In Hanoi, Dong opened a restaurant and a food business that became successful. When the French left Hanoi in 1954 following the fall of Dien Bien Phu, he knew that if he stayed with the communists, he would lose everything since all private enterprises would be nationalized. His previous work with the French would also make him suspicious in the eyes of the Viet Minh. He therefore left Hanoi with only "two suitcases and in a cloud of shock." He was definitely bitter for having to abandon everything — house, belongings, business, customers and friends. So did nearly one million people who left the North for the South. He resettled in the south and restarted from scratch. His business was booming until

1975 when he had to leave a second time following the fall of Saigon. He recollected that in 1954, he was bitter at the French because they promised him a "way of life and a protection of that way of life, and they failed.... In some ways, they were like the Americans" in 1975.[26]

Atrocities

Not everyone was able to get out of communist held areas safely and not everyone escaped unharmed. To stem the flood of people trying to escape southward, the communists applied severe restrictions on civilian movements, including refusing to issue passes, requiring large payments for passes, blocking roads, separating children from their families, firing on departing vessels, and blowing up bridges. Under communist controlled areas, without the required passes civilians could not move freely from one region to another and therefore were unable to escape to freedom. In other places crowds of children and women were organized to block departing trucks carrying refugees. Delaying tactics and legal or illegal maneuvers to hold the people back were simply designed to prevent them from escaping to freedom. These actions contradicted the agreement signed by Hanoi in Geneva.

The communists also used torture and other forms of physical violence against the escapees: old women had their collarbones broken by rifle butts and a priest had nails driven into his skull to make a crown of thorns.[27] Atrocities committed against villagers were frequently noted in communist controlled areas. One or two civilians were usually tortured in front of the rest of the villagers and the example was used as a warning to those who did not follow the rules. The fear of having to suffer from similar treatment caused the frightened populace to run away whenever escape was possible.

The communists saw religion, especially the Catholic faith, as the enemy of the people and the party. In order to induce villagers to renounce their faith, they subjected a few of them to painful experiences. In the village of Bao Loc, North Vietnam they would cut off part of a person's ear with a pincer like a pair of pliers and let it dangle in the air. This treatment was reserved for those who listened to Catholic masses. It served as a grisly reminder to others who listened to or planned to listen to foreign priests.[28] Everything that was deemed "feudal or reactionary" to the Viet

Minh needed to be destroyed: that meant almost everything from ancestor worship to attending mass. Villagers were no longer allowed to attend mass. Christian catechisms were burned and the teaching of religion was abolished. Frightened by the application of the new laws, the Catholic Bui Chu people loaded their boats and sailed toward the armada of foreign ships waiting for them a few miles off shore. About 18,000 escapees were thus saved,[29] although many more failed to escape to freedom. For learning religion, children in another village had their eardrums rammed with chopsticks. They screamed, wrestled, and suffered horribly. The teacher had his tongue held with a pair of pliers and cut with a bayonet. After the soldiers released him, he fell on the ground because of the pain and blood squirted all around him.[30]

In the village of Cua Lo about two hundred miles from the coastline, the new land reform rapidly turned into family denunciations, self-criticism, and distrust. One neighbor accused another in order to remain in good standing with the police. Tired of the reforms and not knowing whether they would be the next targets for denunciations, many villagers simply ran away. One group's plan was ingeniously simple. While Thinh, a somewhat retarded villager, diverted the attention of the police by creating a disturbance on one end of the village, the others ran to their boats that were moored along the river and escaped. The communists vented their rage on Thinh: they tied him to a tree, beat him, sprayed him with gasoline, and burned him to death.[31]

Those who escaped from the North to the South in 1954 were thus well aware of the atrocious behavior of communists for having lived under their rule. Therefore, as soon as the northerners started their spring offensive in 1975, the 1954 escapees were ready to escape again. Southerners who did not know the communists at heart were slower to react and tended to give them the benefit of the doubt. The first wave 1975 refugees therefore included more 1954 escapees than native southerners.

Civilians could go to the port of Hai Phong, North Vietnam, for transfer to the ships or directly to the foreign ships that waited for them at sea if they had access to boats. In accordance with the cease-fire agreement, an area around the city-port of Hai Phong served as the evacuation zone for all those who wished to go south instead of living under communism. That open zone was gradually returned to the communists by mid–May 1955. Getting to the boats or to Hai Phong from communist-controlled areas proved to be the most difficult and challenging task, as all the roads to freedom were either blocked or tightly controlled by the communists. Passes were not easy to obtain because of their unavailability or their outrageous prices. Without these passes, civilians were forced to remain where they were and therefore lost their freedom.

Boats from many foreign countries were anchored at sea, ready to pick up any refugee and to assist with the relocation. On many occasions, however, people who were lucky enough to reach the shore found themselves without any sampan or means to get to the foreign ships; they remained stranded on land until the communist police or soldiers caught them and sent them back home. Fishermen were the luckiest among the refugees. They could use their own sailing junks and fishing boats for their escape. They could either go directly to the ships or just follow the coastline in a southward direction if they felt comfortable with their sailing skills and their boats.

The communists did interfere with the free flow of refugees by blocking the roads to freedom and by inflicting physical and moral harm to the escapees. Many more people would have left North Vietnam had these interferences not happened. People were treated like numbers or materials to be used in the building of the communist nation. They were not treated as human beings.

3

RESETTLEMENT

The transportation of a million people to the South required a great deal of logistical work. Then came the resettlement process, which was not easy but required a lot of effort, coordination, goodwill and deep pockets. The refugees had lost everything during the process and not only needed food, clothing, land, housing, and seed money, but also a lot of moral comfort. Some had even lost their relatives during the flight: these emotional wounds unfortunately took a longer time to heal.

Screening Process

In the beginning, refugees were immediately brought onboard the ships where they received a bath, DDT spray, and medical care. As the number of escapees grew in size, camps were set up around the port of Hai Phong complete with showers and open-air toilets. New arrivals frequently did not know how to use these toilets and had to be taught. They were quartered in the camps, fed, screened and treated before being sent to the waiting ships. Many escapees suffered from medical problems and wounds during their inland travels. Bruises, cuts, and injuries from mines or gunshots were fairly common. Tropical diseases were also encountered during that period.

The majority of refugees arrived on their own at the gates of the camps. Americans also went up the river aboard LSTs (landing ship tanks) to pick up stranded escapees and bring them back to the camps in Hai Phong. Some LST's could carry up to 3,000 people at a time. DDT was used liberally to kill lice while people waited to climb aboard the ships.[1]

Modes of Transportation

Various modes of transportation were used during this exodus, which turned out to be well organized. Since allies knew the time frame of the process (nine months), they were able to commandeer ships to get the people out in time. This was a controlled exodus, unlike the 1975 diaspora where the Americans had only two days to get the people out of Saigon.

Trains. Rails were also used but only occasionally. The North-South route one was long and interrupted at various places during the long war between the French and the Viet Minh.

Planes. During the height of the operation, a French plane took off from Hanoi then Hai Phong every 10 minutes, night and day. A total of 213,635 people were evacuated aboard French planes. Nga was lucky to be able to escape from Hanoi in 1954 aboard an American plane. Her father, having worked for the French, decided it was time to leave the North and its communist rulers. Nga was ambiguous about leaving in the beginning but when everyone in the family left for Gia Lam airport, she too came. Her father told the family members to stick together, otherwise the communists would split them apart. They were allowed 40 pounds of luggage but no furniture, only gold. They landed in Saigon and lived in Cholon, Saigon's Chinatown, where the locals only spoke Chinese. They crammed, nine of them, in a two-bedroom apartment. At night the baby would wake everyone up with her cries. There was a public outhouse outside where people had to wait in line for their turn. Nga was so shy she had to wake up at 5 A.M. to go to the bathroom.

She noticed that northerners worked harder; they also tried to save as much as they could to buy gold for future protection. Southerners on the other hand spent all their wages. They did not take life seriously and did not plan for the future. Her mother was furious at her because she wanted to go to work and be independent.

Working as a secretary for the Americans in the late '70s allowed her to make the evacuation list. She took the plane out of Saigon after first being refused entry to the Tan Son Nhut airport. She landed in the Philippines aboard a C-123 then flew to Guam and Fort Chaffee.[2]

Boats. The majority came aboard foreign boats that were anchored outside the port of Hai Phong. This was a simple, easy, cheap means of mass transportation that could hold thousands and thousands of refugees at a time. Ships departed as soon as they were loaded. As of August 12, 1954, the sealift was scheduled to transport 100,000 escapees to the South monthly.

The refugees were brought onboard landing crafts that then ferried them to the waiting ships. The speed of the crafts, the fresh salty air from the ocean, and the lurching of the vessels across the incoming waves made them feel queasy and uneasy. This was for a long moment the meeting and clash of civilizations. As they closed in on the ships, they became terrified at the sight of the huge cargo containers they had never seen before in their lives. They looked at the ships, these iron dragons, as some kind of monsters that could only exist in their wildest dreams. These were peasants who had never ventured outside their villages in their lifetime, let alone traveled on an iron ship. They were the Neanderthals, relics of the past, who carried their meager belongings on balance sticks over their shoulders. Their dark and dirty clothes floated around their thin and emaciated bodies that let bones jut out. Anxious looks could be noted on their weary faces, which were partially hidden behind their conical straw hats. The refugees were often "covered with open sores. They bore scars and disfigurements of mistreatment."[3] In their haste to escape, many did not carry any belongings, except for a bundle of clothing, while others were obviously poor and had nothing to take with them. One man held a wooden crucifix while another pressed a framed picture of the Virgin Mary against his chest. Their long journey across the communist held lands did not leave them time to wash themselves. The smell was so awful it made the sailors gag. They had never used bathrooms before. One mother who gave birth on the shore bit off the umbilical cord and washed her child in the dirty river.[4] One account described:

"Miserable, filthy, lame, blind, crippled and war wounded come aboard.... Eighty percent were old men and women, and others are infants, all swollen with malnutrition and starvation, and literally dozens without limbs. They have a few paltry bags on sticks, called yokes, with two bags on each end. This is the only thing they have left in the way of possessions."[5]

Communist propaganda had warned these peasants that the Americans would play tricks on them, take them to the South or abroad to sell them as slaves. The refugees did not know what communism was about and whom to believe in. On the other hand, the communists were so good in their propaganda that they even fooled the experts in the field.

As soon as the escapees heard these stories, whether true or not, their self-preservation instincts made them careful in dealing with the Americans. They therefore stood in the landing crafts not knowing whether they should climb aboard or not. On one side was the fear of the unknown and on the other the danger of staying behind and being swallowed by the red tide. Risks were big on either side. The leaders stood confused right in front of the stairs that led to the ships and blocked the path of others. The Americans faced the encounter with a puzzling disappointment; they did not understand what these people were thinking. They anxiously waited for them to come aboard and then faced the fact that the escapees just stood there unwilling to risk their lives in the bellies of the beast.

During this period, the U.S. Navy 7th Fleet also lent hands and carried 310,848 out of the 800,000 evacuees. Cargo vessels and tankers were converted to accommodate the large number of refugees coming aboard. What was characteristic about this exodus was that whole communities of Catholics had been able to organize and escape south with their own priests. The whole village—from the elders to the youngest ones—just uprooted itself and left the north en masse. Although Lansdale, the U.S. adviser to the Saigon government, helped them by broadcasting radio comments like "the Virgin Mary has moved south,"[6] they simply left because of a genuine fear of the communist government. Many of them who were deeply attached to their ancestral homes were willing to stay back, although they could not.

Thousands of other people sailed south aboard their own boats or junks by hugging the coastline. They had either missed the big ships or did not like to travel on foreign ships. Their boats took all kinds of shapes and sizes as people tried to get away with whatever they had in hand. There was no such a scene in history before, as there had never been such a large exodus of people leaving a country or place almost at the same time. It looked like an armada of fishing boats coming from 20 or 30 different villages and going out for a fishing reunion. About 109,000 people escaped by their own means.

Resettlement

In 1954, the U.S. Navy formed Task Force 90 for the purpose of carrying out the evacuation. The operation was named Passage to Freedom.

By the end, the Operation Exodus (as the government of Vietnam named it) shuttled more than a million people to freedom. The total refugees, excluding the military, consisted mainly of farmers (706,026) and fishermen (88,850). There were 794,876 Catholics and 133,276 Buddhists and Protestants.

Operation Exodus from a transportation process snowballed into resettlement of all refugees. The operation had been fairly successful in relocating these people who were persecuted in the North. It also provided a valuable human resource to the South. The North had two million more people than the South (16 million versus 14 million). And many areas in the South, especially the southernmost part of South Vietnam, the land of a very ancient civilization in Oc Eo, were largely underpopulated. This was also one of the reasons why the Saigon government did not want a reunification of the country through a popular vote in 1956. The North would have won it outright with its large population size and its intimidation methods. The newly independent government of Vietnam (GVN) did not have the skilled organization, the military muscle, the political power, and the technical and economical resources to deal with the Hanoi Communist Party, which had been in existence three decades earlier.

The Saigon nationalists, as their name indicated, were a broad coalition of free thinkers, intellectuals, politicians, wheelers and dealers, and religious leaders whose aspirations and ideas were as huge and confused as the fog in early spring. White nationalists came and went as fast as the autumnal winds, the ruling communist party remained united, unchanged and monolithic. If the strength of the nationalists was in their anarchy and rebellious search for pure freedom, the strength of the communists lay in their stubbornness and their single-minded pursuit of liberation. If free meant free spirit, it also meant free fall. If the presence of a cacophony of voices meant freedom, it could also lead to disorder and failure. The multi-talented and multi-voiced nationalists eventually could not prevail against the stern, ruthless, and single-minded communists. In wanting to have everything from freedom and comfort to riches, the southerners eventually lost everything. Southerners and southern nationalists should, however, be proud of the legacy they left behind them. Their ideas of freedom will in time prevail. There is no way to prevent the truth and the free nature of the Vietnamese from emerging.

This was the picture Saigon and Hanoi projected at the heels of the exodus in 1955, a picture of two universes as diverse and opposite as the moon and the sun. This image would lead to a two-decade war between South and North, Ngo Dinh Diem and Ho Chi Minh, Capitalism and Socialism, Freedom and Oppression, and between free and closed societies. This was the duality of the Vietnamese mind; a clash of thoughts that would tear apart two societies, one new and one old, the people of the Mekong delta and those of the Red River delta. If the North eventually won the war, the South won the peace.

Many of the newcomers, particularly farmers and fishermen, were classified as economic migrants, as their main goal was to search for a new and better life in the under-populated South. Life was harsh in the Red River delta in the North, especially coming on the heels of the famine and the land reform a few years earlier. The cradle of the Vietnamese nation had been overcrowded for many centuries. This situation had been the driving force behind Vietnam's southern expansion (*nam tien*) in the 17th and 18th centuries. As a matter of fact, this trend had begun as early as in the thirteenth century.

The boats landed at Vung Tau, a small village at the mouth of the Mekong river 80 miles west of Saigon. Refugees were transported to nearby reception areas then dispersed throughout the south to a network of churches, pagodas, hospitals, government buildings, warehouses, and schools. The ARVN (Army of the Republic of Vietnam) took charge of all the reception centers. The crunch in food and housing became a fact of life. All available buildings were requisitioned and opened as shelters for all these people. In the middle downtown Saigon, the Opera House, the site of many lavish cultural meetings for the French and Saigonese elite, was opened as a shelter for hundreds of refugees. ("The Opera House was later converted into a legislative building (for the House of Representatives) of the Saigon government.") It was therefore not uncommon to find that a family of nine had to squeeze into a two-room apartment and that people slept huddled together in a crowded environment. Dining rooms held wall-to-wall cots at night after serving as eating places and reception rooms during the daytime. Commodities were also lacking and people had to wait in lines to use bathrooms.[7] Life in the beginning consisted of searching for bigger and better housing and higher paying jobs.

If everyone expected to see a few newcomers, no one in the South was ready to face the arrival of one million people, a five to eight percent population growth in just a few months. The large influx of refugees no doubt created a logistical nightmare for the new and young government of Prime Minister Diem. The refugees were on his mind all the time. He spoke about his difficulties with and his resentment toward the French. The latter in the beginning spoke about 60,000 refugees maximum. This number eventually climbed up to 500,000 and leveled at one million (928,152 civilians and 120,000 military personnel).[8] On the other hand, had the French been helpful, Diem thought that two million northerners would have easily moved south. Because of the magnitude of the refugee problem, he had to request financial assistance from the U.S. and other nations.

The refugees on arrival showed incredible misery, although they did not exhibit signs of hunger or starvation, which had been characteristic of post–world war refugees. This had to do with the fact that the trip was short and that the majority had not been under communist control for a long time; those who were had not been able to escape. There were, however, enough troubling signs coming from the communists to cause these people to escape to the South. They were in general well received by southerners who were great hosts and they adapted well in the new society, although conflicts and misunderstandings did occasionally occur. A young girl while strolling at an open market knocked down a seller's fruit basket. The seller was obviously upset at the incident and became enraged when she realized the girl came from the North. She immediately associated the stranger as someone who came down to take away her job, her security and her future. She wanted to beat up on the intruder, but another southerner stepped in and advised her to calm down; the stranger, he said, is a Vietnamese; she had suffered enough and had lost everything in the North.[9]

Northerners differed from southerners by their voices, clothes, and skin color. Elderly northern people lacquered their teeth in black, a millennium-old tradition they had faithfully preserved. The difference in skin color between the two groups reflected the fact that southerners spent a lot of time outdoors under the hot tropical sun. Northerners wore dark-colored clothes that stood out in the middle of southern multi-colored outfits. Their verbosity, pomposity and the way they expressed themselves revealed a certain degree of untruthfulness, which southerners could not share. Southerners were straight talkers and went directly to the subject.

Refugees were given a lump sum of 800 piasters (p.) upon arrival and an additional 200 p. if they settled in the highlands (at 35.5p. for $1 U.S.). They were provided with seven to 10 days of rice and more thereafter until they became self-sufficient. They did not lose their identities in the South, as they came in groups with their own relatives. Whole villages of fishermen came together with their priests. They were resettled in the same area in order to preserve their customs. New villages sprang out of nowhere close to the Vung Tau area with easy access to the ocean. As these fishermen used to sundry their catches, the smell of the rotting seafood spread over a large area. Travelers who drove from Saigon to Vung Tau had to face the memorable and nauseating stench of decaying fish. The Northern peasant, though "industrious and persevering, but slow, stubborn, adjusted poorly to new methods and naively swallowed all propaganda lines." Every one of them demanded he be given a "house, a hectare, a buffalo"[10] as if the Southern government was very rich. These demands caused the southerners to feel slighted because of the government's favoritism toward the new refugees.

The U.S. and many other countries along with private non-governmental organizations participated in the resettlement process. The U.S. contributed $56 million in 1955 and $37 million in 1956. The Catholic Relief Service by the end of 1957 had given a total of 35 million U.S. dollars. It provided rice, trucks, tractors, water pumps, medicines, food, clothing, and so on. It also assisted in the resettlement of 20 villages. A large herd of water buffaloes had been purchased from Thailand to fulfill the agricultural needs of these farmers. The International Rescue Committee under the direction of Buttinger managed to provide food, clothing, and medicines to the refugees. Buttinger also worked hard to help the displaced students and Hanoi University professors who escaped to Saigon. They were the most difficult people to place since they did not want to relocate to the countryside where opportunities for learning were lacking. He looked for temporary jobs, shelters, and food for them. Students ended up working during the daytime and going to classes in the evening. These students and professors would form the nucleus for the University of Saigon. Since Hanoi had the only University in Vietnam, Buttinger was instrumental in helping raise funds for the establishment of the universities of Saigon and Hue.[11] With the large number of refugees arriving in the South, the problem of providing health care to these people was raised. Since Vietnam did not have enough doctors to render medical care to the new refugees, the Philippines provided a team of 105 doctors and nurses to meet the demands. They saw a total of 400,000 patients the first year. The program was later expanded to provide technical assistance in agriculture and fish culture to the newcomers. The tremendous outpouring of help from all these organizations and other countries in the world was instrumental in the success of the operation. Without them, the many personal needs of each refugee would be lost in the shuffle.

About 300,000 not entitled to any assistance or unwilling to wait for it settled on their own, the majority in the Saigon area. Another 462,799 refugees had been resettled to relocation areas by April 1955. The largest resettlement, named Honai, was located close to Saigon. It comprised seven villages with a total of 66,000 refugees. These villages nostalgically bore the names of Hanoi, Hai Phong and so on to remind the newcomers of their lost cities and their heritage. Go Vap, a newly built town in the province of Gia Dinh, held 30,000 refugees. As the result of the influx, Saigon had added many suburbs like Go Vap and Phu Tho, which markedly increased its size and its population. Many adjacent towns had also grown in size within a short time.

In December 1955, President Diem announced the largest resettlement project named Cai San in the Kien Giang province close to the Gulf of Siam. It held 100,000 refugees. Each family was given seven acres of land to farm in this under-populated region. By 1960, the total surface of land reclaimed amounted to 192,000 acres. It became the showcase of the resettlement program, one of the most ambitious of its kind anywhere. Besides rice, which was the main crop, bananas, sweet potatoes, and sugar cane were planted in the Cai San project. Resettlement was then expanded and directed next toward the highland areas, the lands of the minority Montagnards, although its objectives were controversial. These minority tribes resented the Vietnamese encroaching on their lands, which they considered sacred.

This first exodus linked to the takeover of North Vietnam by the communists caused a traumatic dislocation of the refugee population: parents were separated from their children, siblings were split apart, and families were divided. The majority did not know where the rest of their family went. They longed and looked for each other although the separation appeared to be permanent. Some stayed in the North and were forced to work for the communists while others went to the South to enroll into the Saigon government. As Hanoi and Saigon became staunch enemies, so did family members. On many occasions, brothers ended up fighting against each other during the war and waiting for each other's news. They would have to wait until the end of the war to communicate with each other. The wait would last for two decades. Then those who migrated to the South in 1954 were forced to move again in 1975, this time abroad and the wait would continue anew. Some family members would not see each other for three to four heartbreaking decades. One woman who went to the South in 1954 did not want to migrate with her family abroad in 1975. She remained in Vietnam after the war ended to meet her mother, whom she had not seen for two decades. Since the communist government would not let her emigrate, she was separated from her children and husband for another two decades.

The exodus caused a major social shift in the South Vietnamese society. While South Vietnamese were mainly Buddhists or Confucians, the newcomers were fiercely Catholics and non-communists. In the North after the exodus, the number of Catholics declined from 1,133,000 to 457,000, while the number in the South jumped from 461,000 to 1,137,000, one in every 9.6 inhabitants.[12] This large group of northern Catholics, favored by the Diem regime, soon joined the southern army and government and displaced southerners from key governmental positions. They were known to be hard and aggressive workers but intransigent in their views; they thus had the tendency to cause rifts among the locals who were more moderate and easy-going. The locals also stood by powerless as the scarce national resources went to the newcomers, forcing them to scrape by for their living. The refugees projected an image of the Diem government "whose protection and largesse were extended preferentially to Catholics and northerners."[13] The increasing number of these vocal Catholics in an overwhelming Buddhist society polarized the South Vietnamese society and in time would split it apart, leading to an open confrontation between Buddhists and Catholics. The southern society, which was open and less rigid than its northern counterpart, would not be able to withstand this internal division that eventually led to its downfall.

The 1954 exodus of about one million people from the North to the South represented the biggest naval diaspora arising from one country during a single period, although it has barely been mentioned in history books. There was no question that more people would have escaped had they been allowed to go freely. The ease with which the task force was able to transport such a large number of refugees was due to the fact that the trip was straightforward. This was usually a smooth, uneventful, and fairly routine north to south trip that followed the coastline. The allied also had a lot of time to maneuver; having nine months to complete the project, they did not feel the rush to solve all the problems at the same time. No pirates or adverse encounters were expected. As for bad weather and storms, the large cargo ships were able to handle them well. Casualties, which were minimal because the trip was short, were mostly related to malnutrition or old age.

The resettlement was a surprisingly rapid and major success considering the fact that the newly created Republic of Vietnam (1955) had no previous experience, background, or means to deal with this monstrous problem. To successfully handle this crisis at a time when the different branches of the new government either lacked coordination or were not well organized spoke highly of the ingenuity of the various organizations involved. One had to give President Diem high marks for having successfully handled this difficult crisis, the first of his new government, during difficult times. He concurrently had to battle with a rebellious army chief of staff and the renegade well-armed sects of Binh Xuyen and Hoa Hao. A less than confident leader would have been displaced from office right away.

This tremendously difficult work also succeeded thanks to the overwhelming generosity and assistance of many wealthy nations that opened their hearts to these impoverished people. Without them these people would have needlessly suffered under the communist regime for two more decades or starved in a free South Vietnam.

4

THE RUMBLES OF WAR

The story would have ended right there with the exodus of this million villagers from North to South, but history took a different turn because of the hegemonic goals of Ho and his communists. Ho aimed to totally control the Indochinese peninsula and especially South Vietnam for economic as well as political reasons. The communists therefore continued their long and bloody struggle.

For centuries, the cradle of the Vietnamese civilization was localized around the Red River delta in the North. This was where the Vietnamese Bronze civilization, with its characteristic bronze drums adorned with fishing and agricultural sceneries, appeared and flourished. This civilization was rather unique among neighboring civilizations. It did not, however, have time to fully flourish because its mighty northern neighbor China descended on the country and enslaved it for almost a millennium. Vietnam tossed its yoke in AD 939 and remained independent until the late 19th century, when it was again enslaved by a western civilization, France. From the 10th to the 19th centuries, Vietnam, although independent, could always feel China's breath on its neck, for the latter had never fully rejected the idea of controlling the Vietnamese. As a matter of fact it conquered Vietnam for three more decades from 1400 to 1428.

Vietnam, limited by the Lang Son plateau and the Chinese in the North, the highlands on the western front and the Pacific Ocean on its eastern side, had no other way to expand and escape from the Chinese influence than going southwards. From the 13th century onward, little by little, it moved south along the coastline, chopping away the lands of the Chams, an Indianized civilization who occupied the present-day central Vietnam. By 1600 Vietnam developed a fiefdom in the south with its capital at Phu Xuan (Hue) and the Nguyen lords as rulers. The Red River delta region remained under the Le and Trinh kings. Vietnam was thus physically divided into two regions and separated by a boundary going through roughly the 17th parallel. The Nguyen, although fighting against the Le, continued their southern migration (*nam tien*) and from 1600 to 1800 conquered the present day South Vietnam. The land was rich and bountiful thanks to the Mekong River that brought silts and sediments from the Himalayan Mountains all the way down the Mekong delta. Under the diverse tropical climate, a lush array of fruit trees sprang out of the rich soil. Fisheries and rice culture became the staples of the region. Commerce with neighboring countries also opened the minds of the southerners. With a rapidly growing population, the Vietnamese neutralized the Chams and the Khmers who had lived in this region for some time. During these two centuries, southerners began to differentiate from their northern counterparts culturally, religiously and economically. While northerners remained Confucians, southerners by their dealings with the Chams and Khmers became Buddhists. The Nguyen lords made Buddhism the religion of the land, built numerous pagodas, and even converted into Buddhists. In 1802, they reunified North and South and for the first time in many millennia Vietnam as it is known today was born. The North realized it could not survive without the riches of the Mekong delta.

France invaded Vietnam in 1858 and took control of the South first before moving to the North. The South became a full-fledged colony while the North and center of Vietnam remained partly under the control of the Nguyen emperor whose power and palace remained in Hue. The colonization accentuated northern-southern differences and pushed the south toward a western market-oriented economy. The north on the contrary remained socially stationary and imbedded in its Confucian values and old traditions.

Ho and his communists found in the northerners a rich milieu in which to plant and impose their socialist theory. They found in these people the sacrifice, the passion, and the hard-working drive with which to mold them into tough and obedient soldiers. Without these qualities, the monolithic faith of the communist doctrine simply could not survive. Profiting from the disorder caused by the end of World War II, Ho took over Hanoi then the whole North, which was then under the control of the French. Using similar words from the 1789 French revolution and the U.S. Declaration of Independence, he declared his country's independence from the French. A long war ensued. The communists beat the French at Dien Bien Phu, driving them out of Vietnam.

The Geneva Accords did not solve any problems, except for allowing the French to exit peacefully. It did not allow the aspirations of the South Vietnamese, who wanted to live in a free democratic, Western-type society. It did not solve the wishes of the communists, who wanted to control the whole South. They considered the accords as a truce during the long war, which gave them the opportunity to prepare for an all out assault on South Vietnam.

The communists turned around and decided to conquer the south with its rich rice basket and oil fields. They launched continuous attacks on South Vietnam with ammunitions and military hardware coming through the Ho Chi Minh trail that linked North and South. Southerners who were unable to sustain the attacks failed not only because of their character, but also for their love of freedom. Tired of a long and bloody war during which they saw the country torn in ruins, disheartened by the withdrawal of the Americans, economically depressed and financially and physically bankrupt, the worn out country simply collapsed under its own weight like a giant running out of steam. Internal dissentions split the country apart while it disintegrated under enemy attacks. The communists did not have such reservations and second thoughts; they killed people right and left and pretended they did it for the people. They terrorized the locals who submitted to them because of fear. They simply prevailed with their cutthroat philosophy.

The Major Battles

During the next two decades, the North Vietnamese Army (NVA) continued their daily attacks on South Vietnamese forces, cities and civilians. The relentless attacks wore the two sides down physically and morally, although Hanoi never acknowledged its true and huge human cost. Only after the war ended did it finally acknowledge a loss of more than one million men compared to the 250,000 casualties for the South. Being less Spartan than their Northern counterparts, the South Vietnamese endured their fights with courage, dignity and in silence for two decades. As every sacrifice had its limit, the exhausted Southerners finally broke down in 1975, unwilling to fight any longer. The whole Southern society just collapsed like a house of cards.

The major battles that slowly sapped the energy of the southerners included the 1968 Tet Offensive, the 1972 Eastern Offensive, and the 1975 Offensive.

The Tet Offensive. By 1968, Hanoi was convinced that the time was ripe for an all-out assault on the Army of the Republic of Vietnam (ARVN). The North mobilized a total of 84,000 Viet Cong guerillas and troops and mounted simultaneous assaults on 36 of the 44 provincial capitals, five major cities including Saigon and Hue, 64 district capitals and 50 hamlets. This was the largest, bloodiest, and most widespread offensive anyone had ever witnessed during the war. The NVA enjoyed initial successes due to the surprise effect and to the fact that half of the ARVN soldiers were on leave for the lunar New Year. Within days most of the attacks had been repelled, except in Saigon, Hue, Can Tho, Kontum and Ban Me Thuot.

In Saigon, several groups of sappers disguising themselves as field police troopers simultaneously attacked the Presidential Palace, the American Embassy, the Joint General Staff Headquarters, the radio station, the Tan Son Nhut airport and Navy headquarters. At the palace the 34-man platoon attempted to crash through the gates but was repelled. All the men were killed. Three blocks down the road, a 19-man platoon charged through the American Embassy. Although they gained entrance through the blown-up gates, 17 of the 19 were killed on the lawn of the building. The complex was deemed secure a few hours later. At the airport, three NVA battalions were repulsed by paratroopers leaving behind 300 dead. Attacks at other sites were also driven back. Subversive agents introduced almost 15 Viet Cong battalions in Saigon, Cholon and the Gia Dinh province during the offensive. The guerillas broke down into small groups, took shelters in people's houses, high-rise buildings, and pagodas, and waited for reinforcements. None came. They were slowly flushed out of their hiding places.

The most bitter fight was in Hue, the ancient imperial city, which was occupied by the Viet Cong for three long weeks. After an intense barrage of rockets and mortars, the NVA attacked the city forces and settled in the old imperial palace. They freed 2,000 inmates from the local jail and used them as porters or combat replacements. They then systematically rounded up Vietnamese government officials, military officers,

Catholic priests and other "enemies of the people" and marched them off to the jungle. They asked the prisoners to dig large holes in various places, and then shot, bludgeoned them to death, or buried them alive. The graves of 2,800 people were later uncovered and 3,000 other civilians were never seen again. Many of these graves would never have been discovered had they not been pinpointed by Viet Cong defectors later on.[1]

Battles raged on for some time in these cities but eventually the NVA withdrew in defeat. It lost 45,000 men, and 5,800 people were captured. The ARVN lost 2,100 men and the U.S. 1,000 men. For the South Vietnamese the uprising represented a major military defeat for the NVA. It brought the population out of lethargy and gave it assurance and pride. They had seen these young Viet Cong faces full of immaturity and innocence and were not impressed by them. They thought the war was winnable with the Americans around. They had never risen to help the Viet Cong, which they saw as standing for war and destruction. They were appalled by the brutality and the senseless carnage caused by the enemy, especially in Hue. The massacre of innocent people in Hue forever lingered in the minds of its inhabitants. Years later, when the NVA closed on the city, its citizens evacuated in a few hours; no one would accept a repeat of the 1968 Hue massacre. Following the offensive, dissension disappeared by miracle. A general mobilization was passed recalling to immediate duty retired servicemen. The JGS estimated that the armed forces would enroll 260,000 men by the end of the year. But by September, 240,000 were trained and ready for combat.[2]

In the U.S., however, the media portrayed the offensive as a defeat for the Americans. The pictures of burning houses, cadavers and tanks in the city streets, Saigon being attacked, and the American Embassy being infiltrated gave them a feeling of vulnerability as a sense that the war would be protracted. The disaster theme seemed to be exploited for its own sake. Newsman Walter Cronkite returning from a hurried Vietnam trip, called Tet an American defeat. President Lyndon Johnson after watching the news was quoted saying: "If I've lost Cronkite, I've lost middle America." Although it was a military success, the extent and depth of the attacks and the instability of the situation shocked the American audience. It finally lost its patience and demands for an immediate withdrawal out of Vietnam grew louder. On March 28, 1968, the incumbent President Johnson announced he would not seek reelection.

The Paris Peace talks. What bothered Nguyen Van Thieu and the South Vietnamese was U.S. Secretary of State Henry Kissinger's preconception about South Vietnam when he came to the peace talks. In his mind, the fight between Saigon and Hanoi was similar to that between Athens and Sparta centuries ago. Athens used its maritime advantage to offset somewhat for the military might of the Spartans on land. Saigon with the American air power could neutralize Hanoi's forces but not win the war. The Spartans also had that discipline and faith forged by overcoming material strength. After a visit to Hanoi in 1973, the fate of the squabbling Athenians had been sealed. Kissinger had made his choice.

While describing Thieu as a loyal ally, meaning he could count on the president to follow his scheme, it did not matter to Kissinger whether he showed any loyalty to Thieu.[3] For a long time, he had been negotiating behind Thieu's back about obtaining from Hanoi a commitment for a "decent interval" between an American withdrawal and Hanoi's takeover of South Vietnam. With a friend like that, Saigon did not need any enemy. Although photographs of him smiling and shaking hands with Hanoi's leaders were seen in his memoirs, none showed him even talking to President Thieu. In 1969, Lodge resigned as leader of the U.S. delegation in Paris. He felt awkward to be sitting next to the Saigon delegation and being unable to tell them that Kissinger had been negotiating the most sensitive matters behind their backs with the Hanoi's men facing them across the table.[4] After Kissinger conceded that Hanoi did not have to withdraw its troops out of South Vietnam, which was contrary to Saigon's position, the Americans sent an undersecretary to brief Thieu, who was furious at the underhanded way Saigon was treated. Kissinger went on to write in his *White House Years* he had briefed Thieu frequently on his talks. Others analysts noted this was a blatant lie.[5] Thieu knew he could not trust Kissinger, although he did not have too many choices.

By 1972, the CIA had bribed so many South Vietnamese military and political figures inside the government that these collaborators and spies were simply extensions of the U.S. government. General Dang Van Quang (Thieu's advisor) and General Nguyen Khac Binh (Saigon's national police chief) collaborated with the CIA. Even the Presidential Palace and the prime minister's office were bugged. Thieu could not even go to the bathroom without the CIA knowing about it. Quang and Binh "became symbols of the American-inflicted corruption and decadence that ultimately provided the communists with their best propaganda weapon."[6] Finally, when Thieu complained in January 1972 that Kissinger did not discuss the final details of the agreement, Kissinger told Ambassador Bunker: "Thieu must understand that we could have reached agreement over the summer by agreeing to overthrow him."[7]

The NVA began the Eastern 1972 Offensive in response to Kissinger's offer for settlement. Their intent was to break the back of the Saigon government and to show the Americans the futility of supporting that government. Most of the U.S. troops had been withdrawn out of Vietnam except for two combat brigades. The NVA thought they could easily beat the ARVN and thus inflict a humiliating defeat to President Nixon in an election year.

The 1972 Eastern Offensive. The 1972 offensive would cost General Vo Nguyen Giap his job and set back Hanoi's conquest of South Vietnam for another three years. More than 125,000 men were involved—they were divided into 14 divisions and supported by heavy artillery and tanks. It was a three-pronged attack against major cites in South Vietnam: Quang Tri (north), Kon Tum (center) and An Loc (south).

On March 30, under the cover of heavy artillery, the NVA 304th and 308th divisions, three infantry regiments, two tank regiments and four artillery regiments crossed the demilitarized zone (DMZ) in full violation of the Geneva Accords and slammed into Quang Tri. Under heavy artillery attack, the green 3rd ARVN division that defended the city pulled back and regrouped south of town. A column of refugees fled in a disorderly manner southward "away from the liberation army" and under a barrage of mortars and artillery shells. Disfigured and dead bodies lay unclaimed among charred carcasses of trucks and tanks strewn along Route one leading to Hue. The sight of women crying and holding their children was heartbreaking. Wailings and sobbing could be heard among the quietly moving column. In the rear, bombs, shells, and mortars fell on the city, which was covered under heavy black and nauseating columns of smoke. If there was hell on earth, that must be it. A new defensive line was established.

On April 23, the enemy, reinforced by the 325th division, attacked the city again. On May 1, subjected to heavy artillery, soldiers of the 3rd division panicked and abandoned the city. Thieu fired the I Corps commander and replaced him with General Ngo Quang Truong. Truong took charge and made the Marines defend the north and northwest of

Hue while the 1st ARVN division held the western front. The NVA advance had been checked. On June 28 he launched a counteroffensive to retake the Quang Tri province. Supported by massive U.S. firepower and B-52 bombers, the counterattack slowly moved north, routing six opposing NVA divisions. By September 16, Quang Tri was retaken.

On April 2, under heavy artillery coverage, three NVA divisions coming from Laos and Cambodia moved toward Kontum. By April 15, the bases at Dak To and Tan Canh were surrounded and overrun. Kontum was left defenseless. The 23rd ARVN division commander, Colonel Ly Tong Ba, was brought up to take charge of the battle. He reorganized the defense and repulsed multiple NVA attacks supported by U.S. air strikes. On May 28, Ba ordered a house-to-house counterattack to clear the enemy out of town. Two days later, Kontum had been recaptured.

Moving from their bases in Cambodia, three divisions crossed the border into Vietnam and attacked An Loc, a town about 75 miles north of Saigon, on April 2. A forward base was overrun. The 21st ARVN division was sent to the rescue. It repulsed multiple NVA attacks under heavy U.S. air attack. Soon the enemy forces ran out of steam and withdrew back to Cambodia. The 90-day siege of An Loc was over.

The NVA took more than 100,000 casualties out of its 200,000-man invasion force and lost more than half of its tanks and artillery. NVA General Giap was eased out of power. The ARVN fought well but under coverage of U.S. air power.[8]

In the meantime, Kissinger and Hanoi had drafted an agreement in which the U.S. got everything it wanted: withdrawal and release of prisoners of war, while Saigon got next to the worst deal. The agreement allowed Hanoi to keep 13 NVA divisions and 75 regiments — a total of 160,000 troops — in the South, a proposition that Saigon had repeatedly rejected in the past. Thieu wept when he was handed the draft of the agreement. For South Vietnam, the nature of the agreement was a matter of survival. The bargain that had been made with Hanoi was "tantamount to surrender." When Thieu refused to sign the agreement, Kissinger notified Washington and Hanoi of Saigon's reluctance. A few days later, Radio Hanoi broke the news that the U.S. had agreed to sign the accords three times and had reneged each time. The revelation could only embarrass the United States, for it put the blame on the U.S. for having prolonged the war. Kissinger had just "deceived both his enemy and his ally and had the United States into an act of bad faith that can have few parallels in its diplomatic history."[9] Hanoi only returned to the negotiating table after being bombarded 11 days in a row around Christmas 1972. In the end, to induce Thieu to sign, the U.S. promised "swift and severe retaliatory action" if the accords were broken. These promises turned out to be empty words[10] because the Case-Church Amendment prevented any further U.S. military involvement in Southeast Asia. The U.S., Defense Secretary James Schlesinger remarked, was in danger of becoming the "Perfidious Albion."[11]

The Peace Accords were finally signed on January 27, 1973.

Consequences

The exodus for a long time divided the country into North and South. It polarized the Vietnamese society and divided them into hardened nationalists and communists who then had governments to back up their views. Things would never be the same again. Brothers would look at brothers as enemies and the animosity between the two sides just went on as the years of division went by. For the next two decades, war raged on throughout South Vietnam in a relentless manner. No town or city would be immune from Viet Cong or NVA attack. Terror and violence escalated and the number of casualties kept rising. There was no end in sight, as the Paris Accords did not change Hanoi's goal. They just delayed the final ending and made another exodus more likely.

During this conflict, southerners developed an innate fear of the communists who were viewed as Machiavellian robots who just knew how to destroy but not build. They were afraid of the northerners because of their steely character, their lust for blood, and disregard of common laws. They saw the ruthlessness with which communists killed the peasants in the mid–'50s during the land reform, the heartless killings and executions during the 1968 Tet attacks, and their single-minded struggle for 20 years against overwhelming odds to unite the country. Later came the sending of southern nationalists to reeducation camps and their planned conquest of Laos and Cambodia after 1975.

In 1975, 21 years after the exodus, as the communists approached the vicinities of Saigon, they unleashed the same fear they had caused two decades earlier when they took control over Hanoi. Rumors of an overall massacre spread like wild fire around the city as the headless Saigon government rapidly lost its grip over its population. Terrified by fear, the Saigonese ran around looking for ways to get out of town. There were, unfortunately, not many choices left.

Part II

The 1975–1992 Diaspora

5

Prelude to the 1975 Diaspora

Before Saigon fell in 1975, other cities in the western and northernmost regions of South Vietnam came under enemy attacks by the 13 divisions Hanoi never pulled out after the Paris Peace Accords were signed. Fresh divisions coming from the North joined the offensive.

The 1975 Offensive

In the past, especially in 1968 and 1972, the ARVN had been able to fight back with good results. Once the support of the Americans was gone and the delivery of military supplies and ammunitions dwindled following the Paris Accords, the morale of the army went rapidly downhill. "Betrayal" was on the minds of the soldiers and their leaders. In the meantime, the NVA in the South continued to receive floods of heavy military equipment from the North through a newly built all-weather road that went all the way down to Saigon. A north to south trip could take three weeks instead of the usual two months. Shipments moved in convoys of trucks, immune from bombing. A new pipeline was constructed along the road and provided much needed fuel for the North Vietnamese who were ready for the attacks. By the end of 1974, they took control over 500 hamlets in the delta with about 750,000 inhabitants, more than anytime in the previous five years.[1]

In January 1975, they launched an attack on Phuoc Long to test the will of the United Sates. The town fell without Washington lifting its fingers. Only 3,000 civilians out of 30,000 or more escaped communist control. The province, village, and hamlet officials were captured and summarily executed. Hanoi knew the U.S. would not intervene and thus could proceed with the conquest of South Vietnam, which they failed to do in 1968 and 1972. In February, General Van Tien Dung, chief of staff of the NVA, arrived in South Vietnam to take command of the Great Offensive that would lead to the fall of Saigon. Ban Me Thuot and the highlands were attacked on March 8, 1975. The NVA blocked highways 19 and 21, preventing ARVN forces from coming to the rescue of the city. Then, using tactical superiority, the NVA overran Ban Me Thuot's local forces.

Overstretched and undermanned, the southern forces could not react effectively and forcefully enough. In a tactical move President Thieu ordered General Phu, the II Corps commander, to withdraw his troops from the highlands. Phu delegated the job to his assistants and flew to Nha Trang with his staff. The poorly organized retreat turned into a disaster. Of all the roads, the ARVN chose the heavily mined 7B, a 135 mile-long road through jungles and mountains. That road had not used for quite some time for good reason. Anxious family members tagged along with the soldiers and scores of frightened civilians followed the military convoy. A column of trucks, buses, cars, motorcycles, and oxcarts followed behind. Everyone was fighting for his own life. Mutinous Montagnard soldiers turned against government units and fired at them. They were upset that the government had abandoned the highlands and their families. At Cheo Reo, the column easily fell prey to the NVA, which indiscriminately slaughtered soldiers as well as civilians. NVA soldiers fired mortars on the convoy and machine-gunned all the people without exception. Children and elderly people were not even spared. "The sound of roaring artillery and small arms, the scream of seriously wounded people at death's door, and children, created a voice out of hell" wrote a reporter who accompanied this Convoy of Tears. The picture was similar to a scene from Dante's hell.

The convoy was held back for five days when the NVA blew up a pontoon bridge on the swift Song Ba river. People ran everywhere, up and down the riverbanks and into the river, where many drowned. The guerillas had in front of them what amounted to a "shooting gallery." Soldiers and civilians were massacred by machine-gun fire after trying to surrender and hundreds of bodies floated down the river.[2] In a nearby clearing, one worried infantryman holding his two children was looking for the remaining six who had disappeared in the middle of the attack on the convoy. An old woman frantically searched for her 32-year-old injured daughter. Food and water were almost non-existent, as no one had planned for a long trip. Many refugees had not eaten anything except leaves and roots during many days of this 11-day trek. ARVN helicopters flew 80 missions a day to drop bread, give gunfire support, and evacuate the injured. By the time it reached the coastline, the II Corps army had ceased to exist. Only 20,000 of the 60,000 troops and 100,000 out of 400,000 civilians made it to Tuy Hoa and neighboring areas where they found no food or shelter.[3]

Soon the cities fell one after another like unwanted dominoes. The result was a massive flood of refugees that poured out of the highlands and the northern provinces to the central coastal areas. Ships were dispatched to pick up civilians and soldiers stranded in towns along the coastline. The 1975 diaspora had begun.

Sealift

As the NVA attacked Ban Me Thuot, other units probed the defenses of the Quang Tri area. These attacks alone caused 50,000 civilians to flee from Quang Tri to Hue, the first of what would become the largest and most tragic flight of the war. President Thieu then decided to abandon Quang Tri, the northernmost city of South Vietnam close to the demilitarized zone. He ordered general Ngo Quang Truong, commander of the I Corps, to send the Airborne division back to Saigon. Three brigades pulled out of their positions west of Hue and Da Nang on March 16. The subsequent pulling of the Marine division out of Quang Tri panicked the general population and triggered a massive evacuation of civilians and the military. By March 23, government units began to melt away around Hue. Hue citizens evacuated themselves before the NVA arrived, in an attempt to avoid a repeat of the slaughter of the 1968 Tet attack. One schoolteacher was quoted as saying: "We cannot live with the communists. We must escape from them."[4] Streets that were normally bustling and crowded became empty and the sampans were gone from the river. An old man with a wispy beard and wearing a worn out mandarin tunic quietly and steadily wept. Quietness had fallen down on the ancient imperial city. Hue became dead like Pompeii before the volcano eruption took place. The city surrendered itself without a single shot.

These redeployments coming on the heels of the debacle in the highlands broke the morale of the ARVN First Division and other locals units. Soldiers, their families and other civilians escaped en masse to the next city, Da Nang. Although not much fighting was going on at that time, civilians had figured out that without the protection of the Marines and the Airborne divisions, the local units would not be able to fight against the NVA.

Saigon sent every available ship up north to pick up the remnants of the marine brigade at the port of Tan My in Thua Thien province. Scores of nervous and unruly civilians followed. Everyone pushed and shoved and fought to get onboard the overcrowded ships. This spectacle would repeat itself again and again over the next three months. By March 24, at least 500,000 refugees flooded the city of Da Nang waiting for food, shelter and sealift. World Airways planes were chartered to pick up about 40,000 people. When the first plane landed, it was mobbed by untold number of refugees who rushed onto the runway. Planes were forced to leave in a hurry with their back door, loading steps, and wheels still down. The operation was cancelled and only 1,200 out of the planned 40,000 had been evacuated. American Defense Attaché General Homer Smith procured and sent all tugs, barges, and cargo ships to the Da Nang and Nha Trang areas to pick up soldiers and civilians.

On March 28, the 13,532-ton freighter SS *Pioneer Contender* picked up about 6,000 refugees from Da Nang. The refugees filed up the ship's single gangway "in a seemingly endless, tattered line uncoiling from the mass of humanity below like a strand of yarn from a pile of wool."[5] Marines disarmed the soldiers, carried babies and helped the sick and elderly up the ladder. The ship soon steamed away and the USNS *Andrew Miller* took on another 7,500 refugees. Other ships followed. Crowds became unruly as the NVA troops headed toward the city. Altogether 90,000 people were evacuated by sea, 16,000 of them were soldiers. This was all that remained of the I Corps forces. Da Nang fell in the hands of the enemy on March 30. Government policemen were beheaded, groups of soldiers were tied together and killed with grenades, and security personnel were liquidated.[6] The refugees who were previously dropped off in Nha Trang were taken to Vung Tau or Phu Quoc Island.

The *Greenville Victory,* with 7,000 Cam Ranh Bay refugees on board, steamed towards Vung Tau but was refused landing. Although refugees became unruly, the ship continued its trip towards Phu Quoc. On arrival, the refugees refused to step ashore and some even threatened to blow up the ship if it did not go back to Vung Tau. The captain cooperated and the soldiers threw away their guns and ammunitions. When the ship landed at Vung Tau the next day, all the refugees all left peacefully. Three new U.S. citizens were born during the trip.

The *Contender* took on refugees at Cam Ranh on April 3. Attempts to confiscate arms from the refugees were unsuccessful in the chaotic crowding. Riots occurred when food was served the next morning. Out-of-control soldiers even robbed civilians of their belongings and some even sold water at gunpoint to the other refugees. The Phu Quoc authorities did not know what to do with the newly arrived refugees. Afraid of communist infiltrators, the refugees were left on board for six steamy, long days. One crewman collapsed from exhaustion. Aboard the crowded ship, riots occurred and two women and five children were crushed to death on the first day of arrival. Many more would die because of thirst and starvation. Others had pneumonia and infected wounds. Robberies and black-market profiteering occurred. Two hundred men jumped overboard trying to swim ashore but were caught by the Navy. Viral epidemics broke out, causing diarrhea and fever among the refugees. Many also had conjunctivitis. Riots occurred again on the second day over food distribution. The ship was finally allowed to unload its passengers three days after its arrival. It took another three other days to disembark the full 16,700 refugees. This was the biggest cargo load during all the wars. Between 200 to 400 people, mostly children, died of thirst, heat, disease and violence. The Phu Quoc Island commander had five renegade soldiers shot on the beach, two on April 5 and three more the following day, for crimes at sea. The summary discipline worked; the island remained quiet for the rest of the month. Overall, 40,000 refugees landed in Phu Quoc. The main problem became a logistical nightmare: how to provide and deliver food and water to this new population.[7]

By the end of the first week of April, American ships had picked up 95,612 refugees and other foreign ships carried over 40,000 people. Another 750,000 people fled the communists aboard river and coastal boats, land vehicles, or on foot. There were stories of people and soldiers walking 50 to 100 miles on foot and with any means available to get back home. This was a repeat story of the Convoy of Tears. What sustained them were their will to live and the desire to be with their families.

Moral Dilemmas

Many factors caused the ARVN to suddenly collapse during the last stretch of the war. The long war years had finally caught up with the soldiers. They felt they could not do their duty any longer. The withdrawal of the American forces, which could be equated as abandonment, had something to do with the low morale among the troops. They felt vulnerable without the support of the U.S. Air Force and the provision of military supplies.

The "family syndrome" played a major role in the disintegration of the ARVN. Families were allowed to live near the bases to boost the morale of the soldiers. Families also provided additional financial support, as wives often took on secondary jobs. Having families around was a way for the government to compensate for the soldiers' ridiculously low pay. This was a compassionate move that had its own risks. Soldiers' pay was meager at best and could not cover the cost of raising the average family with three to four children. Soldiers fought well during the 1968 and 1972 uprisings when they knew their families were safe at the home bases. In 1975, however, when the troops were ordered to withdraw without any mention about their families, the soldiers immediately took them in tow. Soldiers who usually fought with courage when unburdened by their families became more circumspect with loved ones around. They no longer thought about waging a real war when distracted by other considerations. The cruelty of the NVA was obvious when they just machine-gunned or shelled everyone indiscriminately. The responsibility rested on their commanding officers to make the correct moral judgment. War being war, the indiscriminate slaughter of unarmed civilians could not be morally supported; it could be viewed as a war crime.

The other factor was the deep-seated fear of communism and communists. Southerners were more sensitive to moral matters than northerners. Civilians and soldiers knew too well about the cruelty of the communists. In the beginning there was the ruthless killing of peasants during the land reform and the obstacles created by the communists to impede the flight south in 1954. There were the slaughters of the 1968

Tet offensive where 3,000 civilians alone were executed in Hue, the killings during the uprising in 1972, and the slaughter of the Convoy of Tears. In between those times, untold cruelty was noted at all levels and in all provinces. Not a single day passed by without mention of communist-induced casualties. If war rendered soldiers cruel and insensitive, the steely cruelty of the communists at times reached sadistic levels. They just killed before even asking questions. A survey of 70 refugees in Vung Tau about the cause of their becoming refugees revealed clear-cut answers. Forty one percent feared communists' reprisals and 29 percent were unwilling to live under communist control — a total of 70 percent cited communists as the cause of their flight.[8] There was no significant difference between Catholics and non–Catholics. These simple answers revealed the state of mind of southerners towards communists.

Another factor involved the soldier himself. An infantryman holding two children was running around in Tuy Hoa visibly angry and upset while looking for milk for his starving and malnourished three-month-old baby. Father and child came down from the highlands with the Convoy of Tears and the child had not tasted milk for a while. The man was also upset because he was not able to locate his wife and two other children in the shuffle. He was angry at the whole system and for feeling vulnerable and exploited. Soldiers like him were angry first at the Americans, "at the government that had ordered their retreat, at the generals who botched it, at their own officers who had deserted them ... at themselves for leaving the wounded, for robbing and terrorizing helpless civilians on the trail. The disaster was not their fault. But the shame bit deeply just the same." That was the shame the soldiers experienced in a disorganized escape. That was the shame of proud soldiers who were not permitted to fight the war and die in the full glory of a battle. That last stand had been taken away from them. Their pride had been mortally wounded.

This was the moral picture of these poor soldiers who for two decades silently, cynically, and courageously stood by their government. Unlike American soldiers who rotated out after a year of service, they remained drafted until they died or the war was over. They soldiered on year in and year out with calm dignity. Resignation was plastered like a mask on their bony, war-hardened faces. "The endurance of the Vietnamese soldier was something one came to take for granted. After suffering so much for so long and for so little reward, these soldiers had now experienced a betrayal that even their remarkable resilience could not bear."⁹ The soldiers were devastated for having done so much and ended with nothing—no house, no food, no reward, no leaders, and nowhere to hang on.

The leadership was obviously at fault during this collapse. If a few generals did remain in place to guide their soldiers, the remaining officers had deserted their divisions. Had they remained at their posts, the collapse would not have been that dramatic. Even communists predicted that South Vietnam would at least resist for a year and a half before falling apart. On the philosophical point of view, had the fight gone on longer, the number of casualties would be enormous and the bitter feeling between the sides—who knows—would be irreversible.

General Le Minh Dao fought bravely at the last battle of Xuan Loc. When he finally surrendered, he had only 600 men left under him against 10,000 NVA troops. He was sent to a northern reeducation camp for the next 17 years. General Ly Tong Ba, the hero of Kontum in 1972, fought valiantly and was incarcerated for a total of 13 years. General Nguyen Khoa Nam, IV Corps commander, and his deputy, General Le Van Hung, killed themselves instead of surrendering to the enemy. So did General Le Nguyen Vy, commander of the 5th ARVN division, and General Tran Van Hai. These were some of the last heroes of the Vietnam War.¹⁰

Operation Babylift

In 1974, a total of only 1,352 orphans had been adopted by American families. Of South Vietnam's 900,000 orphans, only 21,000 lived in orphanages and few of them were adoptable. The rest lived with their extended families. In 1975 with the war coming close to Saigon, the adoption process had been speeded up and with the green light from various departments Operation Babylift was immediately set in motion.

The first batch of orphans was airlifted aboard an Air Force C-5 Galaxy on April 4. When the plane took off, the cargo doors blew open and the plane had to return to the airport because of decompression problems, only to crash in the nearby muddy field. All passengers in the lower deck died while those on the upper deck survived. The disaster was laden with a sense that the "Americans somehow were cursed in Vietnam, fated to bring only tragedy even when trying to do good."¹¹ The airlift went on despite the tragedy and by April 8, 1,300 children had been airlifted. By April 28, 2,700 children had been evacuated along with a number of adults. There were some abuses; some children were not really orphans and many adults were wives or girlfriends of Americans.

Well before the massive diaspora of May 1975 got underway, a large number of refugees (135,000 by sea) from central Vietnam had been relocated either to Vung Tau or Phu Quoc Island in the first few months of 1975. Another 750,000 people escaped with their own means on land. This was one of the largest unplanned resettlements of refugees during any war. This phase could be termed exodus number two. There were also 2,700 orphans relocated to the U.S. in the last days of April. These actions were just rehearsals for the real thing to come.

6

THE 1975 WAVE

> We glimpse their blood-red flag — hair stands on end.
> We peek at Uncle's photo — sweat breaks out...
> "Heaven, they're coming! Let's clear out, and quick!"
> — Luu Van Vong[1]

Before 1971, only a few thousand Vietnamese lived in the United States. By April 21, 1975, when South Vietnamese President Nguyen Van Thieu resigned, 3,000 additional Vietnamese had been evacuated to the U.S. With the NVA closing on Saigon, Washington thought about saving the endangered people. This included Catholics, Buddhists, government officials, landowners and capitalists, especially those who worked for the U.S. government and their families. Members of the ARVN surely would have to make the list since the NVA considered them enemies. Washington and Ambassador Martin argued back and forth about the exact number of endangered people. By April 9, the Interagency Task Force suggested the number of 197,000.

On April 15, 1975, Philip Habib, assistant secretary of the State Department, told Congress in a closed door session that the U.S. would evacuate 17,600 Vietnamese who were actually working for the U.S. government. The total number would rise to 130,000 if their dependents were counted. The department would ignore the rest of the population, although the probability for mass murder by the communists would be high. Two days later, Kissinger told Ambassador Martin to start the evacuation not only of Americans, but also of 200,000 Vietnamese.[2] Martin was "headstrong and absolutely impervious to persuasion.... He was thought to be the next best thing to a B-52" and had been sent to Vietnam to hold the line. Having lost an adopted son, a combat soldier in Vietnam, he was the last person to be willing to concede defeat to the communists.[3] He believed in a last minute deal with the North Vietnamese and worked feverishly behind the scenes with the Polish and the French. He did not activate the evacuation process until April 29. By that time, it was too late.

Fall of Saigon

The last battle between North and South was waged at Xuan Loc, a town of 38,000 located about 40 miles northeast of Saigon on route 1. After two weeks of fierce fighting during which nothing was spared, the North Vietnamese overran the completely demolished town on April 22, 1975. The roads to Saigon were wide open. By April 27, at least 140,000 communist troops had encircled the city and soon blocked off all the exits out of the capital. They shelled the city, causing fires in certain neighborhoods, destroying houses and creating a deep uproar among the already scarred Saigonese. The city's inhabitants ran around eagerly looking for ways to get out of the country. There were only three ways of escaping from the besieged city: airlift from Tan Son Nhut airport, airlift from the rooftop of the American Embassy, or escape by boat from the port of Saigon. The port could be closed anytime.

Between April 21 and 29, 35,000 Vietnamese, most of them women and children, had been airlifted aboard American aircrafts. Although families of high-level officials were evacuated, bargirls and housemaids connected with the G.I.s also made the trip. It had been estimated that only 20 percent of this group could be deemed as high-risk people. This fact caused quite a few eyebrows to raise, although it was short lived. Everyone was preoccupied with finding a way out and no longer bothered to look at his neighbor's problem. The situation became critical in Saigon as the enemy's brutal shelling of the city's Tan Son Nhut airport caused it to shut down on April 29, disrupting the evacuation by fixed wing aircrafts. Operation Frequent Wind IV was finally activated with the purpose of flying Americans and some Vietnamese officials out of Vietnam. Helicopters were used instead of fixed wing planes. Despite their limited capability to carry people, they were able to land in places where other aircraft could not: rooftops and courtyards. The song "I'm dreaming of a white Christmas" was heard on the radio followed by "The temperature in Saigon is 105 degrees and climbing." This was the coded signal for the Americans to go to the 13 designated areas to be picked up.

At the almost deserted compound of the JGS at Tan Son Nhut air base, Marshall Ky met General Khuyen, chief of staff, who told him General Vien had left the day before. A colonel told him to leave, as the NVA were approaching the airport. He met General Truong, former Corps I commander, and invited him to come on the trip. Truong and Ky's entourage piled into his helicopter, which took off. The sky was filled with airplanes. Ky told some of pilots who were enquiring on the distress line to fly to the fleet, or if they had enough fuel to fly to Thailand. He flew to the USS *Midway*, which had picked up his distress signal and guided him in. He was later transferred to the USS *Blue Ridge* (Butler 85: 399–400).

Many more could have been evacuated had the order gone out earlier. People working for the Americans were told to gather at various places around Saigon where they could be picked up. These plans were later cancelled due to the risks involved in landing airplanes in the middle of the city. Many thus waited and waited, and since no one came to pick them up they tearfully realized they were left behind. They slowly and sadly picked up their belongings and silently walked home. There was nothing else they could do and were resigned to meet their fate, whatever it would be. A lot of people faced the same scenario. Seventy Vietnamese working as translators for the U.S. Central Intelligence Agency (CIA) were holed up in a hotel waiting to be picked up and flown out. The CIA agent assigned to assist the group had evacuated himself and left them behind. After the communists took over Saigon, they machine gunned most of the Vietnamese at the hotel.[4]

Van Tran, an employee of the USAID and the CIA, was told to be present at Lam Son Square right in front of the Tran Hung Dao statue in the center of Saigon. This was one of the designated landing spots where Vietnamese working for the Americans would be picked up by helicopter and transported out of Saigon. At the last minute, the spot was no longer considered safe for landing and Tran was told to board a bus heading to the airport. He at least felt lucky to be picked up and hopefully evacuated. At the gates of the Tan Son Nhut airport, confusion arose due to the fact that everyone struggled to force his way into the terminal. The disorder caused the guards to fire at the incoming buses. At the same time a 130mm North Vietnamese mortar hit the airport runway, sending everyone scrambling for shelter. Entry was further restricted. The South Vietnamese were separated from their American guides and advised to go to the U.S. Embassy where a pick-up was likely. They turned around and headed back to Saigon where heavy rains fell that Thursday, cooling the hopes of the freedom seekers.

Despite the rain, thousands of people surrounded the embassy and fought to get into the compound. Each person had to walk through the restless crowd all the way to the slightly opened gate guarded by Marines. There was a lot of yelling, shoving, pushing, crying, and swearing. A few people attempted to climb over the eight-foot fence and its barbed wire, only to be pushed back by the Marines. Parents lifted their children above their heads and attempted to shove them to the guards, hoping the guards would pick them up and take them to safety. They no longer cared about themselves since they could not get in, but they at least would be happy if their children could escape alive. Since Tran and his family were on the list of evacuees, they were allowed to get through the gate and told to sit in one corner of a room. Outside the shouting and yelling continued unabated while on the roof, the rumbling noises made by the helicopters on landing and departing broke the silence of the evening. Gunfire was also heard outside. Tear gas thrown by the guards to keep the unruly crowd under control made breathing difficult. Eyes were burning and tearing. The air conditioning and the elevators broke down; the heat was intense. The incinerators on the roof were working full blast as the ambassador himself tried to shred secret documents at the last minute. The gusts of wind generated by the landing choppers blew open bags filled with half-shredded secrets, sending them down the courtyard and up into the trees. Discarded weapons taken from the evacuees as well as luggage piled up in the hallway and courtyard.

The embassy was evacuated floor by floor and people were shifted from room to room and up to the roof. Only one CH-46 at a time could land on the roof while the heavier CH-53 had to maneuver into the cramped parking lot. Dangers and difficulties multiplied because of darkness. A 35mm projector was turned on to illuminate the courtyard's landing pad each time a CH-53 arrived. When asked about the number of remaining refugees to be evacuated and no matter how many choppers had taken off, the embassy's answer to the headquarters in Thailand and Hawaii remained the same 2,000 to go ... 2,000. It felt like trying to empty a bottomless pit.⁵ An hour before midnight, the skies over the embassy became quiet. The air crews had flown for 10 hours straight and had been grounded. General Carey argued that the airlift should go on because Saigon would be in the hands of the communists by daylight. His tired pilots climbed back into their aircraft and headed back to Saigon. Ambassador Martin promised everyone would be picked up, although more than 1,000 people remained. Among them were a German priest and 10 Koreans including Brigadier General Rhee Dai Yong, deputy commander of the Korean expeditionary force in Vietnam. Only 19 flights were allowed. Then came a White House order for Martin to board the last plane out. There were 700 people left when the CH-53 stopped coming. Tran and his family were finally allowed to climb the stairs up to the landing pad.⁶

By 4:30 A.M. the limit of the 19 flights had been reached with 500 people remaining in the embassy. The White House advised Martin that it would step in if Martin did not end the airlift. The ambassador and his staff flew off. By 5:30 Colonel Madison flew off, leaving behind 420 people after having promised them a safe evacuation. Only the Marines remained. It was only later that the 420 people in the compound realized they had been deserted. The communists jailed General Rhee the next day despite his diplomatic status.⁷ Thousands of Vietnamese were still seen in the streets, desperate but oddly silent. In the horizon, the ammunition dumps at the Bien Hoa airbase were still exploding, sending big fumes in the air, while at the periphery of the city the amber lights of the North Vietnamese army convoy prepared for the assault. They were so cocky they did not even turn the lights off. Tracers flew toward the chopper, which gained altitude and veered east toward the coast. Forty-five minutes later it landed on the USS *Okinawa*. The landing pads of this and other ships had been busy receiving an armada of U.S. as well as Vietnamese choppers during the last 21 hours. In the beginning, Vietnamese pilots were told to jump out of the planes before crashing them into the sea. Attempts to perform the trick turned out to be dangerous and pilots were allowed to land on the ships. They landed with a cargo of men, women and children — their families in tow. The ship's crew then ran a steel cable from the ship's crane around the skid of the Huey and slid it across the flight deck, and tipped it over the side. The waste was inevitable, as room was needed for other planes to land.

At 5:30 A.M., North Vietnamese Tank Brigade 203 crossed the Newport bridge and began entering the outskirts of Saigon. The airlift had ceased by order of the president and in Washington Secretary Kissinger announced during a press conference that the evacuation had been successfully completed. U.S. involvement in Vietnam had ended. The war "ended just as it had been conducted by the Americans, with an often total disregard for the lives at stake."[8] An aide, however, whispered to him that a few Marines were still stranded in the U.S. compound in Saigon. Order was given to get them out immediately. At the same time a small crowd of Vietnamese continued to wait in the courtyard. They were quiet and subdued, knowing well they would be left behind. Stoic resignation had replaced the disorganized attempt to get into the compound. A last request to send out six more choppers to rescue them failed. A helicopter dropped on the embassy roof at 7:30 A.M. to pick up the last Marines. They slammed the huge oaken doors shut, barred them, ran into the stairwells and up into the plane. The last chopper took off at 7:53 A.M. April 30, 1975.

Seven thousand people (1,400 Americans, 5,600 Vietnamese and 85 third-country nationals) were thus airlifted on April 29 and 30 from the rooftop of the American Embassy in Saigon. A fleet of 70 choppers and 865 Marines flew over 630 sorties during those last 18 critical hours. This was probably the most intensive and short-term airlift out of a small helipad in the Vietnam War history. This number, however, was small in comparison with that of past and present employees of the embassy and their families — over 90,000, according to the State Department. There were also 400 members of the Special Police Branch, 400 working members of the CIA, scores of clerks and radio operators, agents, translators, waitresses and maids, and especially the 30,000 counter-terrorist agents trained with the Phoenix Program.[9] Thus only a fraction of this high-risk group had been evacuated.

Those who did not have American connection or were unable to get into the U.S. Embassy ran around to find a way to get out of the anarchic city. A small group of unhappy people vented their anger and began vandalizing and looting the stores. They also set fire to houses. Groups of people were able to sneak into the port of Saigon and get onto the few remaining ships that were still anchored. Places were limited, however. They fought against other escapees and forced their way through sheer strength and violence onto the boats. Others swore and yelled. The few lucky ones stepped onto the deck. The last boat finally cast off as the first North Vietnamese tank rolled through the gates of the port. Shouting and gunfire were heard. The enemy tank stopped, positioned itself and fired two shots that luckily missed the boat. The escapees, their heads bent, heard the whooshing sound going by and breathed big sighs of relief. The boat steamed along the Mekong River, as the escapees continued to fear for their lives during the length of this trip. They knew any shot fired from the riverbanks could hit the ship and put an end to their escape.

By the time Saigon surrendered on April 30, a whole armada of supply and patrol boats, landing craft, fishing boats, trawlers, tugs, ferries, and anything that could float headed toward the sea. The sea, which was usually empty, became crowded and filled with floating vessels that day. One hundred small boats gathered around the sealift freighter *Greenville Victory*. The captain decided to take no more than 6,000 people in the bay of Vung Tau. In the beginning, ladders were used to bring refugees aboard, then cargo nets. As many as 20 people were hoisted inside each net at a time with many more hanging from the outside. As the limit was reached, the ship took off followed by a flotilla of boats. Twenty-five minutes later, it was allowed to pick up 2,000 extra refugees. The limit was raised to 10,000. But people kept coming. The captain asked for assistance but no help was given. There was no room on board but 60 boats were still decked alongside the freighter asking to be picked up. The *Boo Heung Pioneer* and tug *Chito Maru* picked up about 6,000 in the port of Saigon from several bus convoys organized by junior embassy officers.[10] Overall, U.S. ships along the coastline picked up a total of 60,000 refugees in the following days. Another 20,000 Vietnamese headed to the Philippines aboard a flotilla of 32 ships belonging to the South Vietnamese Navy. A total of 125,000 Vietnamese left Vietnam during the last weeks of the war and most of them were relocated to the U.S.[11] At most 60 to 80,000 of Saigon's three million citizens escaped from the city itself and the rest came from the ports the on coastline and from Phu Quoc Island. Among the evacuees were the inhabitants of one whole fishing village. During this phase of the evacuation, the majority of heads of household who had escaped had lived in North Vietnam prior to 1954[12]: they were ready to leave Vietnam as soon as the communists arrived at the outskirts of the city. Some startled fishermen working on their daily routine at sea were told to "come aboard," only to realize that the next land they saw was Guam.

The majority of Saigonese (98 percent), however, were trapped inside the city because of local imposition of curfews, government refusal to grant exit visas, and scarcity of modes of evacuation. They had nowhere to go. The city was encircled and they would eventually form the bulk of the second-wave migration. What was difficult to understand was that many low-risk people were able to get out, leaving genuinely endangered people behind. Only about 55,000 of the evacuees fit the parole guidelines. The remaining people were fishermen, farmers, soldiers, housemaids, small merchants, bargirls and others who could not be characterized as high risks. The presence of the Seventh Fleet off the coast of South Vietnam had been helpful in saving tens of thousands of people who otherwise would end up sailing by themselves to foreign soil on rickety boats.

Around 10 A.M. on April 30, a column of NVA T-34 tanks strolled down Thong Nhut Avenue and passed by the American Embassy where a few hours earlier the last helicopter took off from its roof. The NVA did not seem to know or care about the embassy. They headed straight down the road in the direction of the Presidential Palace and passed by the Saigon Catholic Cathedral. Military parades used to drive through Thong Nhut Avenue. What was unusual about this military column was that the tanks were T-34 with a red flag and a yellow star in its center. The uniformed soldiers wore pith helmets and looked small and young. This was definitely not the normal parade group: the enemy had arrived in the heart of town. The first T-34 slammed into one of the wrought-iron gates closing on sandstone pillars. The gates shook but did not give way. The tank backed up, roared forward and slammed again on the gates, which came off their hinges. Half an hour later, Duong van Minh and his staff surrendered to the leading NVA commander.

The North Vietnamese who conquered the city seemed to be "so immune to normal human doubt and despair and want and fear" that many Westerners found them chilling — on the border of inhumanity. Liberation to them meant different things, but "never the freedom of the individual consciousness to doubt, question, dissent, argue, or search for a private path to truth.... To their ungentle hands, Vietnam's future was now committed."[13]

Causes

Luu Van Vong's above verse summarized the morbid fear the southerners experienced towards the communists. As soon as they saw the red flag propping up, they ran away to avoid being caught by the enemy. They knew too well the communists were heartless and ruthless. Strongly anticommunist, they did not want to surrender to the enemy after having fought against them for almost two long and painful decades. Surrender meant putting an end to their lives and dreams. It meant reneging on the sacrifices made by so many of their friends and relatives who had fallen to defend the freedom of South Vietnam. It meant loss of pride and faith in freedom itself. Nothing would illustrate this fierce feeling better than the action of this father who "poisoned his entire family, shot everyone, then blew his own brains out" the day after the fall of Saigon.[14] He would rather die than live under enemy control. And there were many such examples throughout South Vietnam at that time.[15]

These staunch anticommunists also included the Catholics and northerners who came south after 1954. Their main reasons for moving south were their dislike of communists and their willingness to continue their fight against the regime. They knew well how the communists behave back in the '50s and therefore did not trust them. The nagging suspicion prevailed over the decades and led them to attempt to escape before the communists showed up in town.[16] Many of the escapees were high-level officials who had worked closely with the U.S. in the past and were at high risk for reprisal. The future proved them right, for those who were not able to get out of town in time would eventually be sent to reeducation camps for a long time. Others felt they were simply unable to live under communist regime, having witnessed too many atrocities committed by the communists.

Many southerners did not want to see the communists come in and steal their lands. Their forefathers came to this southern region three centuries earlier, worked aggressively on the land, and transformed it into lush paddy fields. For them, the communists had nothing to do with and in the South. Their action was pure aggression, a land grab. However, they were somewhat morally divided — one group included staunch communists while other people were rather easy going and lenient, as most southerners were. They thought the North Vietnamese were also countrymen and therefore would not cause them any harm. Although they were afraid, they did not think about leaving their native country yet. This might explain why a higher percentage of northerners than southerners escaped during this first wave.

These ambiguous feelings were later confirmed as the communists strengthened their hold on the South. Many southerners had their personal reasons for not wanting to move abroad. They did not known any foreign language, they were middle age people and did not want to uproot themselves, retrain and relearn everything before getting a job. They did not know whether they could even get a job in a new country. Vietnam had been their homeland for so long they did not want to abandon it. Since all their relatives lived in the country, they would miss them badly if they had to migrate to another nation. They also did not know what life would be in the new land; therefore, they thought it would be a big gamble to escape.

Vietnamese were brought up to remain with their families and to work and live as a unit, as multiple generations sometimes stayed under the same roof in the same building. Since they shared the same vision and supported each other during difficult times, they did not feel it necessary to go abroad. To be willing to escape, they had to suppress all these basic instincts that kept them anchored to their ancestral land. They also needed to have a sense of adventure and a will to uproot themselves. Like other people, they were attached to their homes, families, environment, lands, and friends. Although they might not have the best house in their neighborhood, it was theirs: they built it, earned it or bought it with their sweat and work. When forced to leave everything behind on the spurt of the moment, they were stunned and afraid to leave. They could not understand the reason behind the move. They debated and argued among themselves and found decisions were hard to make. In the end, pushed by events that worsened with time, they escaped with nothing except a few pairs of pants or shirts.

Escape

The escape could start in Saigon itself or in one of the many sea or river ports which housed boats. When the Saigon government surrendered, boat owners and common people alike rushed to the docks to get onto one of the few remaining boats. They loaded them with whatever they could put their hands on while others just jumped onto the boats carrying nothing except a few shirts or pants. They did not know where they were going. They were not prepared for any foreign trip and did not have the means to survive or even to communicate in these countries. All they cared about was getting out of the country.

On Phu Quoc Island about 60 miles off of the southwestern coast of Vietnam stood a large refugee camp. About 40,000 refugees from central Vietnam who had escaped the advancing communists had been relocated there since early April. Local fishermen and inhabitants dealing with fishing-related businesses populated the island along with a moderate-sized navy compound. The island was calm and quiet, although islanders had discussed their options during their daily coffee breaks. They would stay put as long as the Saigon government remained in power. If it fell, they could always head to their boats and seek asylum in neighboring countries that were a few days' travel by sea.

As soon as Saigon announced its surrender around noon local time on April 30, swarms of people rushed to the shoreline and scrambled onto the two to three dozens of fishing boats that lay lazily on the beach. They stashed their meager belongings, asked their family members to jump in, and headed to the sea. In the compound, navy personnel also loaded their families onto their patrol boats and took off. Swarms of helicopters from nearby provinces loaded with airmen and their families negotiated their slow descent onto the local runway. There had never been so many airplanes flying above the island in a single day; it looked like an air show was about to begin. All the parking areas were soon filled with airplanes. The next helicopter had to land and park on the beach, causing sand to swirl around like sandstorm. Phu Quoc Island became the staging area for present and future escapes. Remote and isolated, the island gave its people a few days of respite before the communists could come from land to take over the place.

Each boat loaded to the maximum with untold number of passengers (no one wanted to be left behind) headed to the seas toward the unknown. Everyone was quiet and no one was talking. The only noise came from the roaring engine. Their eyes were locked into the vast horizon and the blue sea. They did not know what this trip, which they thought was crucial, entailed and where they were going. This was their first trip abroad. They were all serious for they did not know what would happen next. They just left everything in the hands of *thuong de* (God).

Luckily for the Phu Quoc islanders, they did not have to sail very far before reaching an American ship. They were totally surprised to encounter a ship ready to pick them up. "Fate is on our side," murmured a few. Unbeknownst to them, the United States government had ordered a few ships to anchor outside Vietnamese territorial waters and to pick up any escapee: operation New Life had begun. The escapees steered their boats toward the big ship and as they came closer, they saw men and women slowly climbing the flimsy ladders to take refuge in the hold of the cargo boat. As the waves bounced against the boat, the ladders started swinging back and forth, scaring the uneasy and unprepared climbers who reacted swiftly by gripping the ropes harder. The islanders who had not climbed any ladder in years were asked that day to swing on ropy ladders as they had in their younger years. Although the exercise was scary, they managed to complete it because this was the only way they could get out of the country. From below, one could see the same saddening picture of tired and scared people climbing the stairs that either led to the helicopter pad of the U.S. Embassy in Saigon or to the decks of the boats moored in the middle of the seas in an attempt to get out of the country. The transfer was lengthy, as islanders climbed up the ladder one at a time.

Once the refugees were picked up and settled either in the hold or the deck, the boat steamed in the northeastern direction. That direction could only mean Saigon. That night many refugees could not sleep fearing the ship captain would turn them back to the new government in Saigon. The fear was real, because they thought they would be punished for having tried to escape the country. By the morning they indeed had arrived at Vung Tau at the mouth of the Saigon River. They were relieved to see the armada of the U.S. Navy Seventh Fleet that had been assembled to pick up anyone willing to escape Vietnam. They knew they would not be dropped back to land. They only felt safer when the boats sailed eastward, most likely towards Subic Bay base in the Philippines, to unload their passengers. A big smile lit up their faces. The large number of refugees arriving from everywhere soon overwhelmed the handling capacities of Subic Bay base. The remaining ships were then advised to steam straight to Guam with their human cargo.

Aboard the boats, the refugees were fed twice a day. Idle and bored, they lay in the cargo bay or on the deck usually on a piece of cardboard or whatever sheet or towels they had been able to bring with them. They braved the hot weather during daytime and got to look at the starry sky at night. They tried to imagine what their relatives had been doing under the new regime. They felt guilty for having abandoned them to their fate during this unexpected flight: many who were soldiers living hundred of miles away from home when Saigon surrendered simply did not have the chance to swing back home and pick up their relatives. They were all orphans without a homeland — abandoned and rejected by their own country. Many became real orphans, as they left without or lost their parents or families during the escape.

The trip took about a week, during which they spent time looking at the ocean or the sky day and night. Occasionally they would see a few passing ships or some dolphins frolicking in the water. They were lucky not to encounter any high winds or storms during the trip, otherwise they would have spent a few miserable days in their wet clothes. Many refugees just had the clothes they wore. They finally landed on the island of Guam in the middle of the night. From afar, the lights of the island cast such a bright whitish glow on the horizon that even a child could tell land was in sight. They stood up as it was about past midnight and gazed at the light that came closer with time. The ship finally docked and everything on the pier was bright, quiet, and clean. They were screened and filled out forms before being dropped to a tent they shared with three to five other complete strangers. By that time, it was almost dawn. It was the first time in more than a week they slept on firm land. They just dropped on their cots and slept soundly until noon.

The refugees lined up to get their daily food rations and to apply for relocation. The first thing they did on American soil was to learn to wait in line. They had rarely done this in Vietnam, where people would just conglomerate around a vendor or distributor. Staying in line was not something the Vietnamese could do naturally. After meal times, they wandered aimlessly around the camp not knowing what to do and what the future had in store for them. There was the beach with its amenities, but no one was in the mood to take a sunbath at that time. There were so many things torturing their minds: family, future, job, money, homeland, language barrier, and so on. The worst thing was the agonizing lack of news from their relatives from home. Reports coming out of Vietnam were sketchy at best. No one knew what happened to Vietnam and to those who were left behind. Then there was the nagging homesickness that tortured them day and night. This was the first trip abroad for almost all of them and they were very much attached to their native land. A few thousand people decided they had had enough of freedom and wanted to return home to reunite with their families.

Now that they felt more stable with a roof over their heads and a cot to sleep on, although it was temporary, they tried to analyze the deep sadness that followed them everywhere and clung to them day and night. Many just felt sad for having lost their homeland; they still did not understand how they could lose the war in such a short time. They fought valiantly for 20 years and then lost it in just a few months. They were stunned, too stunned to share their deep feelings, their anger, and resentment. They could not imagine that scenario and could not believe the war had ended, and ended in infamy and defeat for them. That was just impossible and too painful to bear. They had to live with that pain and that feeling of failure in their minds the rest of their lives. They also asked themselves why the Americans did not help them in their moment of crisis. The U.S. could have at least stemmed the red tide. Then they felt bad for having left their comrades and friends behind. But what could they have done? The war was over and they just ran away to avoid being caught by the communists. All these thoughts twirled in their minds like clothes in a washing machine. And the same questions and thoughts came up again and again. Enough to give them a bad headache. There were too many questions that remained unanswered. And there probably will be no final answer, ever...

At the Guam camp, as men and women shared the few bathrooms, women were so shy they would only go at night. During daytime, they would water themselves with a can as in the market. Rice was cooked in a mushy way minced with fish. The smell was so horrible that even hungry children would stay away from it. The Vietnamese liked their rice fluffy. If any refugee had money, there were "meals on wheels," carts from which they could buy sandwiches, ice cream and hot dogs.[17]

The island of Guam was 32 miles long and four to 12 miles wide with a population of 80,000 people. It ended up housing more than 60,000 refugees at one time, almost doubling the size of its population overnight. There was a sketch in the local newspaper at that time depicting the island slowly sinking into the ocean under the weight of its people and the refugees. Luckily no such a thing happened. On the other hand, the camp was simply unable to sanitarily dispose of three million gallons of sewage generated daily and human fecal material was found floating in the ocean and washing up the beaches. Swimming was forbidden. The refugees also brought with them an infection caused by the Dengue virus and transported by mosquitoes. Many children as a result died of hemorrhagic fever, although local physicians and the CDC worked hard to prevent the spread of the disease by controlling the breeding ground of mosquitoes.[18] The authorities also worked hard to spray the insects to prevent the spread of the disease.

Refugees were then screened by the volags (voluntary agencies). The goal of these organizations was to match the refugee with a resettlement country. In the beginning, there were no criteria for resettlement and refugees were dispatched on a first come, first served basis. Then each country set up its own criteria: "Norway took the heart patients. New Zealand took single women, Holland took the blind, Switzerland took the severely handicapped, France took the criminals and psychiatric cases, and the United States took all the farmers and fishermen."[19] In that moment of despair, many did not know what resettlement meant or could afford to be choosy. Many took whatever was offered to them and as long as they could live under a roof with four walls around them, they would be happy. In their simple minds, one country would be equivalent to another, as they had never been abroad before and therefore could not made an informed decision.

Thus each refugee was sent from Guam to his or her host country. It would be a long flight to the new country as one went to Canada, the other to Europe, the third to Australia and so on. The refugees were divided again, this time for good, as they were scattered all over the world. Ho Chi Minh probably did not realize that a byproduct of his conquest of Vietnam was to scatter Vietnamese genes all around the world. This was in essence the principle of international communism. A young woman refugee was sent to a French psychiatric hospital for being a little wild. She realized that "being in that asylum in Correze, France was the same thing as being dead and buried."[20] She struggled hard to follow orders and was treated with sympathy by the psychiatrist. She in the end was allowed to leave the asylum and to return to civilian life.

The Camps

Four reception centers were opened in the U.S.: Camp Pendleton in California, Fort Indiantown Gap in Pennsylvania, Eglin Air Force Base in Florida, and Fort Chaffee in Arkansas. The centers were transition areas where refugees were processed into immigrants. Camp Pendleton was the first to fill up, as the majority of refugees made California their first choice because of the state's climate. Refugees who came later were simply directed to the remaining camps.

In the camps, all the refugees were equal in status: they instantaneously and spontaneously lost all their titles when they climbed aboard the ships. They began anew in life on the same starting line. This was a humbling experience, the first of many, for those who had occupied a position of power in the past. The fact that everyone had to sleep on similar bunk bed, go to the bathroom and stay in line for his meals within a certain time period took away the power or status of a person. It rendered that person similar to the guy next door. There were no longer professors or housewives, bosses or employees, only refugees. The other eye opener for the refugee was that he was dispossessed of any material wealth. He no longer had any house, car, motorbike, suit or fancy outfit, or money. He was stripped down to the bare minimum. He had lost everything. And for the first time in his life, he realized he could survive without all these material things. This situation brought him back to his own nature and self, something that would stay with him and that no one could take away.

At the Fort Chaffee camp, a general was recognized as he was going about his business. During the war, he was known to accept bribes from people who did not want to get enlisted or be transferred to the battlefield. A mob of women came up to him and beat him on the head with their wooden shoes. "Because of you my son, my husband, my brother was left behind," they shouted angrily. All the pent-up anger had to be released one way or another. They beat him up until the MPs arrived and pulled him out to safety. This incident probably would not have happened in Vietnam, but familiarity and closeness in the camps bred contempt.

The refugees learned fast which food was good. Word spread around immediately when beef was served, but they would stay away a while longer on canned fish day. For those who came penniless, any food was good: it was a blessing compared to the days when they ran for their lives and did not have anything to eat or drink. Those who had money could afford to buy sandwiches, candy bars, and ice cream from a small snack bar. They all enjoyed free outdoor movies. When time came to leave the fort, they had made friends with other people and began to like the fort's lifestyle.[21] This was a sheltered and pampered life, as they did not have to do anything to get their meals. Everything was provided. The only worries in their minds concerned their future: getting sponsored and getting employed. The rest would come after these problems were resolved.

Many refugees were flown from different places to Harrisburg International Airport and then driven to Fort Indiantown Gap on small roads.

Along the way locals cheerfully waved at them. This was the first time during their ordeal friendly people had greeted them. This simple and spontaneous welcome lifted the hearts of the tired refugees. The flight from Guam to Harrisburg through Honolulu was a long and tiring one. Overall this had been a long trip from Vietnam all the way to the U.S. The change in scenery and social life had been astounding. Everything was new to the refugees — the long boat trip, the clean and well-organized camps in Guam, and the large airplanes that took them to the mainland, the airports and the hills and meadows of middle Pennsylvania. The transition from one world to another lasted less than a week for some and more than a year for others. Everything was so peaceful, nice and beautiful in the U.S., not like Vietnam, where the sounds of gunfire, rockets, and airplanes could be heard at every moment of the day and where disfigured bodies of the soldiers were taken to the morgue every day.

A block of nicely arranged barracks in the camp, the limits of which had been delineated by a yellow police tape, had been reserved for the refugees. One could easily walk out of the camp but no one did because no one knew where to go. There was no barbed wire or fence either. This was so unlike Vietnam, where everything had to be fenced in to prevent the Viet Cong from sneaking into vital areas or sandbagged to protect the people from mortars. The refugees entered a huge mess hall converted into a reception center where hundreds of others were gathered. They sat and chatted nonchalantly while waiting for the officers to come and explain the regulations. They were then assigned to a barrack and led to their dwellings. In front of the reception center, a few ladies from the Salvation Army handed out snacks and drinks, as they knew that by midnight everyone was hungry. These ladies with their lovely smiles put some warmth in the refugees' hearts. They could not believe that some ladies would actually wait for them until midnight to hand out snacks and drinks. It was a cool, misty, early June night and the refugees never forgot the ladies' smiles. They then went to bed all dressed up, for they were too tired from the long transatlantic flight to get changed.

The daily routine started with breakfast at the mess, after which everyone was free to run around, look for friends, or visit other buildings. This was the time to exchange information about the whereabouts of friends and relatives and to congratulate a refugee for having received good news. Nothing was more heartwarming than to share the news with a family or person who had found a sponsor. These people were happy and excited about being able to get out of the camp for the first time in many months and to feel free again. There was nothing like the freedom of doing the things one wanted at the time of one's convenience. Then came time for lunch and refugees had to line up again to get their meals. Some more free time followed lunch, then came time for supper. The routine set in and was interrupted only by notifications of resettlement by the volags.

The average length of stay in the camps was several months and all first-wave refugees were released by December 1975.[22] There were nine volags and they did a remarkable job in resettling the refugees in a short time. Some refugees were luckier than others; a few remained in the camps a few days to weeks before finding their sponsors, while others languished a little longer. Some had superb sponsors while others were not that lucky. Overall they were happy to find any sponsor who would get them out of the camp. Volags were given grants of $500 for each refugee resettled and by December 1975, when the last refugee had been resettled, a total of $36 million had been spent on the project.[23]

When the refugees were released from one of the four U.S. camps between 1975 and 1980, the U.S. resettlement program planned to disperse them equally throughout all the states. The goal was not to assimilate the refugees but to limit the cost of social health and educational services incurred by counties with large numbers of refugees. From the refugees' point of view, up to that point their main goal was to gain resettlement while living in temporary makeshifts or tents. Now that they became a little more stable by holding temporary jobs and living in a community, they began their "grieving phase." And there was no better way to grieve than with someone who would understand them. They, therefore, started moving around (secondary migration) looking for reunification with kin, friends, and compatriots in states with warmer climates and better social welfare programs. Feeling lonely and isolated within the assigned communities no matter how friendly they were, unable to speak the local language and to find the right job or the right type of food and spices they were used to, badly homesick, depressed for having lost the war and a homeland, and separated from friends and kin, they tended to congregate around certain areas where they could find compatriots in order to vent their emotions and frustrations. And there were a lot of emotions to vent at the French, the Americans, the generals, the leaders, the system, their wretched lives, and at themselves too.

The five states with the largest refugee populations in 1975 were California (20.9 percent), Texas (7 percent), Pennsylvania (5.5 percent), Florida (4.1 percent), and Washington (3.2 percent). By 1990, Florida and Pennsylvania had been replaced by Minnesota and New York. The new list included California (39.6 percent), Texas (7.5 percent), Washington (4.7 percent), Minnesota (3.7 percent), and New York (3.6 percent). Almost half of the refugee population lived in California and Texas, although a good number of them still lived in New York, Washington, and Minnesota. California's share of the refugee population increased from 21.6 percent in 1975 to 31 percent in 1979 after secondary migration.[24] Most of the refugees gathered around Little Saigon, an enclave bordered by Westminster and Bolsa avenues in Orange County, California. They slowly spread to adjacent streets.

The first and second wave individuals had ties with the Americans. They had fought along with the Americans who did not persevere to help them win freedom for their country. Some felt that assisting them with relocation was not only a moral obligation, but also a means of dealing with the national guilt.[25]

Although the first wave refugees were fortunate enough to have everything set up for them when they got out of Vietnam, from boats to the camps in Guam and the U.S. and to the volags, life in the new country was not simple or easy. Multiple hardships awaited them around the corner. They faced an uphill battle to retrain themselves, learn the language, make a living, and improve their future.

7

THE POST-1975 WAVES

Since the 1975 American evacuation, the flow of refugees had filtered down to a trickle: 377 in 1975 and 5,619 in 1976; but "by 1977 it became a flow — 21,276; by the end of 1978, a flood — 106,489; and in the first months of 1979, a torrent — 106,604."[1] The numbers spoke volumes about the attitude of the Vietnamese. In the beginning they were too "stunned" by the sudden communists' conquest to react. They opted for a "wait and see" approach toward the new government: if it were compassionate and lenient, they would stay and rebuild the country. On the other hand, if it was unacceptable politically and socially, they could always escape. The spiraling downturn of the political and social events soon pushed them to find ways to get out of the country.

Economic Factors

The following time life analysis evaluated the political and economic factors behind the various emigration waves, taking into account the social and ethnic origin of the emigrants.[2]

May 1975 to March 1978. The imposition of socialism, the establishment of the NEZ (New Economic Zones), and the incarceration of former officials and soldiers of the Republic of Vietnam impoverished the southern society and put a chill on the minds of the locals. Since May 1975, officials and ARVN soldiers were sent to reeducation camps where they were forced to do hard labor under a starvation diet. Some were executed, others were tortured, and many were confined to tiger cages or conex at the slightest infraction. They also underwent thought reform, the goal of which was to transform them into socialists.[3] Their wives became the breadwinners of the families by selling food, vegetables, and anything they could sell at the market. Many civilians were sent to the NEZ where they earned their living by becoming farmers in arid and deserted areas. Many did not survive the change and escaped back to their original locations.

People in general were unhappy with the Hanoi regime because of its poor economic and political conditions. A wife usually waited for her husband's return from reeducation camp before contemplating an escape. Departures, which were minimal in 1975 and 1976 as southerners tried to adapt to the new regime, slowly picked up in 1977 as a sign of growing dissatisfaction.

April to December 1978. Facing growing economic difficulties, the government initiated a program of agricultural collectivization in the Mekong delta. The experiment failed and was abandoned. Heavy taxes, arbitrary arrests, relentless surveillance, political and ethnic oppression, and continuing mobilization into the armed forces created widespread discontent. The number of Vietnamese boat people increased and 160,000 ethnic Chinese escaped overland to China (this number was not counted in data from the United Nations High Commission on Refugees [UNHCR]).

January to December 1979. Vietnam was at war with Cambodia and China. The mobilization of a million men, the expulsion of ethnic Chinese, and the freeing of many former ARVN officers from reeducation camps caused an exodus of boat people. Hanoi fulfilled its hegemonic goals by invading Cambodia. The war in the end cost the country 60,000 lives and drained all its economic resources. It put the country further in debt, from which it would not recover. Mobilization especially in the south caused a lot of local dissatisfaction, for no one wanted to serve in the North Vietnamese army.

January 1980 to December 1981. Other Asian countries forced Hanoi to control illegal departures. A moratorium on leaving the country temporarily cut down the number of departures, which slowly picked up again as economic conditions worsened. The push back policy (refugee boats were not allowed to land but were pushed back to the sea), which was initiated in 1979, was temporarily placed on hold.

January 1982 to December 1987. After a slowing of departures, a new wave began in 1986 and involved mainly unaccompanied minors. Under very difficult economic conditions, parents sent their children away by themselves in order to establish a beachhead in another country. It was expected that the children would in turn sponsor their parents whenever they became successful. This, however, put a lot of pressure on these youngsters who were still immature, uneducated and needed a lot of parental support before facing the world by themselves. If they were unsuccessful, they would forever blame themselves for having failed their parents. On the other hand, if this were the true goal of these parents, the adults probably had faced agonizing and conflicting debates about sending their children away. And they must have been very desperate to do such a thing, for parents usually did not have the heart to separate from their children, let alone send them away on their own. A lot of these children were later repatriated as unaccompanied minors.

Although there were multiple subsequent waves, they could be divided into two main groups: 1975–79 and 1980–86. The multiplicity of the waves could only attest to the fact that the majority of the escapes were spontaneous in nature and individually funded with local governmental approval. Without local agreement obtained through bribes, all these escapes would simply not have been possible.

One has to admire the persistence and the ingenuity of the southerners who, despite difficult odds, persisted in looking for ways to get out of the country. Finding the money to make the trip was not easy, and that was just the beginning. They had to look for a reputable dealer, bribe the bo doi, make the commitment to leave everything behind and risk their lives in that trip. And they kept coming, wave after wave of refugees. For those who chose freedom, it was worth more than death.

Second Wave: 1975–1979

Case 1: Phong took three months to assemble a drum-raft with his children. This job required a lot of logistical work and technical experience, for these drums were not easy to come by. If the bo doi caught the Phong working on this raft, they would immediately jail him and his family. The raft consisted of two rows each of 18 empty oil drums lashed together with metal chains and wooden rods. A floor and cabin were built over the drum. He added two small engines that gave the craft a speed of six miles per hour. He left Vietnam in September 1975 with 13 other family members. A Japanese freighter picked them up four days later 175 miles off the coast.[4] This craft turned out to be the most ingenious floating device ever built out of scrap by the escapees.

Case 2: Due to last minute changes in the schedule, Orchid, her mother and six other siblings could not connect with her father on April 30, 1975. As a result they remained stuck in Saigon. Two other siblings were able to sneak out of the country with their aunt. Her father, on the other hand, became anxious when he did not see his family coming while the communists closed in on the naval compound. Unwilling to leave them behind, he pulled his gun out and took his own life. Unable to locate her father, the 20-year-old Orchid began assuming the leadership of the family, which soon lost its entire savings and a construction company. The new government closed all the banks and shut down all private companies. Essentially broke and seeing her mother struggle under difficult conditions, Orchid took on odd jobs to bring home some needed cash. She woke up every morning at 4 A.M. to travel to the nearby province to get sugar and other commodities that were rationed. She bought 40 kilos of sugar along with other goods, smuggled the merchandise back to Saigon in overcrowded buses and sold them to wholesale dealers. The profits were turned over to her mother to help raise her siblings. She then went to college in the afternoon and at night made extra money by weaving rattan chairs.

Realizing one day that living under these difficult conditions could only lead to a dead end, she decided to escape — against the advice of her mother. On multiple occasions, she went to Mui Ne, a fishing village one hundred miles north of Saigon, to look for ways to escape. The trip by railroad car was hazardous due to lack of security. Bands of thieves roamed the cars, beat the passengers up and stole their money and merchandise. Each trip became a nightmare but Orchid forged ahead because she badly wanted to get out of the country. Many attempts ended in failure along with loss of precious savings. But she never relented. She then fell in love and married into a rich family. She soon enrolled 30 people who paid 10 ounces of gold each to escape. They met in Mui Ne in preparation for the escape, but in the end the police caught them all, except Orchid and her husband and brother-in-law. The boat owner, his extended family, friends and three Saigonese jumped into the boat and escaped, closely pursued by the police. They luckily survived a violent storm that turned their boat around like a yoyo. They sailed for 21 long days, as no foreign ship would pick them up. They survived on one meal and a few cups of water a day and subsisted on whatever compassionate ship captains were willing to throw overboard. They almost died of thirst and hunger on many occasions. They followed the Thai coastline but were waved away. No one wanted to accept them and let them land. They were chased out of one port after another, but finally were greeted by some islanders who took them in. They were then transported to a refugee camp in Djakarta where her brother, who was able to escape to the United States in 1975, sponsored her to the U.S.

Case 3: Trinh Do, his three siblings and his mother, who used to live in a military complex in Vung Tau, had to vacate the government building after the fall of Saigon to make room for the incoming northern communists. The family of five squeezed into a filthy outhouse that consisted of a bedroom and a storage room. His father was sent to a reeducation camp. Without any income, his mother resorted to selling vegetables at the market for a living. Do's job at the age of 11 was to baby sit his brothers, haul water, wash clothes, find firewood for fuel and cook for the whole family.[5] He, of course, burned many meals before producing something edible. The worst job was to haul water from a well a hundred yards away. The load turned out to be too heavy for an 11-year-old boy's shoulders. During his spare time, he planted vegetables in the family's small plot to get additional food. For three years he went to the local school where he studied under teachers who were more versed in politics than academic knowledge. Because of his father's anti-revolutionary background, he was not allowed to move from middle to high school. He was dismissed from school for refusing to finger point the students who during a prank smeared feces in the classrooms and on Ho's pictures. His mother used the occasion to send him abroad with his cousins from Can Tho. He never saw his parents again; they escaped last and died at sea. Being an orphan, he felt like a man at age 14.

Southerners who missed the April-May 1975 escape looked for ways to get out of the country at all costs. Their decision to emigrate dated back to the fall of Saigon. If they had money, they would buy a good, functioning boat and start practicing with it. If not, they could build their own boat out of scrap like Phong's. Those linked to the Saigon government continued to escape at a slow but steady pace. The pace did not really pick up until mid–1978, when storms and floods wreaked havoc on the harvests, causing a severe economic downturn and an increase in food rationing. These natural disasters occurred at a time when Hanoi decided to get rid of the Chinese in preparation for a war with mainland China.

In addition, mobilization for the war antagonized many youngsters and their families in the south. They simply did not want to serve on the same side as their oppressors. Even after they enrolled into the army, they were discriminated against because of their southern origin. One southern recruit performed admirably during the war in Cambodia and was even recommended by his northern superiors for further training at a northern military school with a sure and certain promotion. At the school, he was evaluated and found to be a southerner. He was sent back to Cambodia to fight as a grunt and his promotion was gone. During the same period, southerners who came back from the NEZ or the reeducation camps noticed their children were shunned and not allowed to pursue higher education. They felt marginalized, watched by the police, and were unable to get employment. Frustrated, they too decided to leave the country. The majority of this group came from the south. They were in general not as well educated as the first wave refugees and had less exposure to the West. They were later confronted with serious problems of adjustment in their new countries. More than half of the people in this second-wave group were younger than 20 years of age.

Northerners, mostly ethnic Chinese, used the northeast route to Hong Kong. They used slow sailing and antiquated junks or sailboats to hug the Chinese coastline during their journey, which was pretty safe. There were no pirates to worry about. They could always sail back to the shore to hide from any storm. As they used ancient sailboats, their trips took about five to six weeks. Southerners, on the other hand, mainly used the southwestern route to Malaysia or Indonesia and tried to avoid Thailand and its cruel pirates. They traveled by motorized boats that reached up to seven knots an hour and their trips took only five to seven days unless they got lost, had engine failure, or encountered pirates. The difference in sailing techniques between North and South was related to the degree of mechanization between the two parts of the country. The distance from Rach Gia to Trengganu on the western coast of Malaysia was 350 miles, from My Tho in the Mekong delta to Trengganu was 475 miles.

As the years passed by, the refugee tide continued to swell, at times reaching 50,000 a month. In 1978 and 1979, about 300,000 refugees came ashore in various Asian countries. Faced with an inflow of refugees, these countries became reluctant to grant asylum to newcomers for fear they would permanently settle in the area. Malaysia and Thailand, the two leading destinations, began turning away refugee boats. In 1979, 267 boats loaded with 40,000 passengers were turned away. Thai soldiers even forced 40,000 Khmer refugees at gunpoint back into Cambodia along a heavily mined trail.[6] Those who were allowed to stay were placed in camps with marginal facilities to deter newcomers from seeking asylum. In response to the crisis, the United States accepted 167,000 additional refugees between 1979 and 1980.

Another factor came into play in the late '70s. The Chinese living in North Vietnam (also called Hoa) had been crossing the border into China since 1977, but Peking made this an issue only in April 1978. A war of words progressively got worse and the Hoa, afraid of being caught in the middle, began to stampede out of Vietnam. Some contended Hanoi had a policy to drive the Hoa out of the country.[7] In general, Hanoi tried to persuade the Hoa not to leave, because many held important roles in the administration or industry; they were also veterans of the socialist system and respected citizens. Their escape would be felt as a void in the northern society. In the South, the Hoa lived in Cholon, Saigon's Chinatown. They were traditional merchants and good businessmen who did not see any economic role for themselves in the new socialist economy.

Although living and working in Vietnam and intermarrying with Vietnamese, few Hoa adopted Vietnamese citizenship. They felt they were really Chinese and were attached to the Chinese motherland. Only a few volunteered to serve in the communist army. Others, however, having spent all their lives in Vietnam, believed the country was their home.[8]

Mainland China, by closing its border with Vietnam in July 1978, shifted any escape toward the sea route. The month long Chinese invasion of North Vietnam in February–March 1979 brought the animosity into the open. Hanoi started clamping down on the Hoa, forcing them to either escape or be sent to the new economic zones. The Hoa bought boats and sailed toward Hong Kong after March 1979. Although escaping by sea was riskier and more dramatic than going by land, the number of escapees going by sea was much higher.

The Cong An or PSB (Public Security Bureau), which was part of the interior ministry, had been coordinating the Hoa escapes for some time. They screened, approved the applicants wanting to go abroad and gave the final evaluations prior to departure. The mode of transportation was left to middlemen. Through this program, only the Hoa were allowed to exit. Some locals bought false papers and changed their names in order to be eligible.

In the south, the organizer would meet with a PSB agent closest to the departure site to discuss about the number of participants, date of departure, and payment. The fare ranged from eight to 10 taels of gold ($2,400 to $3,000) per adult and four to five taels for children aged five to 15. Children under five years of age traveled for free. Half of the money would be handed over to the PSB about a week prior to the departure date and the other half would cover the cost of the boat, supplies and bribes; the leftover belonged to the organizer. Sometimes the organizer claimed that he needed to bring in additional passengers to recover expenses. The initial number of escapees could therefore double by the time of departure.

The organizer would contact potential escapees and ask them for a down payment. He would go to the state-controlled shipyard to buy or refurbish a boat. He then looked for an experienced boat captain as well as a few assistants. He also had to buy fuel and supplies on the black market.[9] The whole scheme would take a few months to complete. A few days prior to the scheduled date, the escapees were gathered in a waiting area and then ferried out to the boat. Occasionally, the local PSB agents would add a few more passengers they had themselves recruited. They kept the passengers' fare for themselves. If the organizer refused to accept the newcomers, the PSB would hold the ship back. Escapees had to sign a declaration waiving any future claim against the state and donating their properties to the government. All valuables, except two taels of gold per person, were confiscated. Corruption was therefore more prevalent among southern than northern PSB agents, since the Hoa were much richer in the south than in the north. Later, to increase their take, the PSB colluded with Chinese organizers from abroad to use freighters to bring the Hoa out of Vietnam. The higher the number of escapees, the higher the returns.

On September 19, 1978, the 950-ton freighter *Southern Cross* cabled the UNHCR office at Kuala Lumpur, Malaysia, that it had rescued 1,200 refugees at sea and requested permission to drop them at a camp in Mersing. Since the ship was short of food and water, Malaysian authorities had to ferry supplies to the ship. Malaysia, however, refused to let the refugees land unless a country would immediately come forward and accept them. The *Southern Cross* broke the deadlock by steaming toward the deserted Indonesian island of Pengibu and dropping the refugees there. Indonesia decided to grant the refugees asylum and proceeded to relocate them. Although a French newspaper reported that Vietnamese officials had allowed the Hoa to buy their way out of Vietnam with more than half a ton of gold, the incident was soon forgotten.

The following year on May 9, 1979, Ross and three partners were charged with trafficking in Hoa refugees with the complicity of Vietnamese authorities. Ross revealed that on August 25, 1978, the *Southern Cross*, belonging to Seng Bee Shipping company, steamed out of Singapore heading northeast with an empty hold. On this trip, Ross, a Seng Bee employee, was responsible for the cargo and was to keep an eye on a 51-year-old Singaporean Chinese businessman named Tay Kheng Hong. Tay was married to a Singaporean woman. While doing business in Saigon in the early '70s, he took a second wife with whom he had two children. Trapped in Saigon when the communists invaded the country, he was able to bribe himself out in 1978. His goal was to return to Saigon to get his wife and two children out along with $110,000 in cash he had entrusted to her.[10]

A few days later the *Southern Cross* lay anchored about 30 miles from the Vietnamese coast, off the port of Vung Tau. Contact was made and the next morning a Vietnamese pilot came aboard to guide the freighter through the Saigon river estuary. It docked on the Saigon wharf two hours later. A man in a khaki army uniform came aboard and talked with Tay. On September 5, two other visitors came aboard and Tay told Ross they wanted to load the ship with eight hundred passengers. The following day, the ship steamed slowly toward the entrance of the Saigon River. On September 7, three fishing trawlers loaded with refugees arrived and the refugees boarded the ship, which then sailed toward Indonesia. Four sacks of gold were also brought on board. Tay told Ross each passenger paid the Vietnamese government six to eight taels of gold to leave the country and paid one to two taels to Seng Bee Shipping. Several days later not far from Singapore, the gold was transferred to a yacht that was waiting for Tay and Ross. The crew was later paid off and Seng Bee Shipping's share on this trip was $210,000.[11]

On October 15, 1978, the *Hai Hong* steamed out of Singapore on what was supposed to be her last voyage; she was sold to a Hong Kong buyer for scrap. On October 31, the *Hai Hong* appeared out of the blue at an Indonesian port. It was supposed to steam to Hong Kong but changed course because of a storm in the South China Sea. The captain radioed UNCHR office claiming to have picked up 2,500 refugees stranded in the middle of the ocean. The ship was ordered to leave Indonesia but she managed to slip into Port Klang harbor, Malaysia. Malaysian officers noticed that after two weeks at sea, the passengers were dehydrated and listless, children had open sores, and the stench on the boat was horrible. Authorities became suspicious of the captain's story and began investigating. They pieced information together about the *Southern Cross* and the *Hai Hong* and realized the two ships were trafficking in refugees. The captain was later accused of concealing a "planned migration of a sizable number of people from Vietnam." Among the people arrested was Tay Kheng Hong. Tay stated that the *Hai Hong* was supposed to pick up 1,200 refugees in Saigon, but the authorities forced him to take an additional 1,300 passengers. At 10 taels per person, the communists had levied about $4 million for the *Hai Hong* trip.[12] Tay's take was $60,000 while the boat owner pocketed $300,000.

The third ship involved in massive trafficking of refugees was the *Huey Fong*. On December 19, 1978, the ship captain claimed to have rescued boatloads of refugees off the Vietnamese coast. The *Huey Fong* was crammed with 3,318 refugees as she was anchored outside Hong Kong harbor on December 23. The methods involved in this case were similar to those of the *Hai Hong* except that the port of destination was Hong Kong instead of Singapore. The Vietnamese agents involved in this case belonged to the PSB.[13] The other ships involved were the *Ky Lu* (or Sky Luck) and the *Sen ong* (or Seng Cheong).

These cases illustrated the fact that ethnic Chinese inside and outside Vietnam in conjunction with the Hanoi government colluded to export the Hoa people from Vietnam. The Hanoi government handsomely benefited from this approach at the expense of the impoverished and frightened refuge-seekers.

Causes

Deception and Marginalization. Right after April 30, 1975, southerners were ruthlessly dispossessed of their houses, bank accounts, lands, and jobs.[14] All banks were closed and the accounts were frozen overnight. A few days later, the doors opened again but people were only allowed to withdraw a one-time minimum amount of money for their needs. A life of work and savings just flew by like a nightmare. People went from having some cash reserve and material riches to being penniless in less than 24 hours. A few, unable to tolerate the emotional and economic roller coaster, killed themselves. Private businesses, enterprises and drug stores were closed. People's livelihood was gone, as was their self-worth. Freedom was taken away from them and many were jailed. They were no longer citizens in their own state, just mere appendages.[15]

Such was the case of Hoang Cuong. He was a 49-year-old businessman and taught administration at Dalat University in the southern highlands. Since he was too old for military draft and did not get involved in politics before 1975, he felt sure the communists would not bother him. After 1975, however, he had to surrender his share in a radio and television assembly plant in return for a job on the factory floor. He then realized he had no future under the communist system and nothing to work for anymore. While before 1975, he was somewhat influential, after that date, he was just an assemblyman like any other employee. The communists pushed him aside and neither used his skill nor his knowledge. This led him to decide to escape. It took him three times but he finally succeeded. His brother-in-law had to work as a fisherman for six months, selling his catch to a cooperative in exchange for fuel and food. In that capacity, he was able to collect and save 60 gallons of scarce fuel for the escape. When time came, 11 people gathered in a 33 foot boat powered by a 10-horsepower engine and took off from Vinh Binh close to the coastline. They arrived on the northeast coast of Malaysia, were given food and fuel, and advised to continue toward Singapore, where they were towed away and left drifting in international waters. They restarted their engine and came back to Malaysia where they were taken to one of the camps.[16]

Northerners just used their own people in all positions, although they were not technically qualified for these jobs. A physician returning from reeducation camps noticed that Saigon hospitals were no longer run by physicians, but only by northern communist nurses who had been promoted as physicians. Medical disasters were common, as these nurses had not received adequate training. Former southern physicians who used to run the hospitals and deliver healthcare to the population were in the meantime sent to reeducation camps. Disillusioned, southerners came to see the communists as "manipulators and liars interested only in controlling people for their own ends."[17] Not that they did not know that fact beforehand, they simply did not believe northerners were that bad. They felt they belonged to "a despised underclass of highly educated and intelligent men with no prospects for a productive future in Vietnam either for themselves or their children."[18] Dispirited, they felt they could not live in that environment and their only choice was to leave the country.

They had been taught to "bear their feelings stoically and alone.... We Vietnamese do not wear our hearts on our sleeves. We carry a lot around inside our heads that we do not tell anyone, even our closest friends and family members."[19] As such, they were seen as haughty and emotionless or people without feelings, but the reality was different. They simply did not want to complain or bother other people with their personal problems. They did not want to show off either; they were more introverts rather than extroverts.

Even schoolchildren were indoctrinated. They were taught communists' mottos and the history of the party and its leader, Ho Chi Minh, instead of the usual math and science curriculum. They then had to learn northern patriotic songs, which they mischievously distorted to show their discontent.

> Last night I dreamed of Uncle Ho
> His beard is long, his hair is so white
> I'm so glad, I kissed his cheek
> Uncle Ho smiled and told me I'm a good kid.
> Uncle Ho smiled and told me I'm a good kid.

The lyrics were changed to:

> Last night I dreamed of Uncle Ho
> His legs were long, he was pedaling a cyclo
> I saw him, I called a different cyclo
> Uncle Ho nodded at me "To reeducation camp you go, son"
> Uncle Ho nodded at me "To reeducation camp you go, son."
> Last night I dreamed of a money bag
> In the money bag, there were four thousand dollars.
> I was so glad, I told Uncle Ho
> Uncle Ho smiled at me, "Give all the money to me."
> Uncle Ho smiled at me, "Give all the money to me."[20]

Oppression. The communists sent more than a million southerners to reeducation camps following their conquest of Saigon. The length of imprisonment ranged from a few days to 22 years.[21] Between three to four hundred thousand people spent more than three years in various camps strewn from the north to the south. Northern camps were worse than southern ones as far as treatment and mortality were concerned. It has been estimated that about two to three hundred thousand people died in the process.

The goal was to "reeducate" them through hard labor and thought reform. The treatment was harsh and inmates were beaten, isolated, confined to conex for weeks or months in a row, and starved. Food was marginal in quantity as well as quality. Inmates felt hungry all the time and had to hunt for extra food in form of rats, snakes, berries, corn, and so on. Camps completely lacked medications, leaving inmates susceptible to infections and diseases that killed them rapidly and in a horrible fashion. They were then harassed, verbally assaulted, told they were worthless, and forced to praise socialism and uncle Ho. This form of physical and moral harassment rendered the inmates bitter and drove them away from the Hanoi regime. The harassment continued even after release from the camps.

When Bich came home after 13 years in reeducation camps, 12 of these years in the north, a policeman would be watching him from across the street every day. Whenever he opened the door, the policeman would be there. And every month a policeman would come down from Hanoi to visit and check on him. Under these circumstances, he could not do anything. Whenever he heard a scratching at the door at night, he would wake up in sweat. He dreamt about the communists taking him back to jail.[22] Such was the psychological effect of reeducation on these former inmates.

The NEZ system became a political means to get rid of unemployed or semi-employed people, traders; those who had capital; officials and personnel of the old regime; relatives of those undergoing reeducation; the Chinese; and skilled machinery workers. The NEZ were primitive and life in these camps was harsh. Newcomers had to build their own homes, dig their own well for water, and cultivate infertile lands without seeds or machinery. The workers were malnourished due to lack of food. Diseases like dysentery and malaria were rampant. There was no medicine: healthcare and sanitation were absent and contributed to the high mortality among infants and the elderly. The NEZ were the civilian equivalent of reeducation camps.[23] The majority of the people escaped from the NEZ on the first occasion and returned to the city.

Any civilian who did not tow the line was sent to the NEZ or a reeducation camp. The idea of a reeducation camp was waved every day in front of the common citizen who felt threatened and no longer dared to challenge the authorities. In the end he could not enjoy his work or his life any longer. He just shriveled down and lived like a snail fearful to make any move. The punishment was harsh: banishment to the unknown for the next untold number of years.

Corruption. Favoritism and bribery were two of the forms of corruption. Those who were connected to the state apparatus could possibly avoid reeducation. Bureaucrats set a high price for the right to move freely and for services rendered by the government, thus strengthening the despotism and control of the state agents.[24] Anything could be bartered with money (or sexual favors, if one is poor), as greasing agents: the right to locate a spouse and see him in a reeducation camp, the right to buy a bus ticket, to own a house, to keep a few belongings, to buy a pound of meat or rice, to send a child to school, to obtain a permit to see relatives in a nearby town and so on. Permits were required everywhere and permits only meant more money to cough up and more misery for the local population.

After Sang had been accepted for immigration to the States under the HO (Humanitarian Operation) program, the communists in the exit department asked him for money to speed up the process, otherwise it would take him forever to leave the country. Depressed and dispirited, he gave them two thousand dollars his parents had sent him from the U.S., the only monies he had left.[25]

A government patrolling boat approached a refugee boat as the escapees reached the high seas in their attempted escape. The communists shot in the air, advising them to return to land. One refugee threw them an ounce of gold, which was immediately returned. The remaining refugees chipped in, giving their bracelets, gold, and cash. The new package, which was thrown onto the communist boat, was rapidly acknowledged, accepted and the communists steamed away, letting the refugees continue their trip.[26]

The Chinese Factor. The Chinese came to Vietnam in the 19th and 20th centuries. They settled mostly in the south (1.4 million) but also in the north (0.3 million). In the north they became farmers, fishermen, coal miners, manual workers but also small merchants. Many were also members of the Vietnamese communist party. In the south, they mainly engaged in business and commerce. They monopolized the rice trade, buying paddy cheaply from poor peasants, milling it, transporting it and selling it overseas. They controlled banks, transportation companies, and insurance agencies.

In order to hasten the socialist revolution and get ready for a clash with the Chinese, the Hanoi government decided to get rid of all the Chinese inside Vietnam. In March 1978, 30,000 youth volunteers conducted a house-to-house search in Cholon, a suburb of Saigon, confiscating dollar bills and gold bars, inventorying property and closing businesses. Prior to the crackdown in Cholon, thousands of Chinese had fled North Vietnam into China by land. When China closed its border with Vietnam on July 1978, more than 160,000 Chinese had left for China.

Third Wave: 1980–1986

Between 1980 and 1984, a quarter million refugees arrived in the camps. The last major crisis was between 1988 and 89, when more than 120,000 refugees came ashore. By this time, a lot of nations were reluctant to accept any newcomer. UNHCR decided to evaluate the demographics of this new wave of refugees and found:

- The majority were unaccompanied minors younger than 15: they were labeled as students (51 percent). UNHCR officials suspected they were sent by their parents to establish a beachhead in a third country. It was also possible that their parents, being oppressed by the Hanoi government, were so poor they could not afford to give them a better future in Vietnam and decided to send them away to try their luck somewhere else.
- Persons closely linked to the previous regime (10 percent). These were high level military, police, and officials of the former Republic of Vietnam. Many had returned from the reeducation camps.
- Fishermen (10 percent) and farmers (9 percent). These people had

large families. They represented 19 percent of the cases and 36 percent of the individuals involved.
- Professionals — doctors, teachers, nurses, architects and administrators — totalled three percent. Non-professionals — bricklayers, mechanics, drivers, carpenters, and so on — made up 16 percent of the cases.

The asylum seekers coming from the Saigon area and southern provinces usually migrated to Malaysia and Indonesia.[27] Those traveling to Hong Kong came from northern and central Vietnam. The group was composed mainly of fishermen (75 percent) and students (25 percent).

Therefore, the composition of asylum seekers after 1980 significantly changed over the years and in the last waves involved essentially students, fishermen, and non-professionals. Many countries considered them as "economic migrants" instead of refugees, therefore not eligible for resettlement. They decided to send many of them back home after screening.

By 1979, the first-wave refugees were well established. They were South Vietnam's skilled and better educated: "37 per cent of household heads had completed high school and 16 per cent had been to college."[28] Almost two-thirds could speak English with some fluency and many were westernized to some extent. By December 1978, 94.9 percent of those included in the labor force had jobs. One third of the workers earned more than $200 or more a week. The dark side of the story was that many worked at levels below their potential: generals were washing dishes and teachers worked in garment factories.

The second-wave refugees tended to be less educated and less skilled than the first ones. Forty percent of the newcomers were ethnic Chinese who were mostly merchants, storeowners and dealers without a lot of education, although they had business skills. Since they bought their way out officially, they came with their families, parents, grandparents and friends. They were shipped out aboard big cargo ships and did not suffer from pirate attacks. Although they were crammed in the boats, their ordeal was not as bad as that of the real boat people who struggled by themselves against sea, storms, hunger, and thirst. Although the Vietnamese government had confiscated most of their savings, many had managed to smuggle out gold, jewelry, and other objects of value. With these savings, they could claim to have a leg up on many other refugees. The fact they could pay their way out spoke highly about their wealth.

Others were soldiers in the Army of the Republic of Vietnam and had spent time in reeducation camps before escaping. They also spent more time in the refugee camps abroad where conditions were not always optimal. Having struggled for their lives in the reeducation camps, they languished in Saigon for some time before escaping. They then faced the gloomy outlook of waiting for a sponsor in the camps while living in shacks or straw huts. Their lives in the new camps were similar to the ones in Vietnam, except they could roam freely within the confines camps without being watched by the police. Having resided in many camps and surviving on meager rations, they were sicker and had more diseases like tuberculosis, parasites, skin diseases, and malnutrition than those who came earlier. They were less educated than the old timers and also faced an ailing economy, a tight job market and rising unemployment when they arrived in the host countries. They faced growing antagonism from America's poor, who claimed the new arrivals took away their jobs and housings.[29] They were less accepted than old timers because of "compassion fatigue."

The third-wave refugees did even more poorly than the second group. They came much later and had received minimal education under the communist regime. For years they had been shortchanged and impoverished: they were sent to reeducations camps where they languished for many years and struggled to just remain alive. After being sent home, they remained under police surveillance and were able to only do menial jobs, as they remained suspicious in the eyes of the communist regime and could not compete for lucrative or high paying jobs. They probably had received money their relatives sent them from abroad to supplement their meager income and they thought money was easy to earn in America. When they saw the cars and houses their relatives told them about, they did not know how hard the relatives had worked to get there. They simply thought that if the relatives could buy a car or a house, why couldn't they?

When the newcomers arrived in Western countries, they noticed that those who arrived earlier had over the years achieved economic stability. When the newcomers also wanted to own cars and houses, they realized they had to start somewhere and that somewhere began with taking on menial jobs for a living. There is no shortcut to riches. They immediately felt a wide economic gap separated them from the old timers. They were not only placed at the bottom of American society, but also behind the other Vietnamese who came earlier. Mistreated at home, they felt like economic pariahs in the new society abroad. They also felt they were perpetual losers, in Vietnam as well as abroad. Once a pariah, always a pariah, they felt. As a result they became frustrated and believed early comers had achieved the American dream that still remained elusive to them. It was very hard for the newcomers to catch up with those who came earlier and that gap was widening with time. No matter how hard they worked, they felt they would not be able to catch up. Then came frustration, despair, resignation, and quitting. They became resigned to their lot and refused to dream any longer: they joined and swelled the ranks of the unemployed and increased the number of homeless and beggars in the streets of Bolsa and Westminster in Little Saigon in Orange County, California.

8

THE PLANNING

One could say that if the first wave refugees did not plan their escapes, the subsequent ones carefully planned their trips in order to get to their destinations. But again, planning had to do with making arrangements for the travel inside Vietnam. Their goal was simply to get out of the country. What would happen next in the camps or during the resettlement phase was out of their control. Had Hanoi allowed free travel movement, there would not be any illegal sea escape.

Careful planning could lead to a successful escape, although this was not always true. Many unknown factors like weather, pirates, and infiltration of the project by the secret police could throw the best plan upside down. Timing and luck also played important roles. Many boats took off at night when the guards were sleepy or not very attentive. A departure half an hour earlier or later might prevent an unhappy encounter with police patrols. The same thing was true for storms. The sea, calm or stormy, was a major unknown in all these escapes, for meteorological data were not available at that time. Half a day difference might mean getting out of the eye or path of a storm and avoiding a disaster at sea. Therefore everything depended on luck or fate, as the Vietnamese liked to believe. If they had fate on their side, they knew they would be able to make it.

Dr. Nguyen Gia Tho's story was that of a carefully planned escape. He was a physician and a major in the South Vietnamese Air Force. After 1975, he was sent to a reeducation camp for three years. He went through the ordeal with patience and courage. Following his release, instead of going back to his former profession, he bought a small boat and went up and down the Saigon River selling cabbages for a year and a half like a newly converted socialist worker. This, of course, involved a lot of dedication and a sharp drops in social standing and living standards for the physician and his family. Everyone around him thought he had lost his mind after the years in the camps. On the other hand, he was free to roam around, for the communists left him pretty much alone: he was one of their rare successes. But the former physician did not lose his time; he carefully studied the stars, the tides, and the currents and even bought false Chinese papers. After a year and a half of sailing practice, he loaded his family (wife, seven children and six siblings) on his boat on January 23, 1980, quietly left Saigon, and safely arrived at Pulau Bidong five days later after an encounter with pirates.[1] His sacrifice had saved 14 relatives from a life of misery.

The causes that could lead to a failed escape were numerous and one remains surprised by the large number of people who were able to escape disasters and to safely arrive in another country. Of course, no one is certain about the real number of lives lost during this diaspora. It was probably high, although the exact figure would never be known. Those who drowned or perished at sea did not leave any trace at all. UNHCR had at one time estimated that only one out of two escapees would arrive safely in one of the Asian camps.

Looking for an Organizer

Case 1: Jade was a college student when Saigon fell. Because all schools and colleges were closed, he returned home to the Mekong delta only to realize the local Viet Cong did not like having an educated person around them; they sent him instead to a reeducation camp. His first job in the camp was to tear up a helicopter runway to make a garden with only axes as tools. His life became a classic case of the bamboo gulag filled with stories of hard labor, starvation, torture, and lack of medical care. He caught crickets or lizards to supplement his food ration and ate them raw on the spot. Otherwise he would be punished had he been caught eating during work.[2] Reeducation was almost synonymous to extermination, albeit gradual, insidious and less violent in nature than a regular execution. He was later transferred to a camp close to the Cambodian border where escape was impossible. The Khmer Rouge one night crossed the borders, attacked the camp and wounded the commander. Jailers and inmates pulled out of the camp and hid in a nearby forest waiting for troop reinforcements. Jade was ordered to take the commander to a regional hospital for medical care. He used the occasion to escape.

He returned to the delta and hid in his friend's house; he was afraid to return to his mother's home where he would surely be detected. The local police still came by and knocked at the door at 2 A.M. to check out his identity. Jade was ordered to report to the police station daily from then on. Like in the reeducation camp, he was told to write down his biography along with his family tree. Jade and his friend Hanh decided the country's lack of freedom was unhealthy for them and it was time to get out. The country, "once the land of waving palms had turned into one of the poorest nations in the world; our people had become homeless beggars."[3]

They got in touch through intermediaries with a priest who lived in Vinh Binh about 40 miles from Sadec. The priest in turn referred them to a boat owner who asked for a deposit equivalent of half of the required amount in gold. Directions were given. Jade was told to come to the Gian Long Market across the river from downtown Vinh Binh the following Sunday at 4 P.M. He had to take a passenger boat to a store that sold coffins, where he would ask to buy two "objects." Jade returned to Sadec bringing back the good news to Hanh. They both anxiously waited for D-day and borrowed three bars of gold each from Hanh's mom and sister. When time came, they went to the coffin-store and asked to buy two. They were placed on a boat that went down the river with a dozen passengers on board. After a two-and-a-half hour trip, they met a larger boat anchored in the middle of the river. They boarded the boat only to find out it was the wrong one. They disembarked and rowed back to the river edge where they anxiously waited for their boat. Children were given sleeping pills to keep them quiet. The silence was eerie, only disturbed by the buzzing of mosquitoes and the rapid motion of bats. They were especially afraid to be caught by the river police, which could only mean a jail sentence and loss of money.

The boat finally showed up, to the excitement of the anxious passengers. The total count on the big boat turned out to be one hundred and 24. The big boat sailed out to the ocean but was caught in two big storms. The engine then broke down. A state fishing boat came by. The Viet Cong were given 30 gold bars along with jewelry but complained that the bribe was not big enough. They towed the boat back to land

and jailed all the passengers, who were released two weeks later because the Viet Cong wanted to cover their actions. Jade attempted a second escape; his boat was caught in another storm and began leaking. The engine broke down and half of the 30 passengers died of starvation and sickness. The third time turned out to be a charm, although the boat engine also broke down and they had an encounter with pirates.

Case 2: In another escape attempt, Kien and his aunt were picked up at the scheduled date on a rowboat in Nha Trang and taken to Turtle Island. They encountered a dozen other people and were told to wait for a big boat that would take them to Hong Kong the next morning. They waited and waited. Five days passed without any sign of the boat while they barely survived on berries. They decided to return home, realizing too late the trip was a scam. They forced two lumberjacks who were working on the island to drive them back to land on a motorboat. During the trip the men fought back and a fight ensued. Kien and his aunt jumped overboard to escape. He survived while she drowned. He ended up in reeducation camp PK 34 reserved for escapees who were caught trying to escape.[4]

Escapees were the frequent victims of swindlers. Their obsession about escaping blinded them from the empty promises of organizers who would say anything in order to get money from their victims. Many were cheated not only once but multiple times until they became broke. There was no way to be certain the organizers were real and would deliver what they promised. All the deals were done secretly in order to avoid police detection. As such, it was impossible to check and crosscheck references and connections to avoid scams. Those who were cheated out of their money could not even complain to the police because they would be jailed immediately for attempting to escape.

Looking for a Boat

The simplest way to escape was to look for an organizer who would take care of the trip and boat at the same time. Those who desired to escape by themselves or could not afford the high fees of the organizer had to hunt for a boat as well as an engine. Desperate people even had to repair and put to use old leaky boats that had been sitting in their back yards for quite some time. The price of a boat had been skyrocketing since 1977 because of increasing demands. Buying a boat did not appear to be a simple matter because the business was controlled by the PSB. All sales had to be approved by the PSB. The buyer had to justify his need for a boat (fishing or selling products on the river) and to show the police he was selling products (cabbages, like Dr. Tho) for a period of time to deflect their suspicion.

While the economy was spiraling downward, the business of exporting refugees was booming. Towns like Rach Gia, capital of the Kien Giang province on the southwest coast, were bustling because of high demands on boats. Other cities on the coast or along the Mekong delta like Vung Tau, Long Thanh, My Tho, Vinh Long, Tra Vinh, Can Tho, Bac Lieu and Ca Mau were also involved in refugee shipping.

All boats from fishing crafts to old workhorses were spruced up and repaired for their one-way voyage abroad. The new boats had two toilets separated by a small kitchen. Ventilation pipes were required to accommodate the large number of refugees. Rach Gia became the major center for sponsored departures and boasted 50 or more boats specially built for the refugee trade. At the same time, about one hundred more boats were converted for the same purpose with the authorization of the PSB.[5]

Once the boat or organizer had been found and the price negotiated, the next step was to raise money to pay for the ride. Most of the times escapees had to borrow money from their parents or relatives. Since selling property or belongings would attract the attention of the police, they usually would leave the house behind for the government to take over in due time. They could also turn it over to their relatives, although the latter had to explain to the police the whereabouts of the old owners.

The next question would be whether the family would travel as a unit or separately. Although family members often wanted to escape together, the escape fee for a family of five or seven, at three-to-eight taels of gold per person, was astronomical. Many people could not afford to pay that amount at once. In these situations, they usually split the family up in two or three groups and each group would travel at different times, sometimes two to five years apart. On one occasion the father and second daughter escaped first in 1983 and ended up staying in Malaysian camps for many years before being accepted to America. The oldest daughter escaped with her aunt but was caught and jailed many times before getting to the United States. The mother, son, and another daughter finally escaped in 1987. Family members were separated for many years before finally being reunited.[6] They also had to travel separately in order not to attract the attention of the police. On another occasion, a family of four decided to escape. The wife, however, had second thoughts and opted to remain in Vietnam because of her sympathies to the Hanoi regime. Having paid the fees, the father escaped with his two children and a cousin who substituted for the wife. They ended up in Australia while she remained in Vietnam.

Cong An

The PSB was the "eye and ears" of the Hanoi police state. It monitored citizens closely and executed Hanoi's dark wishes. Under the control of the Ministry of Interior, it had broad powers and could jail or dispose of anyone it deemed to be an opponent of the regime. It had many sections and the B-2 section was assigned the management of refugees. Its officers wore plain clothes and were responsible for internal and external security.

PSB agents directly recruited passengers who were interested in leaving the country. In the south, they worked through intermediaries, as southerners did not want to deal directly with them. They set up the price, the date, referred the organizers to the boat builder, and sometimes provided false papers. Negotiations could take six to eight months, as each side was cautious about the other. The PSB agent would like to get the most out of the deal. There would be a registration fee of two taels of gold and the total fee averaged five to eight taels per adult and half-price for minors. The usual split was 50 percent for the government, 40 percent for the boat, fuel and provisions, and 10 percent for the organizer. The PSB agent would solicit a small bribe for himself; it could be paid in gold, furniture, or watches. He also would receive a commission from the bureau.

People were weary of the PSB, and for good reason. They were afraid of a trap and many people had been sent to jail after paying their full fee. The likely explanation was that these agents set up a sham operation on the side to benefit themselves. Refugees were given a few hours to leave: if they had engine failure or were caught by state-owned fishing boats, these same agents who had been previously bought would put them in jail.

The Chinese used the PSB system because they traveled in large groups. They were placed in touch with Ba Thanh, deputy chief of the Rach Gia PSB and director of the B-2 office. Negotiations took place in non-official offices to conceal government involvement. A boat was bought for 80 taels and the refitting cost 220 taels. The organizer then submitted a list of 350 passengers. The payment was 850 taels of gold for the voyage and Ba Thanh took watches and 20 taels of gold for his services. He also set up the time and date of departure. Four different boats departed that day under the supervision of PSB agents.[7]

The PSB agents were also involved in shipping the Chinese out through the *Huey Fong* and other big freighters. The magnitude of this business could come only from someone who wielded a lot of power within the government. It had been traced back to the Interior Minister Tran Quoc Hoan.[8]

Nguyen Long recounted how he bought false Chinese identity cards for himself and his family in order to escape abroad from the city of My Tho. The My Tho PSB agents organized the trip through two middlemen, controlled the departure date, and had all the passengers arrived at a meeting place in town. Passengers were checked, loaded on a ferry and taken to an island in the middle of the Mekong River that flows through the city. They were then transferred to a boat that was moored close to the island. The PSB agents accompanied the boat for a short distance before letting it go.[9]

From Saigon, My Ngoc took a bus to Can Tho, in the Mekong delta about 80 miles southwest of Saigon. Not seeing her guide, she slept overnight on the ground at the bus station. The next morning, her guide picked her up along with other people and took them to his home. He fed them and at night led them to a skiff where he shoved 10 people in. The skiff moved to a medium size boat where 20 refugees were crammed in a small place. They stayed on the boat overnight and were barely able to move. The boat took them to another boat where the crowd grew to 50. The crew piled coconuts and watermelons on one side of the boat to make it look like a merchant boat while the passengers crowded in the middle. They could not eat, drink, or go to the bathroom the whole day.

At night the boat moved down the river and was stopped by the police. Bribes were given and the boat continued its course. A few miles from the shore the boat was stopped by another government ship. More bribes had to be coughed up. The two-man crew did not know the way and had to ask the police the direction to Malaysia.[10]

PSB agents also watched any suspicious person or group that attempted to escape without their approval. Even after being bribed, these agents could turn on their victims and round them up at the last minute. Orchid attempted multiple escapes, all of them ended unsuccessfully. On one occasion she went to Mui Ne about one hundred miles north to Saigon, where she bought a boat and the service of a fisherman and his family. She returned to Saigon and secretly enrolled 30 people who each paid 10 taels of gold for the trip. She screened each of them carefully to make sure they were willing and trusted partners. The job was hard because any breach in secrecy would land all of them in jail. The escapees traveled in small groups to Mui Ne and stayed in different houses for many days waiting for the day of travel. They were, however, secretly followed by the local agents, as they were strangers to the area.

On D-day, they were led in small groups to the rendezvous. The weather was cool, foggy and rainy. The bad weather it was hoped would keep the PSB agents in their offices. From the road, the escapees had to go down the stairs to reach the beach; they then had to swim to the boat that was anchored one hundred feet from the shore. Women and children were taken to the boat aboard small transport carriers. As the first batch of escapees reached the beach, gunfire broke out. PSB agents, who were already bribed, caught all the escapees standing on the road waiting for their turn to descend to the beach. Only Orchid, her husband and brother-in-law, the fisherman and 20 family members and friends managed to escape. They jumped into the boat and steamed out to the sea in the middle of the storm, which luckily prevented the PSB agents from pursuing them. The boat turned around like a yoyo after the anchor broke loose. Passengers thought they were going to die any time. They prayed and prayed and hung on. By dawn, the sea was calm and the weather was beautiful again. They knew they had luckily escaped another certain death. They sailed for 21 long days before being accepted as refugees in Indonesia. Ships went by without acknowledging their S.O.S signals and their cries. As they approached the Thai shores, villagers waved them away. They landed in Singapore and were allowed to remain in the harbor long enough to have a woman, who had miscarried, treated at the local hospital.

Causes of Failure

These stories showed how risky an escape could turn out. Death or jail sentences could be the tragic consequences of a failed escape. This did not include loss of homes, belongings, jobs, and money. The most well designed plan could unravel at any single stage from the beginning to the end. Factors causing failures were multiple and sometimes unavoidable. Any trip with 30 to 40 complete strangers was bound to be complicated. Even being alive on a foreign soil did not mean the end of the ordeal.

The most important task was to get connected with a boat handler. Since everyone was eager to get out of Vietnam, groups of organizers had mushroomed all over the country to provide means of going abroad. Some were trustworthy and well organized while others were downright sleazy and disreputable. Of course, no one knew for sure which organization could be trusted until a customer dealt with it. Since most organizations worked underground to evade the scrutiny of communist agents, that same secrecy prevented customers from checking on the legitimacy of the operation. People were so desperate to get out of the country that they believed whatever the organizers told them. Even if they got cheated, they could not even complain to the government because they would go to jail for having attempted to escape.

The Viet Cong could be aware of the project since the beginning. Although organizers tried their best to prevent leaks or police infiltration, the system was not always completely secure. One passenger might have inadvertently said or done something that might tip off the police. Selling a house or belongings, the household head making trips to the countryside to feel his way around, pulling of kids out of school, or closing a store could make the Cong An suspicious. The Cong An had all the time in the world — all it did was to spy and spy more on its citizens. Its webs were as dense as weeds in a marsh. Once the details of the operation were known, the Cong An agents just showed up at the right time to catch crew as well as passengers. To prevent such a thing from happening, organizers frequently bribed the authorities, which then pretended not to be aware of the project.

Being a police state, communist Vietnam had a lot of informers everywhere. The police could spot any unusual gathering in the village, on the river, or around the coastline and drop by to check out what was going on. The government even placed two of their agents in any fishing boat going on the ocean. Such agents caught Jade's boat in Vietnamese territorial waters. They were given 30 bars of gold along with jewelry but still were not happy about the bribe. They then towed the boat back to land and imprisoned all the passengers. The communists became unhappy with the unequal sharing of the bribes and argued bitterly with each other. To prevent their superiors from launching any investigation into this matter, they decided to release all the prisoners two weeks later.

Children could play the role of spoilers at various stages. Before departure, they could have told their friends in an innocent way that they would not be able to see them again. Once the secret was out, anyone, including the police, would know it. Children did not intend to cause any harm but they could not keep anything secret for long. On the boats, they got sick easily, cried, and threw fits when they were hungry, bored, tired, or unhappy with the cramped quarters. They could not stay quiet for a long time and could easily alert passersby with their cries, especially when the boats were still navigating the rivers of the delta. And the police would show up and foil the attempted escape. Some parents gave children sleeping pills to calm them down. A few escapes were disrupted by crying children or absent-minded teenagers. In one case, a city teenager stepped off an anchored boat and proceeded toward a store to buy drinks, as it was hot inside the hold of the boat. Her modern outfit immediately caught the attention of the villagers and the police, who stormed the boat and detained all the escapees. Had this teenager listened to the organizers and remained on board, no one would have paid attention to the unremarkable boat that was waiting for nighttime to sail away.[11]

Once people from different areas had been assembled and brought onto a big boat, it would be hard and costly to cancel the trip because a storm was brewing in the ocean. People had committed themselves to the trip for quite some time and could not back out easily. They had already sold their belongings or homes and had been absent too long to safely return home. The police had probably secured their houses once they had been absent for more than two days in a row without notifying them. Returning home would entail going to the police station daily to explain their absence. Anyone suspected of escaping would be immediately jailed or sent to the NEZ. Such was the case of a military physician who did three years of reeducation camp after the war. He was released and allowed to practice in Saigon. A year later, he attempted escape but was caught. He was sent to another reeducation for four more years.[12] Therefore, even inclement weather would not deter people from escaping abroad. Already miserable and distraught under communist rule and having mortgaged everything including their fortune and future on the trip, they could not lose anything else except their lives.

Weather is an important factor in the success of the trip. A scorching sun could severely burn the passengers' skin or cause significant dehydration and eventual death, especially if they were exposed to it all day long. If one day under the sun could severely burn a person, a four to five day trip could easily kill that same person. The boats these refugees traveled in did not have a sun-cover for everyone; only the captain's quarter or mid-section of the boat was covered. Calm waters were almost synonymous to successful travel while storms portended a miserable if not fatal expedition, especially if the boats were small in size. Storms were difficult to avoid, as they could occur anytime during the year. Heat building up over the equator could precipitate violent air movements that could travel as fast as one hundred miles per hour. These conditions were ideal breeding grounds for thunderstorms. In this situation, waves two or three stories tall would pound mercilessly on the small boats and smash them into pieces like an egg falling on the ground. The typhoon season from July to November was a dangerous season for sailing. With its dark clouds, torrential winds and heavy rains, typhoons were feared in all Southeast Asia.[13] Since Vietnam did not have good meteorological stations at that time, captains were rarely aware of any storm gathering at sea. They did not even have a radio to listen to any weather station. They often did not have a barometer on board. They were no better than blind men walking across a crowded city street.

Timing was also crucial. An early arrival at the meeting point (a stranger with a suitcase or a family at a deserted area) could arouse police suspicion. On the other hand, many escapees missed their boats by arriving 10 or 15 minutes later. The delay in getting to the rallying point could be due to missed connections, heavy traffic, untimely stops by buses to pick up passengers, or unusually long searches or identity checks by local police. Checkpoints were set up along highways and before the town and city gates. The police usually looked for contraband, escapees, or youths of draft age. Searches could be cursory or very thorough depending on whether bribes were offered or not. They could also take longer if the police were unhappy with the bribe given. Very often boat owners would wait for all escapees to come on board before pulling the anchor, although they sometimes left early because they felt it to be dangerous to linger at the same place too long. Sometimes waiting would mean missing the tide and getting stuck in sandbars.

Engine breakdowns were frequent at that time. Since the fall of Saigon, only government offices were allowed to buy new boat engines. Captains and fishermen used whatever leftover engines they could put their hands on to power their boats. With so many people looking for the same thing, there was an obvious shortage of good engines. Those available on the market were good for powering small riverboats, but not large boats carrying one hundred to two hundred passengers. There was no school of navigation at that time except in the navy, and skippers learned their skills by training under someone whose only experience was to drive barges on the river. The crew, which was not trained in maintenance, could not even service the engine should it break down. Therefore, engine failure would leave boats stranded in the middle of the ocean and passengers had to pray for someone to tow them back to safety. Otherwise they would drift endlessly until they died of starvation or thirst.

Most of the boats that steamed abroad were small and rickety riverboats that their desperate owners took to the seas in order to escape a cruel government. A smart person would not even use such a boat on the Mekong River. But desperation drove people to do strange things. Many refugees built or refurbished their own boats because they could not afford to pay three to eight gold bars each to get out of Vietnam. One refugee used an old 14 by two-and-a-half meter boat that had been sitting unused on a river for a long time. He pulled it on land, scraped the old wax with all the caulking, and then applied a new layer of wax. He installed a Japanese-made F-10 diesel engine he bought in Saigon with fake papers and was ready for a few rides in preparation for the big trip.[14] The boat later carried 20 people to freedom. If many boats capsized in the ocean because of structural damage, small size, cargo overload, or lack of equipment, many escapees owed their freedom to these small boats. Without them and their owners, they would still be suffering under communist control. To risk one's life to get out of the country spoke volumes about the depth of the despair these people lived in.

Fuel was severely restricted by the communists after 1975 to prevent any escape. It was sold only to fishermen who had a good track record of returning after each fishing trip. The volume of fuel allocated depended on the duration of each trip. No fuel was sold for trips longer than one day, except in very unusual circumstances. Anyone planning to escape would have to store leftover gasoline every day until he had enough reserves to take a big trip. The storage area had to be safe, otherwise he would lose not only his fuel, but also his freedom if the police were aware of it. The biggest danger was to run out of fuel in the middle of the ocean and become prey to pirates or storms.

Passengers brought their own food and water. Each person could not carry more than a gallon of water and a few days' food supply because of the weight and volume. Carrying more would alert the police to a possible escape attempt. Besides, there was no room on the boats, which were always crowded with people. With refugees paying four to eight taels of gold per person, boat owners would rather accommodate them than save space for food or water. Therefore, shortages of these crucial supplies were fairly common during these trips that could last from seven to 14 days. Storms, loss of compass or map, and engine failure could markedly lengthen the duration of the trip and endanger passengers' lives.

The crew usually had minimal experience navigating the ocean. They probably had never traveled abroad and did not even know how to use their compasses or maps. Their only experience was to drive a barge or a riverboat. They had no sea experience and did not know how to handle storms in the middle of the ocean. Sometimes storms would knock off their compasses, causing them to endlessly drift around. Most of the seasoned captains had escaped abroad on previous trips; therefore, the experience of the remaining captains was not particularly good.

Escaping by boat was therefore a risky process. Anything that interfered with the trip could put the safety of passengers in jeopardy. And there were many difficulties lying ahead on the escape road. Besides technical problems, escapees could face pirates who could kill them or authorities who refused to let them land and towed them away. The journey was fraught with dangers and risks that were difficult to predict and avoid at times.

Luck therefore played an important role, although many people would not want to acknowledge it. Without it, it would be very difficult to grasp why some trips were smooth and uneventful while others were just nightmares from the beginning until the end. Similarly, it would be difficult to understand why pirates spared some refugees but killed others from the same boat and why some people made it and others not.

Many refugees believed in a higher protection, therefore they prayed throughout the duration of the trip. Once on the boats, their lives were at the mercy of the elements. And it was hard not to think about God or Buddha for the next several days because there was nothing else around them except the wide, empty ocean and the deep sea.

9

THE BOAT PEOPLE

> ... we are the foam
> floating in the vast ocean
> we are the dust
> wandering in endless space...
> —Anonymous

No words could explain the tragedy of the refugees better than the above verse. The sight of these hapless travelers fighting seas and storms and piled up in overcrowded, rickety boats was tragic. They hung on to the railings as the boats surfed above the waves before falling into the after-wave depression. Their clothes were tattered and wet, their mouths burning of thirst, their lips cracking under the sun, and their stomachs crying for food. They floated and floated on the oceans, their faces haggard and their eyes starring into the horizon for a land that would welcome them.

The 1975 to 1992 diaspora involved more than two million people who sailed to other countries or continents to look for freedom that was absent in their countries. They included many different nationalities: Americans, Chinese and Vietnamese, as well as different socio-political and religious backgrounds like soldiers, professionals, nationalists, fishermen, Buddhists, Catholics, communists, and returnees.

The Americans

The first boat people turned out to be the Americans and their co-workers living in the Can Tho area about 80 miles southwest of Saigon.

Early on April 29, 1975, the Viet Cong fired a few rockets from across the river into Can Tho, the provincial capital of the IV Corps, the southernmost part of Vietnam. No major damage was reported and the area turned out to be calm. No Viet Cong attack was noted or expected in the near future.

The news was not that good in Saigon either. The North Vietnamese army, after defeating the last South Vietnamese stronghold at Xuan Loc, about 40 miles northeast of Saigon converged toward the capital, which had been shelled daily. Kissinger and Ambassador Martin had delayed the evacuation until the last minute. Operation Frequent Wind IV officially began at 1108 hours on April 29. Eight thousand Americans and Vietnamese were lifted off by helicopter during the next 17 hours from the U.S. Embassy rooftop to the Seventh Fleet carriers *Hancock, Okinawa,* and *Midway*.[1] That was a rather limited operation for a city of three million people. Its goal was to prevent what had happened in Da Nang from happening again in Saigon: the mobbing of airplanes by scared people. Those who wanted to escape had to find their own way out.

Evacuation from Can Tho had been discussed a few days earlier between the U.S. Consul Terry McNamara and the CIA representatives. The local CIA suggested using helicopters as means of transportation but this would preclude picking up the Vietnamese working for the Americans. The consul favored using boats that would allow the evacuation of a large number of people out of Can Tho[2] while the helicopters would be sent back to Saigon to assist with the evacuation at the embassy. Orders were given at 10 A.M. and evacuation started at noon on April 29. The CIA would use a motor launch and two Boston Whalers while the consulate handled a rice barge and two LCM (landing craft, mechanized).

The evacuees were contacted, brought to the consulate and loaded on the barges after which the trip began. The convoy was stopped midway by order of the IV Corps commander who would not allow any Vietnamese military personnel or civil servants to leave. In fact, there were a few high ranking Vietnamese officers on board the barges. After two hours of negotiations, Commodore Thang, turning the blind eye, allowed the convoy to proceed.[3] Farther downstream, as the river curled around a few islands, the channel narrowed and the convoy passed a few meters from the riverbanks. It was shot at but retaliated without casualty.

The convoy proceeded safely to the high seas. Twelve hours into its trip, it encountered the *Pioneer Contender,* part of the armada that had been waiting out of Vietnamese territorial borders to rescue the refugees. These were the only Americans who used boats to get out of Vietnam in 1975.

The Soldiers

Case 1. After 1975, Lu Van Thanh, an ARVN officer, ended up in reeducation camps in central Vietnam for three and a half years. Following his release, the police constantly shadowed him, considered him like a stranger and treated him as a foe. As he no longer felt comfortable living in his native country, he decided to escape. His first two attempts ended in failure. The third escape from Nha Trang was delayed five times because of inclement weather. The police had stepped up measures to guard the coastline and to watch bus and railroad stations to prevent any escape. The organizers had even paid 45 ounces of gold to communist agents in charge of the area to look away at the appropriate time.[4]

The meeting place was 80 miles north of Cam Ranh Bay. The escapees had to descend from the highway down to the beach that lay one hundred feet below. They had to get into a small ferryboat that would carry them to the 42 by nine foot boat anchored three hundred feet from the shore. Fuel and food came down the same way. As they made their way downhill, shots were heard from the highway. The police, which had been bribed, came by and caught 30 people including the organizing committee. Thanh had to swim to the boat, which then took off. There were overall 59 people on board. They first sailed along the coastline in an attempt to buy some more water and fuel from local fishermen, then headed eastward toward the Philippines on April 25, 1982, at 8 P.M.

After a few days, fuel, rice, and water ran short. The daily ration was half a bowl of cooked chow with two sips of water per person. They encountered 17 trade ships that passed by without stopping. Desperate, they kept going eastward. They then saw a whale emerging from the South China Sea, which according to fishermen was a good sign. On April 30 at 8 P.M., they noticed a small light on the horizon. An American ship showed up, picked them up and transferred them to Subic Bay in the Philippines, then to the Palawan refugee center. Thanh stayed in the camp for almost seven months before being accepted to the United States.

Case 2. Captain Ben Cai escaped from a reeducation camp where he was incarcerated for five years. He came back to Saigon and lived a life of an outlaw at the edge of a captive society. He attempted to escape twice, the first time from Vung Tau and the second time from Vinh Binh; both of them turned out to be scams. The third one was from My Tho, on the Mekong delta. Since Ben Cai and his cousin arrived early, they sneaked into a movie theater to kill time. While the outdoors poster advertised a Western movie, the show was about a Bulgarian farmer who loved tractors. He realized the communists had lied once again. At the 8 P.M. pickup time, no one showed up. They waited almost until midnight but still did not see the organizer. They were almost picked up by the police for missing the curfew. While his cousin returned home, Ben Cai mingled with the homeless in Saigon.

The fourth attempt was from Saigon, but it turned out to be another scam and his parents lost two more gold leaves. The fifth attempt originated from My Tho. Everything turned out fine and the boat had dropped the last regular passenger at the last stop and all the escapees had boarded. A teenager suddenly decided to get off the boat to buy some drinks. The police, noticing a stranger in the area, caught her and immediately stormed the boat. All the escapees were jailed except Ben Cai, who was able to escape using his survival skills. His two children, however, were detained and his parents had to bribe them out. He tried to escape from Vung Tau and then in the Mekong delta without any success. Almost four years had passed since his first escape and his parents had lost close to 20 gold leaves trying to get him out of the country.

During the last attempt, he worked as a skipper of a 33 foot boat with three hundred passengers aboard. He had taken the boat to the mouth of the Mekong River when he realized his wife and two stepdaughters were missing. Distraught and feeling cheated, he wanted to come back to pick them up, but the passengers dissuaded him. They advised him that the truck that was supposed to pick up about 10 passengers, including his wife, did not reach the rendezvous and these people were left behind. Ben Cai decided to sail ahead and the boat reached Trengganu, Malaysia, on July 16, 1984. He had spent a total of five years in reeducation camps and four more years as an outlaw in communist Vietnam.[5] He was sent to Pulau Bidong where more than 60,000 refugees were relocated, some for more than five years.

Ben Cai was probably one of the rare few who successfully escaped from reeducation camps (with bribes) and managed to get out of the country alive. His former training as a ranger and his family's deep pocket gave him the upper hand as he managed to live as an outlaw on the fringes of the society for four long years. Without his survival skills and the liberal use of gold, he would have been caught long before. This is also the story of a courageous and resilient man who braved all odds to attempt to escape abroad. Many people would have simply abandoned their dreams after having failed on so many occasions.

The majority of ARVN personnel who escaped out of the country after being released from the reeducation camps did it in a less flashy manner. Of course, since they did not escape from the camps, they did not risk as severe a punishment as if Ben Cai was caught, although they could still be sent back to reeducation camps. They either bought their way out with four to eight ounces of gold or were flown to the U.S. later through the ODP (Orderly Departure Program). The program allowed ARVN soldiers who had spent more than three years of reeducation to apply for resettlement in the U.S. as part of a deal with the Hanoi government.[6] Doctors who worked as flight surgeons in the ARVN were not eligible for the ODP since they usually spent two and a half years in the camps. They had to buy their way out themselves, like the rest of the people.

The Professionals and Nationalists

Almost all professions were represented in this diaspora. There were politicians, teachers, store owners, businessmen, and professionals. Dr. Cung's story is detailed in chapter 11. A heart surgeon, he was sent to a reeducation camp where he became paralyzed. After his release, he was forced to practice without salary for a while before escaping in a boat along with more than 600 people. As pirates attacked his boat, he directed the defense by encouraging the escapees to fight back with courage and persistence. The pirates finally gave up and the boat successfully landed at Pulau Bidong with only two casualties. Without his courage and leadership, a lot more people would have died during this attack.

There were also many professionals who were nationalistic and wanted to remain in Vietnam to rebuild the new country. Alas, they too became disappointed with the Hanoi government. The dean of the Saigon law school felt safe to remain in Saigon after 1975 because he did not get involved in politics during the war. The communists thought differently and sent him to jail, where he was tortured. His whereabouts were unknown.

Tuan, a 60-year-old former professor at the University of Saigon, decided to stay back after 1975 because he wanted to rebuild the country. Nam, a 45-year-old architect, returned to Vietnam in 1972 after finishing his study in France. Although he disagreed with the communists, he decided to stay to help his country. After a few months under the communist regime, both of them changed their minds. Tuan wanted to leave three months after the fall of Saigon, but it took him six years to get out. Nam realized he had lost all his freedom under the communist regime. He had to have a resident card and a special permit to simply visit friends and relatives. All his movements and activities were closely controlled.

Manh, a 40-year-old architect and faculty member of the University of Saigon, thought he could help his country by remaining in Vietnam after the war. A year later, he was ordered to assist in relocating the population of Saigon to the NEZ. The NEZ were virgin and infertile lands the people had to exploit without mechanical devices, fertilizers, or grains. He was terrified about the ill-conceived project and argued that it needed a lot of planning and could not be done in a few months. The communist supervisor simply told him if the Khmers could do it, the Vietnamese could too.[7]

Many had escaped with only their clothes, especially those who fled right after the fall of Saigon. Others had left their homes and belongings behind in order not to attract the attention of the communist officials. In case of failure, they could return back home if the authorities had not noticed anything abnormal yet. Many were so happy to be able to get out of the country that they willingly turned over their houses and belongings to the state prior to departure while others were forced to sign them over.

The Fishermen

Fishermen were the only people who could leave the country anytime they liked. Like in the 1954 diaspora, they usually escaped with their families intact and in many cases made extra money by bringing relatives and friends out of the country.

First Wave. Oanh was a fisherman from Vung Tau, a seaside resort and fishing port 80 miles east of Saigon. Early in May 1975, having seen all his friends leaving the country, he loaded his family on his fishing boat and headed to the seas. He wondered whether he should stay back and enjoy his life in Vietnam or join the wave of refugees abroad. As an uneducated fisherman, he did not know how he could make a living in an advanced country. As a believer in the saying that if *Ong Troi* (the Creator) created the elephant, he also allowed grass to grow to feed the elephant, he decided to leave Vietnam confident he could survive in another country with the grace of *Ong Troi*. This was a big gamble for him but between freedom abroad and oppression under the communists, he opted for freedom. His trip was uneventful as a ship picked his family up in international sea-lanes. He later relocated to a seaside town in Connecticut and worked as a custodian for the local church. He dutifully took care of the church and the grounds and cleaned them after Sunday masses. The family of nine lived in a large house belonging to the church and the children went to local school. After a few years, they migrated to Little Saigon, California, to be close to his friends.

Second Wave. Tuyen was a cocky fisherman's son. He was an uneducated teenager who did not even know his birth date, although he was skilled in fishing and navigating boats. The communists took over the family boat in January 1979. Although the family could still use the boat to fish, they had to sell their daily catch to the government at a ridiculously low price. Tired of being exploited, they decided to escape. One night as the three soldiers guarding the port were dining, Tuyen, his nephew and five other friends took off on the boat and landed in Hong Kong a week later. His parents still remained in Hoi, a town in central Vietnam. In their rush to get out of Vietnam, they did not have time to store enough fuel for the trip. They arrived first at Hai Nan island and were towed into the port. The Chinese gave Tuyen 180 gallons of fuel for his trip to Hong Kong and 68 refugees who had escaped from Phan Thiet, Vietnam, one week earlier but had to land in Hai Nan because of engine failure. Tuyen arrived in Hong Kong a few days later.[8]

Fishermen were represented in all waves because they were the ones who owned or had access to boats. They knew how to navigate on the ocean, although they did not have much experience with international sailing. This was the least of their problems because many refugees took to the waters without any formal marine training while others had only riverine experience. Fishermen and farmers formed the majority of the third-wave refugees.

They and the handlers were the luckiest of all the refugees since they could make money, especially gold, by getting people abroad. Some charged three ounces while others charged eight to 10 ounces of gold per person. Of course, they had to spend a small amount to bribe the local officials. Once in the U.S. they could use their gold to buy a new boat and start their fishing business in the gulf.

Buddhists and Catholics

Many Catholics, especially northerners who had fled the communists back in 1954, had no choice but to escape again. They knew they would not be able to live with the communists. They thus formed a high percentage of people leaving during the first wave.

The Buddhists who were allowed to protest under the Diem and Thieu regimes found themselves isolated: their leaders were silenced and sent to remote areas; pagodas were shut down and religions were disbanded for a while until a new leadership subservient to the state was chosen. Thich Thien Quang, a Buddhist leader at the An Quang pagoda in Saigon, fled by boat in June 1979. He claimed the communist regime was so oppressive that "we cannot exist at all."[9] He also related that Thich Tri Quan, a outspoken opponent of the Thieu and Diem regimes, became crippled following an 18-month incarceration at the famous Chi Hoa jail in Saigon. The communists, in an attempt to silence and break him down, placed him in a cubbyhole in which he could not sit or stand up and was let out for only 15 minutes each day to relieve himself and bathe. Tri Quang's muscles became atrophied from disuse and could not hold him up any longer; as a result he remained confined in a wheelchair for quite some time.

Bao was a Buddhist priest who was a proponent of peace. He preached reconciliation and negotiation with the North under the Diem and Thieu regimes. After the war, he thought he would be well accepted by the communists, until he realized the behavior of the conquering troops. As he went out to meet the northern soldiers, they threatened him with guns. One soldier struck him with his rifle and spat on him. Another soldier shot one of his fellow priests dead. They then tore apart the temple he held sacred. They riddled the Buddha statue with bullets and slashed the altar cloths with their bayonets. They told him to sit in a corner and took turns urinating on him. Bao was aghast with the communists' behavior but could not do anything.

He was taken to a holding area along with other educators, priests, and local politicians. As they reminded him that he had painted the communists as reasonable people, he felt he had misjudged the communists and fell in a deep state of depression. He was only one of two monks who survived the destruction of the temple. He decided to escape on the grounds of religious persecution and arrived in the United States in 1990.[10]

The Buddhists finally realized the Diem and Thieu regimes treated them more deferentially than the communists.

The Chinese

In 1978, about four hundred wealthy Chinese gathered in Rach Gia, a seaport in southwestern Vietnam close to the Cambodian border. They each paid about $4,000 and $5,000 for the chance to get out of Vietnam. Their lands and belongings had been confiscated and their sons drafted to fight the war in Cambodia. They felt they no longer could live under an oppressive communist regime.

At sea, their 90-foot boat almost capsized under a storm and the engine suddenly quit. The boat drifted back to land and the bribed communist guards gave them five days to fix the engine. No one was allowed ashore, although a few escaped to return home. Five days later the boat headed back to the Gulf of Thailand. After a four-day trip, it reached a Malaysian island. They sank their boat when the authorities ordered them to sail to another country. The refugees were taken to a local jail and then to Pulau Bidong, an uninhabited island, which served as a dumping ground for more than 60,000 Indochinese refugees at one time. They waited for over a year to be allowed to emigrate to the U.S.[11]

The Chinese, especially those from the South, were probably the richest of the escapees. Coming under an almost legalized and sanctioned escape, they had been able to bring their riches with them in form of diamonds or gold. Although communist officials forced them to declare their riches at the time of departure and although they were allowed to take only two ounces of gold per person, many had found ways to transfer their money in some other form. In 1978, a Chinese jeweler from Cholon, a suburb of Saigon, came to Malaysia with uncut diamonds worth $1.25 million. He hid them in a can of lubricating oil, which he placed in the boat's bilge. Of course, he probably owned the boat and had placed the can without the knowledge of the crew. Anyone who carried an oil can aboard the boat instead of the usual luggage and food would become immediately suspicious in the eyes of the escapees and crew. Another Chinese businessman requested Malaysian authorities to take custody of $200,000 in gold and $350,000 in currency. A woman arrived in Darwin, Australia with a specially designed corset containing $250,000 in cash, jewelry and gold.[12] These cases were, however rare, as the majority carried a few hundred to a few thousand dollars at most. All their savings had been used up to survive under a communist regime and to buy their way out of the country for them and their family. Northern Chinese who had lived under a communist regime from 1954 to 1975 were most likely impoverished, as were the fishermen and soldiers.

By contrast to the Vietnamese, the Chinese had been able to buy their way out in an official or semi-official way: they dealt directly with the PSB or local police and got fairly deferent treatment. They traveled with their families and in large groups of a few hundred people. The Hanoi government even loaded them by the thousands in the *Southern Cross*, *Hai Hong*, *Huey Fong*, and other ships. Since they traveled in groups, they were not subjected to pirate attacks and therefore suffered much less than other boat people. Many of them were lucky enough to be transferred to third countries without vegetating in the camps for a long time.

The Communists

They also had to escape the communist regime when they felt threatened by their comrades and the system they lived in. This only suggested that although dissent was frequent within the party, it was able to hide these dissensions by discarding or eliminating the rebels.

Case 1: Truong Nhu Tang, director of the Sugar Company in Saigon, joined the Viet Cong in the early '60s in their fight against the Saigon government. After the fall of Saigon, he came back to become the justice minister in the Provisional Revolutionary Government. He witnessed arbitrary arrests, a total of three hundred thousand from 1975 to 1976.[13] Although he appealed to the Hanoi government, nothing was done to correct the problem. He soon had enough with this lawlessness and disregard for basic rights. He believed problems in communist Vietnam were related to "ideological ruthlessness and a contemptuous disregard for human dignity and rights."[14]

He decided to escape in 1977, two years after the fall of Saigon. If the justice minister could not even live under a communist government, it is unlikely that the southerners could survive under the same ruthless system. Tang linked up with his wife's brother-in-law, Dr. Ton, who fought with the Viet Minh against the French during the first Vietnam War. Ton then moved to Hanoi in 1954 and only returned to Long Xuyen around 1977. There he became disappointed with Hanoi policies and he too decided to escape. Both of them and a businessman pitched in and bought a 35 foot long river freighter which was used to haul merchandise between Long Xuyen and Camau.

By August 1978, everything was ready. They started at 4 A.M. on Sunday, August 26. They were five to start with and were led to the hold of the boat. Soon 25 other people were added. The area was cramped and the air heavy and hard to breathe. Twenty-four hours into the trip, they arrived at the mouth of the Mekong River. The businessman turned pilot in less than two months ran up onto a sandbar. Everyone jumped out of the boat and tried to dislodge it from the sandbar. The job was completed when dawn crept up and fishing boats with patrol boats returned home. If they moved forward, the police would search them. Therefore, the skipper decided to return to Long Xuyen and try again the following morning. This time, they were successful, although the propeller got caught in fishermen's nets. They luckily freed themselves without problem and proceeded toward the sea.

On the fourth day, they encountered pirates who stripped them of their belongings but did not harm them. The next morning they ran into an oil rig where they were allowed to stay. They sank their boat in order not to be forced to sail away. The following morning, a Singaporean freighter picked them up and transported them to Galand Island camp. It was six more months before Tang was allowed to emigrate to France.

Case 2: Nguyen Son, a northern communist soldier, had always dreamed of going to South Vietnam or America because life was so wretched in North Vietnam. He was conscripted into the North Vietnamese army but deserted seven months later. He learned to navigate in the waterways of North Vietnam while planning for the escape. With his friends, he collected money to buy a boat. In 1989 at the age of 25 he left Hai Phong for Hong Kong on a boat with his brother, sister and 47 other friends and relatives.

Eight hours into his trip, he already missed Vietnam and cried heavily. He knew he was risking his life, but wanted to live in a free society rather than in a communist country. He knew that Hanoi would never forget nor forgive him if he failed in his escape. Returning to Hanoi meant imprisonment or a bleak existence. He landed in Hong Kong and was sponsored to the United States.[15]

Case 3: Among the refugees at the Pulau Bidong camp in Malaysia resided a communist. When he got off the boat he looked very heavy although he was actually skinny. Malaysian police patted him down and found a couple pounds of gold around his waist. He also carried a K54 pistol he said he could use against the pirates in case he met them. He was a district chief in communist Vietnam and collected a lot of money in bribes. He one day decided to run off with his gold. His superior, knowing he was a bad apple, told the local people he was a U.S. agent who had sabotaged everything in the district. People in the camp shunned him. No free country would accept him, except Norway.[16]

There were many communists and socialist-leaning people like Tang who finally saw Hanoi's true face and decided to leave communist Vietnam. There were a few corrupt communist officials who after having extorted money from people decided to run away before they were caught. There were reports of a few who melted into the groups of refugees, escaped abroad and worked as moles within the Vietnamese community. From January to mid–August 1979, almost 46,000 refugees coming to Hong Kong were North Vietnamese. After leaving North Vietnam they hugged the coastline of China where they could shelter from the rough weather. The boats were twin or single-masted vessels with a raised stern and "sails as ancient as the hand-hewn plank holds" crammed with men in khaki-colored pith helmets, women in their conical hats and children. The trip from Hanoi to Hong Kong took six to eight weeks.[17] Fifty-six percent of these people were ethnic Chinese.

The Returnees

After arriving on the island of Guam in May 1975, a group of refugees had second thoughts about leaving Vietnam. They either came alone or with their families. They were mostly young soldiers, although some of them were elderly. In the late days of the war and on the spur of the moment, as they saw people leaving Vietnam in droves, they too jumped into boats and escaped abroad. Having been at sea and in the camps for a few months, they decided the escape was not worth the trouble and wanted to return home to their families or country. They were really homesick. Nothing in the surroundings reminded them of Vietnam, with its bustling and crowded cities, its mangroves and palm trees, the rivers with their dark black muddy water, and the closeness of its people. They were not used to living in tents and waiting patiently in line for their meals. They were geared for action, especially disorganized action, and inaction and boredom weighed heavily on them.

They felt they did not have freedom — they were confined in camps with no access to society. Outside the camps, as far as they could see while they were taken through cities and villages, was a strange world with only English speaking people and culture. They did not know whether they could ever get a job or fit into that society. They also wondered how members of their families remaining in Vietnam were doing. They had not been able to get in touch with them for a long time. They also felt guilty about leaving their country and about never being able to return home, the land of their ancestors. In their simple ways, they felt if they changed their minds and returned home, the communists would accept them back into their society.

About 2,000 signed up to return to Vietnam. The Task Force referred the problem to UNHCR, which later communicated with the new government in Saigon. As progress was slow, a few impatient soldiers burned down their barracks at camp Asan in Guam and U.S. marshals were sent in to restore order. They also threatened to cut off their fingers and to mail them to President Ford. They later received a radio message from the communists advising them it was all right to come home. The *Viet Nam Thuong Tinh* boat (Vietnam Commercial Bank) on which they arrived on this island was refurbished and loaded with food and water. On October 16, 1975, one thousand five hundred 46 refugees steamed back to Cam Ranh Bay along with an American escort.[18]

On arrival on their native soil, they were immediately confined in another camp until a decision was reached about their fates. Men were separated from women. The latter were kept for one week and then released. All males were sent to a sub-camp of the maximum security A-20 camp.[19] The communists, in their narrow-minded ways, were always suspicious of people who did not share their views. Having never been out of their country, they could not conceive that people could miss their country so much they just wanted to return home. They, therefore, suspected the returnees of having been trained as spies for the Americans in Guam and sent them to reeducation camps. Naval lieutenant Vu Tien Hai was executed as a spy shortly after his arrival. This ended the saga of the *Viet Nam Thuong Tinh* refugees who did not want freedom in America but finally ended up in jails in Vietnam. After their release a few years later and after realizing the dark intentions of the communists, a few bought their way out of Vietnam, completing the full circle they had taken a few years earlier.

The whole Vietnamese society was represented in this diaspora, although in the third wave members of certain professions were more prevalent than others: soldiers and fishermen, for example, had direct and immediate access to boats and planes. Women and children were also represented in high numbers during the first wave (30,000 were evacuated between April 21 and 29, 1975). There were the wives of high-level Vietnamese officials and many were bar girls and girlfriends of the GI. One in five refugees arrived during the first wave. Another one in three came during the peak crisis in 1979 and 1981. The number of refugees coming to the U.S. leveled off to less than 27,000 a year after 1983. In the '80s a large proportion of refugees were detainees released from the reeducation camps.[20]

The first-wave refugees were more educated, spoke more than one language, and were better off than the second or third wave refugees. There was also a higher incidence of professionals and high level officials associated with the Americans. The second wave had more soldiers and Chinese while the third wave consisted of a higher percentage of low-income workers, fishermen, and military personnel returning from reeducation camps.

This was a war-induced migration; no one including the Vietnamese themselves expected to land on Western soil. They just ran for safety and hoped some neighboring countries would accept them. There were totally unprepared for the migration itself; they did not study any foreign language nor prepare for the trip. They did not bring any identity card with them nor carry any warm clothing. They just uprooted themselves and left.

This was a migration of unexpected proportions. No one had predicted the U.S. would receive such a large contingent of refugees. Back in 1975, the government and Congress talked about paroling at most 150,000 to 200,000 people. The number has now ballooned up to more than one million people. Within three decades, from a few thousand people, the Vietnamese became the third or fourth largest migrant minority in the U.S.

A whole section of the Vietnamese society therefore had been transplanted abroad and its effect is beginning to be felt on the host country. In the beginning, they were confused with the Chinese — they were all short, yellow people with slanted eyes. However, as their number increased, they acquired their own identity and were perceived as having a different and unique culture. They had their own cooking with their *pho* (noodle soup) and crusty and tasty *cha gio* (egg roll). They wore their distinct Vietnamese *ao dai* (dress) that looked like no other oriental dress. Unlike the Chinese, who came to the U.S. a long time ago as migrant workers and merchants, the Vietnamese looked for freedom. These and other differences made them unique among other migrants and Orientals.

10

THE ROUTES

Unlock your hearts and let them come inside.
Give those who've lost their country, lost their all,
A chance to live out their expatriate lives.
— Ha Huyen Chi[1]

How did these refugees arrive in their host countries? The routes were convoluted, at times unpredictable, and most often left to the mercy of the winds, the oceans, and the pirates, as all these trips were unplanned and unprotected. The refugees could use the land or sea routes. In case of the land routes, half of the trip was made on land and the second half by boat. The majority of people, however, still favored the sea route as their first choice.

Land Routes

There were only two land routes: north toward China and west toward Thailand through Cambodia. Northerners tended to go to China while southerners moved west through Cambodia. These trips could be completely overland or half of the trip toward Thailand could be done by sea. The trips through Cambodia were technically more difficult, as the refugees had to deal with Cambodian handlers who could abandon them in the middle of the countryside, rob them, or even kill them. Language became a barrier whenever they needed help or needed to buy something like food or drinks. The refugees usually traveled in small groups of three or four, never in large groups of 20 or a hundred, in order not to attract undue attention of the police at various checkpoints. This type of escape placed the refugees completely at the mercy of their handlers.

Overall there were far fewer refugees using land routes than sea routes. Part of the problem related to the fact that westward lay Cambodia and the vicious Khmer Rouge who did not like the Vietnamese at all. Falling into their hands meant a sure death, although no one knew the exact number of refugees who lost their lives in the fields of Cambodia. Besides, there were Vietnamese communist soldiers also stationed in Cambodia. Encountering them meant deportation back to Vietnam followed by jailing. A lot of Chinese living in North Vietnam went northward back to China. No one knew how these people fared in China, as they so far had not written any account about their trips.

Case 1: Lan Nguyen, her mother and brother along with two cousins rode the first leg of the land route from Saigon to Tan Chau, east of the Cambodian border, by bus. They then waited until nighttime to cross the border unofficially. From the west side of the border, they rode on motorcycles to the capital Phnom Penh. They hid in a house for three days and were not allowed to get out for fear of being detected. On the third leg of the land route, they took another motorcycle ride to the beach. Because the handlers went to the wrong beach, the refugees missed their boat and had to return to Phnom Penh to hide and wait for the next boat. One week later, they were brought to another beach where they boarded a small boat. The boat ride took the whole night and at dawn they were dropped on a rocky beach on the Thai side about two miles from an unknown town. To reach the town, they either had to follow the rocky coastline or go through a dense forest. The cousins volunteered to cross the jungle to look for help in the adjacent town. Thai navy men later came by to rescue the refugees with their boat.[2]

Case 2: Kim Ha, her husband and four children took the bus from Saigon to the western town of Tay Ninh. After crossing the Cambodian border illegally at night, they rode on the back of bicycles to Soai Rieng, then on the bed of a truck to the outskirts of Phnom Penh. They crossed the Mekong River on a small boat among suspicious natives and entered the city from the South. They rode to Battambang on the roof of a train fighting sun, smoke and heat. Their guide then abandoned them in the middle of a forest after they refused to give him extra money. They walked around without knowing their way and ran into thieves who stole their bags and clothing. They lost the rest of their money to a Cambodian guard at a checkpoint, and rode on smugglers' oxcarts to the Thai border.[3] Their ordeal appeared almost unbelievable as they traveled on all kinds of vehicles available to them from oxcarts and bicycles to trains or simply walking on foot.

The Thai border had been closed since March 25, 1980, because Thailand would not accept any new refugees. The Para soldiers set up a camp on the Cambodian border where they could control and search the refugees for jewelry and gold. Although Vietnamese women covered their faces with mud or scarves to hide their fair complexion, they were easily spotted. The soldiers came back at night to take young women away for a gang rape.[4] They sometimes returned a shivering, tearful, scar-covered girl in tattered clothes the following morning. Non-returning women were presumed killed. The soldiers later traded each refugee to the Red Cross whose office was located on the Thai border for 10 50-pound bags of rice. Kim Ha and her family had witnessed all the horrors associated with land escapes, including murders, rapes, and killings. They flew out of Bangkok on October 16, 1980, after a dangerous six-month trek through Vietnam and Cambodia and many Para and Thai camps.

The safest route could be divided into four sections or legs: the first section inside Vietnam itself, the second leg to the Cambodian capital, Phnom Penh, the third one southward to the seaside, and the fourth one by fishing boat to Thailand. The most dangerous route was the one that went straight by land from Phnom Penh through the western part of Cambodia to Thailand. The Khmer Rouge, renegade soldiers and many other cruel brigands occupied that unsettled area, where they plied their trades. They held, killed or ransomed those who traveled through that region, including, unfortunately, the refugees.

The underground system in Cambodia run by amateurs was full of loopholes. Many local groups competed with each other for escapees. They were not accountable to anyone and were therefore not reliable. They knew the Vietnamese did not speak the local language and would not report them to the authorities. They were often greedy and attempted to extort extra money from the escapees, pretending changes in the schedule warranted it. They were also ready to steal their money and belongings before dumping them in the middle of the forests.

Most of the escapees therefore used the sea routes. They either went northeast toward Hong Kong, east toward the Philippines, southwest toward Malaysia, Singapore, Indonesia and Thailand, and south toward Australia. They did not need interpreters, as they dealt directly with Vietnamese handlers throughout their trips. They traveled in big groups of 10, 50, or a hundred and therefore could easily argue with their handlers. Their biggest problems were the pirates and the pushback by various Southeast Asian countries, besides the unexpected storms. The other problem was engine failure. Their ordeal could be as complicated and dangerous as that of people taking the land routes. We will follow each of these routes and try to describe the difficulties encountered in each case.

Northeast to Hong Kong

Case 1: Hai Van Le graduated from the South Vietnamese flight school in early April 1975. When the government surrendered, he went to the Saigon River and boarded one of the commercial boats that were still anchored at the pier. Three thousand people — men, women, and children — came aboard with no food and water in their rush to get out of the country. The boat took off and steamed through the meandering Mekong River to reach the ocean. As it passed for the last time by Vung Tau, one soldier, knowing he would never see Vietnam again, pulled out his gun, put it under his chin, and killed himself. A few other distraught people jumped overboard and drowned themselves in the sea. For three days, no one received food or water. A Danish ship found them, picked up women and children and transported them to Hong Kong. They gave food and water to all the men who remained in their own boat and directed them to Hong Kong, where they were reunited with their families.[5] This was one of the first boats arriving to Hong Kong after the war.

Case 2: Pham van Xinh was a security officer with the South Vietnamese Second Infantry division. He witnessed the communists arriving in Da Nang in 1975. They had with them lists of South Vietnamese who had worked with the Americans and when and wherever they got hold of them, they shot them on the spot, execution style. "They just killed them where they found them.... It was frightening. The communists had no mercy." Like during the Tet offensive in Hue where they massacred more than 3,000 innocent civilians, they were ruthless, did not follow any rule and took the law in their own hands.

Xinh was caught a few days later and sent to various labor camps for six years. When he returned home in 1983, he found a man with a small boat. He told the man he would be his navigator if he wanted to get out of Vietnam. He basically traded his work for a free ticket out of the country. This was a risky proposition on his part because if the man reported him to the police he would be automatically sent back to the reeducation camp. The boat owner agreed and gathered 22 more people who paid for the trip and the group set sail to Hai Nan Island in December 1983. The Chinese helped them with food and water and they continued their trip to Hong Kong. The journey took 24 days.[6]

Case 3: A Chinese restaurant owner, his cook and their families decided to get out of Hanoi in February 1979. They paid the Hanoi PSB a $2,045 bribe for permission to travel from the city to Hon Gay to purchase a boat. The local PSB gave the cooperative clearance to sell the boat. The Chinese paid $4,545 for repairs along with six tons of fuel. They also bought $1,818 of food and water. The restaurant owner got 327 other Chinese to pay for the trip. They were finally allowed to leave Hon Gay after paying $455 for a motorized junk to tow their boat to international waters[7] and from there to Hong Kong.

Not too many refugees from South Vietnam headed northeast toward Hong Kong because of the distance of the trip. The majority (70 percent) arrived to this city from North Vietnam mainly during the 1978–79 and 1988 waves. Only one in every 20 boat-refugees from the north was ethnic Vietnamese, the rest being Chinese. The total number of arrivals in Hong Kong climbed from 3,400 in 1987 to over 18,000 in 1988. The trip was usually uneventful, as the refugees safely hugged the coastline and went to shore for hiding when they encountered storms. There were no pirates to fear in this area. This was the safest of all routes.

East to the Philippines

Not too many people took the eastern sea route because it was the most dangerous of all routes due to its isolation. This explained why only 10 thousand out of the three hundred thousand refugees used that route between 1975 and 1979. It was possible that many more did not make it and therefore the true number was unknown. Almost nine hundred and 50 miles (by far one of the longest routes) separated Vietnam from the

Philippines and all of them were in the wide-open seas. Once the refugees crossed the north-south international sea-lanes, the ocean became deserted and no help could be obtained if they faced any mechanical problem. In the second half of the trip, they would encounter a chain of atolls, reefs, and islets that were scattered west and southwest of Palawan Island. These atolls were known as the graveyard of shipwrecks of the South China Sea, as many ships inadvertently crashed onto these submerged islands.

Case 1: Captain Dinh was commanding a PCF (Patrol Craft Fast) with a crew of six when he was ordered on April 29, 1975, to go to Con Son Island for regrouping. Dinh came back to Saigon to pick up seven members of his family along with families of his crew. They were 40 in a 10 by 30 foot boat. His father, who was a former captain of the police, refused to come with him. He thought he was safe because he had retired from the South Vietnamese forces many years ago. The refugees sailed down the Saigon River and stopped a big boat called the *Vong Hong Ni* loaded with 300 Chinese. They transferred to the bigger boat and the group headed toward the Philippines without incident. The trip lasted seven days.

His father in the meantime was sent to various reeducation camps for a total of five years. When he got out, he was disillusioned with the communists. He too decided to escape. He bought his way out but the greedy boat owner overloaded the boat with one hundred and 20 passengers instead of the usual 40. The boat took on water and Dinh's father worked so hard to bail the water that he died of exhaustion. The boat landed in Malaysia seven days later.[8]

Case 2: In Vietnam, Tran Vu was tired of attending nightly communist meetings, doing irrigation work under the hot sun, reading party newspapers, and watching his friends being sent off to Cambodia. Although they had not read *Das Kapital* or the works of Lenin, they knew "from their own retched lives and the terror of last year's purges" they had to leave Vietnam.[9]

On May 29, 1979, using a fake Chinese identity card, Tran Vu got out of Vietnam with a group of Chinese on a planned trip that was cleared by the government. At the last minute, the police added one hundred extra people to the already crowded boat. On the fourth day of the trip, the boat hit something hard. The skipper and the owner argued about the cause of the accident: one believed the boat ran aground while the other thought the propeller was caught in fishing nets. The boat then tipped on one side and its edge became submerged in water. People dumped cans and suitcases overboard in an attempt to decrease the weight. The skipper pushed the engine harder, causing the prow to rear up then fall back onto rocks, crushing cabins full of people.

The boat had run aground on a coral reef. Four hundred people landed in water but luckily no one was killed. Attempts to push the boat back into the water were unsuccessful. For seven days they stayed on the reef waiting for help to come. More and more people died of exhaustion and lack of food. Finally five men, including Tran Vu, volunteered to use a raft to go and look for help. They were burnt by the hot sun and then drifted back to the coral reef. On the 14th day a huge tide swept in and pulled the boat out while passengers pushed it into the water. The skipper turned the engine on and disengaged the boat from the reef. In the end, the boat was able to continue its course to the Philippines.

Case 3: Hue was only 16 when she, her uncle, aunt, and younger brother steamed eastward toward the Philippines. In a moment of panic, her parents and two other brothers were left behind in Can Tho. By the seventh day they ran out of food. The hull started leaking and the boat hit and got stranded on an atoll. They survived on oysters and snails. They valiantly fought against winds, tides, storms, and torrid sun. They, however, died out one by one. No one came to help them out and one month later the 50 passengers dwindled down to seven. The survivors shared food and slept together in one corner of a big wreck. The heat, dehydration, and malnourishment took their toll. They became weaker and weaker and were barely able to get up and move around. They tried to catch seagulls for food. These birds, however, were fast and easily escaped from the tired and slow moving people. There were days when she was too weak to catch anything and had to go hungry. Soon Hue became the last survivor on the atoll. She was not scared of ghosts but only of loneliness. She had no one to talk to. Luckily one navy boat finally came by, rescued her and took her to a navy hospital. Once she got well, she realized she had been on the atoll for five months, most of the time by herself.[10] It indeed was a miracle that she had survived that long.

The west-east trip was rather straightforward if the refugees did not wreck their boat on an atoll or have any mechanical problem. Also there were no pirates to worry about.

Southwest to Malaysia, Thailand, and Indonesia

This was the most commonly used route, but also one of the most dangerous because of the presence of pirates. Since Malaysia, Thailand, Singapore, and Indonesia received the bulk of the refugees, their camps soon became overcrowded and they became the first to use the pushback policy whereby boats were pulled back to the seas and refused landing.

Case 1: Thuy Mac was born in Saigon in 1967. Her mother did not marry her father, who was an American GI. He, however, came back in 1973 and 1975 asking her to come with him to America. She refused on both occasions. After the fall of Saigon Thuy Mac and her mother moved to My Tho, 50 miles southwest of Saigon. Schoolmates found her strange because of her Caucasian traits. Feeling unwanted in Vietnam, she escaped abroad with her aunt's family in 1979 as her mother continued to refuse to leave Vietnam. They sailed from My Tho to Malaysia in eight days and nine nights without encountering any problem. As they approached land, Malaysians shot at the boat to scare them away and in the process wounded a few refugees. The boat captain decided to ask for water, which was given to him. They sailed on to Indonesia where the refugees landed and stayed at three different camps. Her cousins finally sponsored her to the United States in 1981.[11]

Case 2: In 1975 Kim Vinh's father, a colonel in the ARVN, reported to a camp for what was claimed to be a "six-week reeducation." The six-week incarceration became a nine-year ordeal, as he was only released in 1984. She could not get any job or get into college in Vietnam because of her father's background, so she became one of the boat people. She had to sit at the bottom of the boat for six long days during which people on the deck urinated on her. They did not do it intentionally though; as the boat was crowded, people urinated in a bag which was passed around and dumped into the sea. When done incorrectly, the liquid would spill onto the deck down on people sitting in the hold.

The trip turned out to be uneventful. The refugees arrived in Singapore, were given water and C-rations, and told to go somewhere else. They then sailed to Malaysia where, tired of being on the seas all the time, they made up their mind to land. Although local people shot at them with M-16 rifles, the captain decided to sink the ship anyway and destroy the engine. They waddled to the shore. Local people were understandably upset at the refugees but let them live on a soccer field. Three thousand people thus slept on the ground for about a year[12] before being referred to a United Nation camp.

Case 3: Quyet was finally released from a reeducation camp due to health reasons after three years of incarceration. They sent him home expecting him to die with his family. However, he survived his illness and decided to escape in 1979. When his boat arrived in Malaysia in 1979, Malaysian police turned the refugees away when they stated they did not have gold to give. The refugees sailed to another camp but were again turned away. They arrived at Mersing camp, where they were allowed to stay for one month while Quyet helped the local police captain with his language skills. At the end of the month, a navy boat towed them away but their boat capsized and sank. They were taken to the Pulau Permengal camp and given a new refugee boat, then towed to high seas toward Pulau Letung, Indonesia.[13] The Malaysian navy captain then advised them not to return to Malaysia. The refugees settled in a new Indonesian camp that sometimes lacked food and water before being picked up by the UNHCR.

These refugees arrived in Malaysia in the mid-part of 1979, at a time when Asian nations adamantly refused to accept any new refugees. As a result, Quyet and the other refugees were bumped from one camp to another and their boat towed by a navy ship south toward Indonesia. They were even warned about not returning to Malaysia. These were the darkest hours of the boat people, when exhausted, hungry and thirsty following a long sea trip, they finally arrived in view of land only to be chased back to the sea. They hoped to receive a warm welcome but were met with shotguns. They for a certain time felt that these Asians were no better than the cruel communists at home. Indeed, some Malaysian Navy men were ruthless as they even sank refugees' boats. Many more people would die at sea as the result of this pushback policy before it was rescinded.

Southeast to Australia

Not too many refugees planned to go to Australia, partly because of distance and inconvenience, but also because Australians looked so foreign to them. Any refugee could melt easily into a crowd of Asians but not into a group of Australians. And since many Asian nations were convenient for refugees sailing south, there was no need to travel further to Australia unless they were rejected in Asia.

Case 1: Two months after the fall of Saigon, Lam Binh bought and fixed a boat in Rach Gia with the goal of escaping abroad some day. His family of eight people was joined by three friends later on. Rach Gia was a seaport located in southwestern Vietnam close to the Cambodian border with 800 large fishing boats like Binh's and 3,000 smaller ones. Its main businesses were fishing and commercial trade with Cambodia and Thailand. This was also the shipyard as well as one of the escape sites for many refugees. For eight months, Binh studied navigation and began storing away dried food. They set sail in February 1976 aiming in the southwest direction. They arrived in Ubol, Thailand, where six seasick members of his family decided to settle in a Lao refugee camp. The five youngsters aged 16 to 25 moved on but were shunted from port to port. They arrived in Malaysia, Singapore, Sarawak and Sabah (Borneo), where they spent four weeks repairing their boat. They were given food and fuel and told to move on. They continued to Darwin, accumulating a total of 2,200 miles on that trip.

On April 26, 1976 two months after leaving Rach Gia, they arrived in Darwin, northern Australia, in a decrepit wooden boat. Their sixty-foot boat was registered in Kien Giang as *KG 4435*. They left Timor 16 days earlier and had navigated from a page torn from a school atlas. They waited out all night off the coast, as no one seemed to notice them. The following morning, they followed the shoreline, entered the port of Darwin, and anchored at the wharf. The surprised and confused people of Darwin did not know what to do with this group of fishermen who came out of nowhere: they had never seen Vietnamese fishermen before in their lives. The 25-year-old captain, Lam Binh, told the immigration officer who came on board that he and his friends would like to ask for permission to stay in Australia. They thus became the first boat people to sail from Vietnam to Australia.[14]

Case 2: A group of 56 people took off on *PK 504* from Cam Ranh Bay on October 28, 1976, while the remaining 50 others were stopped at a roadblock and jailed. On the seas, many passing ships ignored their call for help. They then sailed southwest and arrived at Mersing, Malaysia, on November 4 and were given food and fuel and told to move on. They stopped at Tioman Island, scaring away many guests at the beach hotel.

They moved to Songkhla where Thai pirates robbed them of their last tael of gold. They turned south, ran into the edge of a cyclone, and battled with rains and winds for three days and nights. Singapore turned them away and told them not to come back. They sailed south toward Indonesia, were given food and fuel and advised about the safe route to Australia. They finally ended up in Darwin after a five thousand mile trip.[15]

Case 3: Employees from a shipping company drugged three armed communist cadres, whose job was to watch them, on the steel-hulled *Song Be 12*. They then picked up their families and friends and sailed to Australia 3,000 miles away. They arrived in November 1977 carrying 181 refugees and three cadres after refueling in Indonesia.[16]

These were the first of the many boats that arrived in Australia after a long and difficult journey at sea. Only then did the Australians realize that the refugee problem was no longer confined to the Southeast Asian states, but had spilled over onto their continent. In the end, Australia would open its arms and receive the third highest number of refugees in the world.

The choice of the land or sea routes depended on the refugees' personal preferences, proximity to the ocean, and familiarity with geography. Many people chose land routes to avoid pirates, the ocean and its storms or because of failure to escape by sea routes in the past. The sea somehow evoked a lot of fears in certain people: the ocean is seen as huge, dark and bottomless, and sailing on the ocean is like sailing into the unknown because of its violent storms, lack of referral points, and lack of protection. If the boat happened to sink, everyone on board usually died of drowning and asphyxiation, a terrible death indeed. It has been estimated that half of the people died at sea. Although the figure has been revised down to 10 to 15 percent, the number remained astronomical: close to one hundred thousand people had perished at sea.

However, there was no safety in land travel either. The Khmer Rouge and Cambodian bandits turned out to be even more ferocious than the pirates. They maimed, raped and killed without remorse. The ordeal was not over once they arrived in Thailand. The camps in northern Thailand were in general worse than those located further south. These facts, however, were not available to the refugees at the time of the escape.

As the Chinese, chased out of their country, arrived in Vietnam in the late 18th and early 19th centuries to look for a place to live and work, the reigning Nguyen lord allowed them to settle in the Mekong delta and southernmost part of Vietnam. As they arrived by boat haggard, homeless and penniless, the Vietnamese ironically called them *Ba Tau* (boat people), a term that has stuck to them until today. In time they became successful entrepreneurs and merchants and controlled most of the Vietnamese economy. History has a way of repeating itself. After 1975, the homeless Vietnamese had become the new *Ba Tau* in the U.S. and other Western countries. In the new lands, they no doubt would duplicate the deeds of the Chinese in Vietnam.

The diaspora was certainly not a benign and joyful adventure. It was treacherous and full of surprises and tragedies. On one hand there was the sea with its storms and pirates or the land with its cruel brigands, on the other hand there were the angry host nations and their pushback policy.

Those who had survived the sea ordeal felt themselves very fortunate indeed, for the ocean had never released its grip on those it held.

11

THE PIRATES

Pirates had always been prevalent in the straights of Malacca and the Gulf of Thailand for many centuries or even millennia. They hid in the many coves and islands that curled around mainland Southeast Asia. They preyed on isolated ships going through the area. They could be regular fishermen looking for easy prey or cold-blooded corsairs who loved to kill and plunder.

In the beginning, a few of these fishermen did help disabled boaters and lead them to safety. They then found it convenient to make a few bucks out of the refugees. They soon turned into marauding and stealing outright by force, then they engaged in violent acts: killing and raping women. Violence became worse as they became more organized and soon almost no boat escaped safely from their attacks.

Fishermen-Pirates

What started almost as a game in 1975 evolved into a routine business and then ended in the late '80s as deadly and wicked tragedies. When the first groups of refugees took to the sea in the second half of 1975, they sailed through the Gulf of Thailand undisturbed and untouched. As the traffic increased, they caught the attention of Thai fishermen who worked in the area. The refugees might have asked some of them for directions or help with mechanical problems they might have with their boats. They could have asked them for food or water in exchange of gold, for the refugees did not have any Thai money. Gold and money began tempting the hard working and low paid fishermen. They began extorting more money for their help or went straight to robbing the refugees.

The seas were vast and since they were in international waters, no one would be around to police them.

Words spread around that refugees had money and soon hordes of fishermen came around looking for a simple way to make a living. They thought the refugees were loaded with money, while in reality they were not. In the late 1975, a few rich people were able to escape and took with them money and belongings. These cases became rarities when the communists started clamping down on the southern society. Bank assets were frozen, people were evicted from their homes, and businesses along with belongings were taken away from them. Food prices increased and basic commodities disappeared in the socialist society. People became impoverished. They spent their savings on food, which had become quite expensive. They had to bribe communist officials for everything from a fine to a registration card. In a socialist society, everything required permission from the authorities, from going to see a friend across town to buying a ticket. Would-be escapees then had to buy their way out of the country and paid three to 10 taels of gold for each attempt. Therefore, when they left Vietnam, they were down to their last two to three taels of gold. The majority had nothing because in order not attract the attention of the police, they did not sell their houses or belongings. But when the boat was loaded with 10 or 20 escapees, the amount of gold that could be extracted from the group rose rapidly.

Fishermen worked solo in the beginning: they went fishing as usual and once a refugee boat was located, they just went after the boat. As time went by, they became more sophisticated, worked in groups and kept in touch with each other by radio communication. They placed their boats in rings in order to trap the refugee boats inside. Once the boats crossed a ring, the pirate boats would zoom in on their victims. They hounded refugees like wolves around their prey. They attacked small boats and later became brave and organized enough to board cargo boats carrying six or seven hundred refugees. They first used long-bladed knives, daggers, axes, and iron bars, then turned to carrying guns.

What they did was pure robbing in the beginning. They made the refugees come over to their boat and lined them up: women on one side and men on the other. They checked everyone for money, gold, earrings or bracelets. They took their time with the refugees and simply requested the rings or bracelets be handed over. When they saw a woman wearing a necklace with an image of Buddha, they bowed in front of the picture.

If they flipped the picture over and noticed a hundred dollar bill hidden behind, they simply asked for it. When the robbing was over, they sent the refugees back to their boat and took off. They gave the refugees whatever food or water they needed before sending them off. They even left a note for other pirates advising them the boat had been robbed. But the next pirate boat came over anyway and took whatever they could put their hands on. The pirates looked more carefully for any leftover money — they checked the hems of clothing where refugees would hide money or valuables. They asked them to undress for a more careful search. Frustrated for having not found anything, they took the refugees on a ride. They made men work on their boat, throwing out and pulling back the fishing nets. After a few days, they let the refugees go.

The number and frequency of the attacks increased with time. In the '80s, refugee boats crossing the Gulf of Thailand were attacked by pirates almost two thirds of the time and each boat was boarded at least twice.

Violent Acts: RMP

The game soon turned violent. The pirates were no longer content with robbing: they started raping, murdering, and pillaging, the reason for the acronym "RMP" that was stamped on many refugees' files. They no longer asked for rings or bracelets; they demanded them. If the refugees refused or were slow to hand them over, they slashed their throats or killed them with axes or iron bars in order to pocket the valuables. They cracked the skull of a four-month pregnant woman with repeated blows to the head with a shovel because she could not climb onboard the pirate boat fast enough. Her body was thrown overboard. If in the beginning, they killed for no reason at all, in the end they killed in order not to leave behind any trace.

The pirates soon did not limit their work to international waters. They became greedy and went into Vietnamese waters in an attempt to be the first to catch the boats and hopefully get the biggest loot. Greed, however, landed many of them in Vietnamese jails as they were caught by police patrols.

Women refugees had heard about the pirates and their violent acts. That was the risk they were taking when they decided to escape. No one, however, knew how violent the pirates could be until they themselves bore witness to the attacks. Women would smear their faces and skin with soot or engine oil to cover their light complexion in order not to attract undue attention. Some even smeared their faces and clothes with *nuoc mam,* a good but stinking fish sauce, in hopes the pirates would not approach them because of the stench. But the pirates knew about the trick: they simply ordered them to bathe, then raped them. Not happy with just raping their victims, they sometimes threw them into the water to watch them drown.

Case 1: Mai and a few girls were taken aboard a pirate boat and raped over and over again. She fought them, but they just beat her and laughed at her. For the next few days, nine different Thai men continued to rape the girls. They terrorized them, thrust knives at their throats, and forced them to perform sexual acts which the girls found humiliating. As one girl froze because of horror and humiliation, they bludgeoned her to death and threw her into the sea. In the meantime, the pirates continued to raid other small boats and found new victims. They got tired of Mai and her companions and threw them into the sea. She lost track of time and was saved by a refugee boat that by chance spotted her. None of her companions survived.[1]

Case 2: In December 1979, the pirates tied a refugee boat to theirs to stabilize it in the middle of a stormy sea. They asked all the refugees to jump to their boat. A couple of girls jumped and fell in the water but were rescued. One man jumped at the wrong time, fell into the water, and was crushed by the two boats coming together. He was killed instantly. The pirates started robbing the passengers. Three others went to the refugee boat to look for hidden gold. They found a sick girl who did not leave the boat and raped her. The refugees were allowed to go back to their boat, which was pushed away.

The pirates took the compass and maps and broke everything. They even created holes in the hold to sink the refugee boat. Water poured in rapidly. The crew patched the holes by inserting their own clothes into the openings and stabilized the boat. The engine died for being soaked by seawater. The boat was left drifting. Everyone was tired and no one knew the direction. Luckily, two Malaysian Navy ships showed up and food was distributed to the passengers. The people were, however, not allowed to land ashore because Malaysia refused to accept any new refugees. The Navy ship towed the refugee boat close to an island where they stayed overnight because of the storm. The next morning, the government changed its mind and allowed the refugees to be taken to the Pulau Bidong camp.[2]

Case 3: On another occasion, a boat with eight Thai men on board approached a refugee boat at sea. The Thais threw anchors on the deck of the Vietnamese boat and attempted to board, but the refugees resisted. The pirates used rags soaked with diesel fuel and got ready to torch the victims' boat but the Vietnamese hurled gasoline back at them. Sensing resistance, the pirates got mad and summoned another boat that came by and rammed the refugee boat, splitting it in half. All the refugees fell into the water. Not happy with destroying the refugee boat, the Thais fished the refugees out of the water one by one. With their long knives, they chopped off their heads and dumped them into the sea; the water turned red. For days, the few survivors clung onto rafts until a Malaysian trawler picked them up. They were found to be dehydrated, hungry, scared, and looked disheveled. Only 16 out of 76 passengers survived the carnage.[3]

Case 4: The 30-foot long *KG 0729* left Vietnam in October 1978 with 30 passengers. As the crew was trying to fix a dead engine, a Thai boat approached and forced the refugees onto its deck. All men were searched and robbed and a few of them were randomly tossed overboard. The rest were tied and shoved into the refrigerated hold. One man could not get his wedding ring off in time and had his ring finger chopped off. He was bludgeoned to death, then thrown into the sea before the horrified eyes of his wife. Women were taken below the deck, stripped and searched. The young girls were dragged back to the deck and raped for three hours. When it was over, the survivors were shoved back onto the *KG 0729*. A few men who were stiff from being in the cold room for some time were thrown overboard, their hands still tied behind their backs. The pirates then battered the refugee boat's engine with hammer. They finally left with deep sighs of relief from the refugees, but returned a few minutes later and rammed the *KG 0729* twice, creating gashes in the hold. The refugees took off their clothes and stuffed them into the openings. They again attempted to fix the engine and got it working again. Two days later, the dehydrated and abused refugees arrived to Pulau Bidong too tired to ask for help.[4]

Case 5: Pirates also abducted young girls to continue their orgy on land or to sell to prostitution rings. Two young girls were brought to a

Songkhla motel. As a pirate tried to force himself onto one of the girls, she screamed and disturbed guests in adjacent rooms. After the pirate fled, she led the police to the dock where the fisherman's boat was still moored. The rest of the crew was arrested and the second girl was also found. The pirates confessed their intention to sell the girls to the red light district in town.[5]

These were just some of the horror stories recounted by the survivors. There were thousands of others, some more gruesome than others. There were many other vicious attacks no one else knew of because the victims did not survive to tell their stories. Many victims were too ashamed of their experiences or too traumatized by these actions to recount them. Retelling them meant not only reliving these painful and tragic experiences, but also suffering anew. Therefore, some just wanted to bury them for good in the back of their minds, not knowing they would come back and haunt them the rest of their lives.

Ko Kra Island

Case 6: The boat *SS0640 IA* left Rach Gia on December 1979 with 107 people. On the third day, pirates boarded the refugee boat and robbed all the passengers. Twenty-seven people were transferred aboard the pirate boat, which then towed the refugee boat at high speed in a circle. The boat tipped and sank, drowning all 80 passengers. The 27 remaining refugees were brought to Ko Kra, a deserted island about 55 miles east from mainland Thailand. The men were shoved overboard at a distance from land and were forced to swim ashore. This caused seven men to drown. The women were dropped ashore and all parts of their bodies were searched for hidden valuables. For the next eight days pirates came back to terrorize and rape them, even when they lay unconscious on the beach because of exhaustion. A Thai navy boat came by but did nothing. A second navy boat came on the fifth day and took a letter from the refugees to the UNHCR commissioner. The refugees were turned over to the commissioner on the eighth-day. Eighty-seven people died during this incident.[6]

Case 7: Thuy Ngoc was 14 when she escaped by boat with her family from a small town close to Qui Nhon in central Vietnam. The weather was so bad the trip had to be aborted twice. They succeeded on the third try with 38 people on board. They sailed southwest toward Malaysia but ran out of food and water on the first day. Thai pirates stopped them, took their gold and valuables, and raped one lady. Two other groups of pirates stopped the boat on two other occasions and gang-raped another lady.

They took all the refugees to an island and took the women to the bushes to rape them. Thuy Ngoc was skinny and did not know what they did to her at that time, except they "hurt" her. The refugees were left to look for food for themselves on the deserted island and the Thai navy came a few days later to pick them up. She landed in California and was teased by her schoolmates because of her small size and shabby clothes. She tried to kill herself with an overdose of pills when she was in high school. Although she went to the university, she still harbored nightmares about the pirates. She could not be "affectionate, hold hands with someone, or even be romantic." She did not know whether she would try to kill herself again.[7]

Case 8: On October 19, 1979, Nhat Tien steamed out of Vung Tau, South Vietnam, with 80 other refugees. There were university professors, reporters, artists, former reeducation camp prisoners, and mostly students of draft age. The boat's engine broke down on the third day and the boat drifted for one week. Food and water became short and passengers had to drink their own urine to survive. Several ships passed by but ignored their distress signals. Pirates robbed them but helped fix their boat engine on the 10th day. The refugees were attacked two more times, but there was nothing left to steal. They were towed to Ko Kra Island where they had two peaceful days. They planted a white flag with an S.O.S. sign on a high place. A Thai navy boat came by to investigate and promised to be back. Three different bands of pirates came at night with torches and armed with rifles, hammers, and knives; they robbed the refugees again. The last group drove all the men into a cave and raped the women until dawn. A young girl attempted to kill herself by jumping into the water. The following nights and days, the pirates came back looking for the women who were hiding deep in the jungle or in the trees. They hunted the women, pulled them out and raped them again.

Three other boatloads of refugees were dropped about 100 feet from the shore. Sixteen people, including four women and three children, drowned before reaching the shore. An oil company pilot who flew by the island on November 15 saw an unusual concentration of boats around the island. Two days later, the helicopter dropped dry fish, rice and some medications. Ted Schweitzer, a UNCHR field officer, and a doctor came by boat the next day and rescued 157 refugees. He saw women who were so weak they had to be dragged out of their hiding places by their relatives. He would later make two dozen more trips to rescue 1,250 more refugees.[8]

The rescue of the first batch of refugees led to the arrest and conviction of seven Thai fishermen who each received 16 years of jail for rape and robbery. The trial was lengthy and humiliating for the nine women who were courageous enough to press charges against the pirates. Each witness was questioned separately without any other boat people present and without a defense lawyer. The session lasted eight hours a day for many days and the witness was not even allowed to sit down during that lengthy session. One witness was bribed and even threatened to have her resettlement efforts delayed.[9]

Piracy only got worse with time because of a lack of policing at sea. A total of 571 deaths along with 599 rapes and 243 abductions had been reported in 1981 alone, although many more remained unreported.

Resistance

Only in rare circumstances were the refugees able to repel their attackers. In April 1978, 36 escapees overpowered a guard stationed on a government-owned fishing boat. They took his AK-47 automatic rifle and pistol and headed toward Malaysia. When the pirate boat approached the refugee boat in the Gulf of Thailand and pirates started threatening the escapees, the refugees responded by shooting the pirates, who rapidly left the area.[10]

Case 9: Dr. Cung was the heart surgeon at Saigon's Nguyen Van Hoc hospital. He was finishing his operation when the North Vietnamese took over the city in 1975. They sent him to a reeducation camp where his right leg became paralyzed. He still had to do hard labor despite his illness. He also witnessed the killing of two ARVN soldiers who attempted to escape but failed. A year later, as the communists needed a heart surgeon for the hospital they released him and put him to work without a salary. He lived on sweet potatoes and water but eagerly studied maps and charts in preparation for an escape.

He also studied the strategy of the pirates. He knew they formed a five to 10 mile diameter ring with seven or eight boats. As soon as a boat entered the ring, the pirates closed in. He escaped one night onboard a 71 foot boat with 687 people. In the gulf, he entered a pirate boat-ring and was sandwiched between two pirate boats. As the pirates threw anchors onto the refugee boat, Dr. Cung ordered the anchor ropes cut. A few refugees wanted to surrender but he told them to fight back with whatever they had: sticks against knives. The refugees had numbers on their side and fought with courage. After more than an hour of fighting, the pirates left. Cung and his fully loaded boat arrived safely at Pulau Bidong on April 15, 1979, with only two deaths.[11]

Despite the heroics of individuals like Ted Schweitzer, pirate attacks continued. In 1981, the first time UNHCR kept records, there were 881 people listed missing or dead, 578 women had been raped, and 228 had been abducted. The actual number could be higher. UNHCR donated a speedboat to Thai Navy to increase sea patrolling. The German boat *Cap Anamur* and the French *Ile de Lumiere* participated in the rescue of refugees stranded at sea. These efforts, however, were limited and not well coordinated. Finally UNHCR in June 1982 funded a $3.6 million anti-piracy program with encouraging results: there were many arrests and convictions. Although the number of attacks decreased, the degree of violence against refugees increased: "infants were thrown in the water in front of their mothers; people dipped in fishing nets into the sea until they were drowned; people attacked with harpoons and ice picks. The tales of rape — they passed girls around like bees finding a field full of flowers" became more frequent.[12] In 1989, the number of dead and missing increased to 750 and the number of rapes and abductions rose. It appears that a group of hard core criminals had taken over the piracy business and took pains to leave no witnesses.

In the beginning, there were only a few unremarkable incidents. As the flow of refugees grew larger, the number of pirate attacks rose markedly, so did the incidence of RMP. Violent acts became more and more frequent as if cold-blooded corsairs had replaced the "mild-mannered" pirates. One boat had been attacked 10 times and by the time it reached shore, the refugees had been stripped except for their underwear. Pirates not only stole, but also pillaged and murdered. They disabled the engines and put holes in the hulls to sink the boats. They destroyed and vandalized everything on the boats. After pillaging, they turned around and rammed the refugee boats in order to sink them. They slashed throats and severed heads. They tied men's hands behind their backs and kicked them into the water. Premeditated and intentional killing was obvious. The number of mutilations and dead washing to shore increased. In one incident only 16 out of 76 people survived an attack. The upsurge in piracy coincided with the push-back measures initiated by the Thai government, which prompted speculation the government had turned its eyes away from the actions of the pirates. On the other hand, pirates worked in international waters and piracy had been present for years and was difficult to eradicate.[13]

The effects of piracy on women and children were dramatic and long lasting. Children started having nightmares right after they reached the camp-island of Pulau Bidong: having associated nightlights with pirates, they became afraid whenever they saw lights at night on the seas around the island. These fishermen's lights could also be pirates' lights. They became extremely frightened when they had to take a boat even during daytime to go to mainland Malaysia for treatment or relocation. Many like Thuy Ngoc harbored deep, agonizing feelings the rest of their lives; they could not be affectionate or even hold hands. They became psychologically disturbed and many attempted suicide. Thirty-six year old Hue still woke up screaming years later from nightmares of the experience — "the dark skinned men encircling her, the knife at her throat, the hands that clawed, and the teeth that bit, mutilating her breasts."[14] These were horror stories that remained with the victims the rest of their lives.

12

THE CAMPS

> You've never lost and left your land.
> All people share the human shape,
> But human hearts don't beat alike.
> — Du Tu Le[1]

Deluged with the rapidly increasing number of arrivals, the first-asylum states (Malaysia, Thailand, Hong Kong, the Philippines, Indonesia, and Singapore) had opened up a number of refugee camps throughout Southeast Asia. Refugees were then screened and flown to their final destination. After the U.S. closed its mainland camps in 1976, all the refugees were screened in these foreign camps prior to their resettlement in the U.S.

Malaysia

Along with Thailand, Malaysia shared a long and sandy eastern coastline that became attractive landing zones for boat refugees who sailed south or southwest. The Sungei Besi camp was situated on the western coast while Pulau Bidong, Kemunin, Pulau Besar, Marang, Kuantan, Pulan Tengah, and Mersing were located on the eastern Malaysian coast.

Pulau Bidong was, according to asylum seekers, a miserable (*Bi Dat*) place to live. It was a deserted tropical island in 1976 about 30 miles off the eastern coast of Malaysia and within five weeks it became home to 25,000 Indochinese. As the refugees landed on the island, they were noted to be as numerous as the trees in the jungle. They transformed the rocky island into a shantytown from scratch as more and more people kept coming and as their stay became longer and longer. Cardboard, cloth from rice bags, plastic sheeting, leaves, tree trunks, and anything that could shield or cover were used in the construction of the dwellings. Flimsy shacks popped up everywhere without order or style, their shapes barely resembling any modern housing complex and their sizes ridiculously small, although they actually accommodated five to 10 people who lived crammed together like sardines. This was a town completely built by hand with leftover and discarded materials, with minimal support from the government and whose only purpose was to shelter a group of refugees for a short period of time. In the end it became a permanent fixture to the island.

The population of the island at one time rose to 60,000. In the beginning, there was little food and water and life was hard. There were no sanitary facilities, except for the typical "Asian squat toilet: a four-inch hole with two raised footrest[s] in a tin shed. There was no shower or tub, only a dipper floating in a drum of water."[2] The stench — a mixture of stagnant water and stale urine — hung over the narrow paths and made foreigners heave. There were rats everywhere: at one time, the refugees caught 11,000 of them in an effort to control the population and to prevent bubonic plague. These rats either came from the mainland or with the boat people. Over time, they became well fed from the amount of garbage that piled up in the dumps.

Malaysian authorities used to tow the refugee boats to high seas and the boats would sink and people drowned as a result. The next morning the shore was full of bodies — men, women, and children — all Vietnamese. The refugees had to bury the dead every morning.[3] One day a CBS News crew came and filmed the camp. And after the program was aired, the Malaysian government was blamed for the poor treatment of the refugees. Food trickled in by courtesy of the United Nations. A UNHCR standard ration pack consisted of 900 grams of rice, a can of condensed milk, three cans of meat, fish and vegetables, two packets of noodles, sugar, salt, and two teabags. Each pack was supposed to last each refugee three days. There was a shortage of drinking and cooking water, as increasing demands overwhelmed limited supplies. Of 100 wells, only 20 were in use. The rest were dry or polluted.

Bidong was sponsored by UNHCR but run by the refugees themselves. It was divided into seven zones (A thru G), each with its local council. The most expensive houses were located close to the beach, administrative center, and water and food distribution sites. The beach was fouled by garbage rotted by the tropical heat and humidity. The houses were tiny shacks, the frames of which were of hand-hewn timber from the hill. The walls were covered with cardboard, tin, or timber. Although no one was allowed to sell any property, a black market did exist. People who left the island sold their properties for $20 up to $350. This was a considerable amount of money for the majority of refugees who came to the island broke and empty handed after paying the boat handlers or after their encounters with pirates.

Bidong "was a dangerously congested slum; a tropical island ghetto; a chunk of South Vietnamese society pre–1975, unrepentantly capitalist, anti communist and predatory, grafted onto a bit of offshore Malaysia; a shantytown...."[4] Life was difficult, if not miserable for the majority of the refugees. To live on a small tropical island with its unpredictable monsoons and floods, its torrid weather, its stale stench, its disease-carrying mosquitoes and rats, its limited food and water rations, its leaky and crowded shacks, and its lack of amenities and entertainment was highly uninspiring or downright depressing. The dream of freedom that started in an oppressive communist country suddenly ended in a shantytown on a crowded and unsanitary island. Life thus consisted of surviving day by day in this tropical ghetto until refugees heard news from the resettlement committee. And this could take months, and most of the time years. Life was a daily struggle against despair, depression, and insanity. For those who could afford to pay, life was satisfactory. The problem was that no one knew how long it would take the authorities to make their decisions; if they spent all their scarce money in the beginning, they would be left with nothing. Then had to starve like the rest of the islanders.

In the beginning, France's *Isle de Lumiere*, a hospital ship, provided medical care for those who fell sick on the island. Patients were transported to the ship that was anchored a few miles off shore, treated and returned to the island once they recovered from their illnesses. When the ship left, a small dispensary was built to serve the islanders' needs. A few doctors, who arrived like the rest of the islanders as refugees, donated their services and cared for the injured and sick. Severe cases requiring hospitalization or surgical care were referred to and treated at a mainland hospital. Most of these refugee-physicians had been released from reeducation camps and felt the need to escape from the oppressive power of the state.

Entrepreneurial talent flourished on the island. Tailors, barbers, pawnbrokers, moneychangers, cake makers, woodcutters, watch repairers, and artists made a living by selling their skills. The island also had a few restaurants and coffee houses that provided extra amenities to those who could afford them. Taped and live music was also available at one of the coffee houses. A black market provided necessary items that were not available anywhere else. Malaysian fishermen smuggled goods to the island at set up points a few kilometers from the shore. Refugees came out on their homemade rafts to buy these goods and resell them at a profit. There were soaps, shampoo, talc powder, kerosene, lamps, pens, pencils, paper, scissors, stamps, flour, cigarettes, canned drinks, and so on.[5]

There was no question that life favored industrious people even in the harshest camp. Binh was a teenager when he arrived at Pulau Bidong with his younger brother. As he was at draft age in the late 1970s, he tried to escape but was unsuccessful the first time around. His parents saved everything in order to send the two brothers away for the second time; it cost them six taels of gold. The parents stayed home. Binh suddenly found himself responsible for his younger brother. In the camp, instead loitering or wasting his time on the beach, he volunteered as a cook. He had never cooked before when he was home, but that was not a requirement. He soon made progress. Cooking in the camp was not that difficult anyway. A year later, he moved to another camp in the Philippines, where he continued to work in the kitchen and to improve his cooking skills. A church in Boston sponsored the two brothers, but they later relocated to Houston to escape from the biting Boston winters. After graduating from school, he moved to the Midwest to pursue a college degree. He delivered papers in the morning and went to classes in the afternoon. He later graduated as an engineer.

Thailand

The Thai camps along the Cambodian border (Sikhiu, Phanat Nikhom, Site 2: Ban Thad, sections 5 and 19) turned out to be the worst among the Thai camps. The Vietnamese interned in these areas came overland through Cambodia: they were known as "Platform Vietnamese." During their journey, they suffered a lot in the hands of the North Vietnamese patrols stationed in Cambodia, the Khmer Rouge, and the Cambodian soldiers and bandits who controlled part of the country. They had to walk through mined areas along the Cambodian border before arriving in Thailand. Only 10 percent survived the horrendous land trip. Up to 1980, they stayed in Khao I Dang camp, then moved to Sikhiu for refugee processing. After March 1980, new arrivals were moved to Northwest nine (NW9) and later to Northwest 82 (NW82).

Refugees coming overland from Vietnam arrived at the Non Chan camps on the Cambodian side of the Thai-Cambodian border. Renegade Cambodian soldiers, known as Para, controlled the area and the camps. They harassed the refugees who crossed their territories, stole their valuables, raped women, and killed anyone they did not like. Survivors arrived at the Non Chan camps where the Para soldiers traded each of them to the Red Cross for 10 50-kilo rice sacks. Soldiers went to the camps at night to select their victims; they took them away to rape them and returned them the next morning. The refugees got upset and reacted by placing all women in the center of the camp. On April 1980, as the Para soldiers came to the camp as usual, they faced a stiff resistance from the refugees, who drove them away. Fearing the soldiers' reprisal, the next morning the refugees appealed to the Red Cross workers for help. The Red Cross rapidly moved all the refugees to a newly established area designated as NW9 on the Thai side to get them out of harm's way. The Para soldiers got incensed and took revenge on the next batch of refugees who came out of the jungle. No woman, not even a young girl, was spared that day.[6]

NW9 was thus established on April 18, 1980. It was built right in the jungle — trees were cut down and huge tents were set up. Snakes and malaria-carrying mosquitoes were prevalent. As a newly established camp, basic commodities were lacking. Water was brought in aboard trucks and people lined up to get their share; three liters of liquid were allocated per family daily for cooking, washing, and bathing. Water, salt, sugar, and cigarettes became the primary commodities: they could be traded for food. A whole new industry was born, as anything was for sale or trade. Camp leaders, stockroom clerks, and kitchen crews stole food and basic items and sold them to the black market. Girls and women traded their favors for fish, sugar or water. Single women had boyfriends to help them carry water or fight for food. War continued outside the camps and rocket and rifle shots could be heard nightly as the North Vietnamese battled the Para soldiers and Khmer Rouge. To escape from despair and hopelessness, people got involved in romance and fantasy. Life became loose and wild.[7]

The Sikhiu camp in central Thailand was known for its abuse of refugees. Guards beat the detainees, burned them with lit cigarettes, extorted money, stole food and medications intended for inmates, and even killed them. The camp was closed in 1986 because of complaints from inmates but reopened in 1991.[8]

Young Thai men broke into the camps to sneak into girls' huts to rape and kidnap them even though Thai police were around.[9] There was only one well for the whole camp for bathing, washing and laundry. A fire truck delivered drinking water once a week and sometimes it skipped a week or two, leaving the refugees nervous. Fifteen kilograms of rice were given to two people monthly.

The Phanat Nikhom camp was better than temporary camps because of the presence of American and Australian volunteers who worked in the section for minors. It had a play area for children, a market, restaurants, and a movie house. Those who had money could have a fun time. For the rest, life was hard. They were fed a small piece of chicken for four people for three days. The bathroom with its squat areas and its horrible smell was a nightmare for those who were not used to it. They lived in big buildings subdivided into small sleeping places with no privacy at all. They had to carry their own water back to their quarters.[10]

In February 1988, with an upsurge in boat arrivals, the newly arrived Vietnamese were transferred to Ban That and Site two camps, where they would be deprived of resettlement opportunities. They shared the camps with Cambodians. By 1990, the population in Site two reached 180,000. Overcrowding, inactivity, and depression led to increased violence in the camps, which besides hospitals had pharmacies, schools, temples, brothels, and gambling dens. The North Vietnamese regularly shelled the camps, disrupting normal activities while Cambodian bandits came down from the hills at night to kill, beat people and rape women. Thai security guards considered the residents at Site two camps as prisoners without legal rights and abused them at will.[11]

Hong Kong

In the beginning, the Hong Kong camps (Chi Ma Wan, Green Island, High Island, Pillar Point, Shek Kong, Tai A Chau, Whitehead) were known to be the most humane of all Southeast Asian camps: refugees were allowed to work and earn a living while their cases were evaluated. In the 1990s, however, the camps were known for their violence, terrible living conditions, and forced repatriation of inmates. The change reflected the fact that Hong Kong authorities wanted to make life in the camps so miserable that inmates were forced to choose repatriation over resettlement.

The Shek Kong camp was built on the runway of the Royal Air Force in the New Territories. It was a real prison without greenery and trees and was divided into six sections separated by high fences and large corridors where guards patrolled. Refugees lived in big steel hangars in five different sections and in huge tents in the sixth section. The hangars were like hot ovens in summertime while the tents were very cold in the winter. Flies and mosquitoes, prevalent in the camps, hounded the inmates. Life in these big and impersonal buildings of concrete and steel was especially tense. Overcrowding, poor living conditions, boredom, and harassment by guards led to explosive outbursts of rage and violence. Detainees were scared and did not know whether they would be allowed to resettle or forced to repatriate. Unaccompanied children particularly dreaded the violent environment. Some had to suffer in these camps for many years. In 1992, the refugees rioted and the North Vietnamese, who formed the majority in the Hong Kong camps, locked the South Vietnamese in their hangar and burned it down. Twenty-four people died, including 10 children.[12] Friction between North and South Vietnamese also occurred in other occasions and other Hong Kong camps. In the Tuen Mun camp, North Vietnamese, with their advantage in numbers harassed the South Vietnamese, who requested to be moved to another camp.[13]

Life was a daily struggle for many. In order to survive in the Whitehead Detention Camp, Mai a 17-year-old girl from Hai Phong, North Vietnam, had to give herself to an adult male in order to be protected from the many youth gangs that roamed around the camps. There was a complete breakdown of the Vietnamese society, as many knew it: elders became powerless in face of the lawless youth gangs. Then there was the camp administration that was determined to assert its will. Since Mai refused to repatriate after being found ineligible for resettlement, the authorities moved her constantly around the camp with the goal of disrupting her life and forcing her to go home. Then came the unexpected searches for weapons or drugs during which all the refugees were evacuated from their dwellings. Stressful situations got worse day by day. She therefore could not feel comfortable and secure enough to study or look for work.[14]

The Philippines

The Palawan camp was located on Palawan Island while the Bataan camp was situated north of Manilla. Bataan was noted to be nicer as far as food and accommodations were concerned. The Palawan camp, however, was a fairly decent camp compared to other Southeast detention centers. Asylum seekers could freely go from one section to another without any problem. They were allowed to set up shops providing food, refreshments, and services to other refugees. Schooling and vocational training were available.

Conditions deteriorated in the early '90s because of repatriation problems. Children complained about the lack of food. They did not eat breakfast, and the ration, which was not enough for one person, had to be divided among three refugees. The fish they got was usually rotten and had to be thrown away.[15]

An economically depressed socialist Vietnam after its lengthy war against the U.S. spent all its dwindling resources invading Cambodia and fighting against China. It embarked on a socialist mission, sending former southern officials to reeducation camps, nationalizing industries and businesses and socializing agriculture. Farmers and fishermen who were used to work in a free market system were unwilling to work for free for the government. People who were sent to unproductive new economic zones became deeply impoverished. Corruption under socialism was worse than the pre–1975 years because the communists wielded absolute power and were not liable to anyone. Agricultural production markedly decreased, leading to overall poverty and famine. Parents were unable to feed their children or even to send them to public school, where tuition was required. Out of desperation in the late '80s or early '90, they sent their 14 or 16 year old children away, expecting they would be resettled in another country then help the family later on. Younger children were also sent away. One child who was four escaped with an aunt and an uncle; she was separated from them in the camp and labeled as an unaccompanied minor. As such, she could be easily repatriated.

The heavy burden of helping the family fell on the fragile shoulders of these children. This was a daunting task for these youngsters who were not ready to tackle life's problems. They were very immature and still in need of nurturing since most of them had not even finished high school or had any vocational training. And when they were rejected for resettlement for the simple reasons they did not have relatives in third countries or came after the Comprehensive Plan of Action deadline, they became devastated. They felt they had failed their parents' trust and were ashamed to return home. The pressure that had been building up in them for some time blew up. They cried and cried but did not even have the comforting voices or reassuring affection of their parents to lean on. They did not even understand it was not their fault. Many became depressed; they would not eat or drink. One youngster set herself on fire. Others became rebellious, violent, and participated in riots. They would not want to go home because they did not know how they would be received. The problem got worse when a girl faced an unexpected pregnancy. Since abortions were not legal in the Philippines, she would end up with a child. If she were repatriated, a youngster and a child would represent two extra burdens for the parents in Vietnam. She therefore had a double reason to fear returning to Vietnam.

Indonesia

There were two separate refugee areas, Galang I and Galang II, on the island. There was even a café, a fruit market, a supermarket and a theater for those who had money. Newcomers stayed in Galang I, where they were lodged in a big house with 50 other people. They slept on benches that stretched from one end of the room to the other. They were given eggs, green beans, rice, flour, and sugar.

Life was better in Galang II, where Ha Nguyen's family was given a whole house. They even planted vegetables in their garden and shared them with neighbors. Sometimes there was not enough food to eat but there was minimal violence in Galang II and children were free to go to school.[16]

In the Galang I camp, where 20,000 refugees huddled under difficult conditions on a 10-square mile island, an unaccompanied girl talked about her hopes of being relocated. One day, she was advised she would be resettled. The decision was, however, reversed a few days later. Distraught by the news, she set herself on fire and died.[17] The guards were known to beat the refugees and sexually assault the women while officials took bribes before recommending resettlement.[18] The camp had a higher than normal resettlement rate among all the camps.

Singapore

The Hawkins Road camp never housed more than 120 to 150 refugees because they were not allowed to remain but were quickly sent away. Singapore was very strict with refugees: it would not allow anyone to land who was not accepted beforehand by a third country.

The camp was located at the site of an old British Army barracks. The quarters were therefore spacious and comfortable. The camp contained ample food, clothing, and medical supplies because of the low number of refugees. The detainees were treated well; they had ample space to move around, and many amenities including schooling for the children and an excellent library. This was by far the most gentle of all camps and with the highest standard of living, even more than Palawan in the Philippines. Yet the detainees were stressed because they knew they were temporary residents who would be repatriated to Vietnam.[19]

Camps, even the best among them, were restrictive in nature. They were similar to jails. Asylum seekers were limited by the boundaries of the camps and were not allowed to get out of these camps. Their freedom was taken away from them. They would like to live a normal life, but life in the camps was nowhere near normal. They were limited by the choice, quantity, and quality of food. They could not complain even if the fish was rotten or if the rice was not well cooked; as refugees they were expected to be happy with what was given to them. Since half-cooked rice was inedible, refugees tended to re-cook it. But that simple act was even forbidden in the Hong Kong camps. Drinking water and basic medications were lacking in many camps. People had nothing to do most of the time (no television, no library) except starring at the horizon. They were bored and did not know where the future had in store for them: resettlement or repatriation. They were at the mercy of camp officials, UNHCR, and third countries for everything, including food, water, medicine, relocation, or repatriation. They did not have any choice at all. Some camps were worse than others because of the gangs or harassment by officials. Over a period of time, boredom and stress would build up. A stay in the camps of less than two years would cause tremendous amount of stress, although it was reversible. A stay of longer than two years, however, had been shown to cause psychological disturbances, especially in children.

Camps were designed as temporary refuges for newcomers. But as refugees kept coming and old timers had not been resettled in third countries, camps took a life of their own and became permanent. Camp officials not only did not think of upgrading the amenities to accommodate for overcrowding, but also decided to make life harder for the refugees hoping to force them to repatriate. Food rations were cut and threats spelled out. Life in the camps over time became worse from a combination of hopelessness, neglect, compassion fatigue, and harassment by officials.

These were some of the camps asylum seekers ended up living in while they were processed for resettlement or repatriation. As they were only transition areas and as the host countries did not feel they had any obligation toward the refugees, the care provided in these camps left a lot to be desired. Although some camps were acceptable, especially in the beginning, others were a nightmare to live in. Camps thus became places where they were victimized once again. Food and water were not only lacking, security was also inconsistent and abuses (sexual and otherwise) abounded. Some camps in Hong Kong were good places until the government changed its policies. It made the camps a terror center to force the refugees to repatriate. Asylum seekers felt like prisoners inside these camps. Besides, there was the imminent threat of repatriation, which made life harder for these refugees. They knew that if they were rejected for asylum, they would also be rejected and discarded at home.

Life in the camps was therefore difficult and stressful, especially after any harrowing escape by sea. However, this was only the second stage of the ordeal, one they had to go through before getting to the next level.

13

INTERNATIONAL RESPONSE

From 1975 to mid-1979, 700,000 people had left Vietnam as part of the diaspora. These included 125,000 first wave-evacuees, 235,000 who fled north into China, 277,000 boat people since mid-1975, and 21,000 who had fled overland to Thailand. Two hundred thousand people remained in the camps at that time. This did not include the Laotians and the Cambodians. Faced with the unending flood of refugees, the foreign ministers of the five-member Association of Southeast Asian Nations (ASEAN) meeting in Bali warned that if the refugees were not resettled, they would be sent out. Despite new funding pledges, refugees kept coming and pushed the asylum system on the brink of collapse.

Compassion Fatigue

In the late 1970s, with a large backlog of refugees in their own camps and with major European countries refusing to take on more refugees, Southeast Asian countries began closing their doors to newcomers. They blamed the refugee problem on the inhumane treatment of people by the Vietnamese communist regime and the U.S. war policies of 1968–1975.

Local governments refused to take any refugee picked up at sea by tankers or ships. One family picked up by an Italian tanker journeyed around the world for almost two and a half months before being dropped off in Italy.[1] In June 1977, the Israeli freighter *Yuvali* picked up 66 refugees 60 miles off the coast of Vietnam aboard a sinking boat. Among them were a professor of geography, a surgeon, two dentists and a bank director. Japan, Hong Kong, Thailand, and Taiwan refused to take them. They were taken to Israel, where they were accepted as refugees.[2] Shipping companies advised their skippers not to pick up any refugee at sea; boat escapees were left at the mercy of storms and seas. This explains why many boat people did not receive any help from ships or tankers and were left wandering around the gulf.

The *Sibonga* was going from Bangkok to Hong Kong to deliver its cargo when the crew sighted distress flares 100 miles south of Vietnam. The ship turned around to investigate the problem. It encountered a 60 by nine foot boat with a tiered deck for maximum capacity and loaded with 600 escapees. The boat had been out to sea for three days and had run out of water. Two children had died and the conditions of the other people were not great either. They crowded in their own dirt and filth. Many were hardly able to stand on their own feet and had to be lifted aboard the ship. After picking up 600 refugees, the ship spotted another boat carrying 300 people. The captain also picked up these people. When the count was completed, the tally was 1,003 with 403 children under the age of 16.

The *Sibonga* was not allowed to drop its human cargo in Hong Kong unless the refugees were accepted for relocation in the rescuing ship's home country. Only a dozen countries, including the United States, France, West Germany, Italy, Denmark, Norway, Holland, Belgium, and Australia, guaranteed that refugees would be accepted by the ship's home country if they had no other place to go. Britain and Japan on the other hand shifted these responsibilities onto the ship owners. Singapore would not accept any refugees picked up at sea unless UNHCR agreed to resettle them in another country. If not, the ship had to post a $5,000 bond for each refugee; the bond was forfeited if anyone jumped ship.

"Flag of convenience" countries like Panama, Honduras, Liberia, and Greece would not accept refugees on behalf of the ships on their registries. Many ship captains, however, offered help to refugees out of compassion by providing food, water, medicines, and maps. Between 1975 and September 1979, 90 commercial vessels dropped 4,800 refugees in Singapore alone.[3]

Because of "compassion fatigue," Singapore was the first state to turn seaworthy boats away after refueling and re-supplying them. In June 1975, the Thai cabinet introduced the "shut, but slightly open" door policy. Refugee boats would not be allowed to land on Thai coast, but if they did, refugees should be confined to displaced persons' camps. The policies, however, were not rigidly enforced. By late 1977, Thailand also regularly rejected refugee boats that later ended up in Malaysia.

These nations' navy ships received the order to tow the boats to high seas and let them drift to another nation or somewhere else. They sometimes did not even help the refugees when their boats sank. Sixty people died in one occasion.[4] In case of mechanical failure, they repaired the boats and pushed the refugees back to sea. If a Singaporean fishing boat helped save refugees, the fishing boat's owner had to post a $4,000 bond for each refugee saved. He would get his money back only when the refugee was pushed back to sea.[5] Some local people would lend hands to the refugees, although others would threaten or shoot at incoming boats to prevent them from landing.

Horror stories were reported in the press. Thieu (unrelated to the late President Thieu) escaped from Ca Mau on the southernmost region of Vietnam on April 17, 1979, with 33 relatives and friends. Pirates attacked their boat on the first day of the trip and robbed them of their valuables. The engine broke down and the boat drifted in the Gulf of Siam. Thai fishermen later towed them to about 15 miles from the Malaysian coast, then turned around and robbed them. Malaysian authorities towed them to a temporary camp and allowed them to stay. On May 11, the 33 were put on another boat with a disabled engine and towed to the seas. They were cast adrift about 10 miles from Bidong Island. The boat started drifting and they ran out of water. Two young children died of dehydration and the other 12 were close to death. Sixty ships passed by without offering any help until a Norwegian ship took them to Singapore.

Some push backs, or actually pull aways, were very traumatic and even deadly. On March 22, 1979, the Malaysian Navy boat *Kris* intercepted the 59 foot *MH-3012* carrying 237 Vietnamese heading toward the Malaysian coastline. The *MH-3012* was towed south for 36 hours, cut loose, and told to head to Indonesia. The Navy officials knew the boat's engine and water pump were broken and a newborn baby was on board. The boat drifted for four more days, causing 10 people — one elderly man and nine children aged two to six — to die of dehydration. Each passenger was allowed two spoonfuls of water a day. On March 31, it encountered a second Malaysian Navy boat, the *Renchong*, which tried to tow it further south. The refugees refused but had to finally agree after one refugee was shot in the arm. The *Renchong* then pulled the boat at high speed for one hour in a zigzag manner, causing it to take on water. During one of these turning maneuvers, the *MH-3012* rolled over and capsized, throwing all the refugees into the water. Instead of rescuing the refugees, the *Renchong* circled around the wreckage for half an hour taking pictures before pulling out 124 survivors.[6] One hundred and four refugees died during the incident.

When the *SB-001* carrying 269 refugees tried to sneak into Singapore in February 1979, two Singaporean Navy ships rammed it at a 90-degree angle. The *P-81* maneuvered alongside the refugee boat while the *P-74* nosed it midship on the other side. A heavy swell lifted the *P-74* up and let it crash down on the stern of the refugee boat, killing one passenger on the spot. Fourteen others were thrown overboard. The patrol boats released one life raft and left. The *SB-001* was taking on water and had to rush ashore. The refugees thrown into the water held on to the raft and one person drowned during this incident.[7]

Four hundred-sixty five refugees who landed in Mersing camp were placed into four boats carrying 30, 30, 100, and 305 people respectively. That night, the *PT-47* towed the four boats south at high speed. The wakes caused the two small boats to be tossed up and down dangerously. One of the ropes broke and the passengers of the two small boats were taken aboard the *PT-47*, stripped of their valuables, and some of the women were raped. The towing continued throughout the night and by dawn, they encountered an Indonesian cruiser. After 30 minutes of discussion with the cruiser crew, the *PT-47* clustered the four refugee boats together and raced around them at a high speed creating huge waves that shook the small boats. The *PT-47* left 20 minutes later and the four boats raced toward Indonesia. Had they not encountered the Indonesian cruiser, someone would have died from the ride.[8]

A Malaysian task force (Task Force VII) was created to decrease the number of boats arriving on its western shores. Its other goals were to look after the boat people and to see that they were resettled. As the number of arrivals ballooned to 63,000 in 1978, the number of push backs jumped to 4,959.[9] In the first six months of 1979, 267 boats carrying 40,000 refugees were towed out to sea; for the year 1979, a total of 51,422 were assisted out of Malaysian waters. Those people who sneaked through and beached on the coastline were isolated and prevented from contacting UNHCR. They lived in limbo on the beach not knowing whether they would be sent to a refugee camp or dropped on a boat and towed to sea. About 10,000 refugees faced that dilemma in 1979.[10]

Neighboring Indonesia saw a 20-fold increase in the number of refugees from 2,800 in 1978 to 49,000 in 1979 as a result of these push backs. In May 1979, 13,500 people were pushed out to sea and according to UNHCR records, 20 to 40 of the hundred boats that subsequently landed in Indonesia were victims of pirates. By the time these refugees arrived to Indonesia, they had been at sea for so long that they were malnourished, dehydrated, exhausted, and devastated by pirate attacks; many were barely responsive.[11]

No one knew the exact number of people who died trying to escape by boat. Between the corrupt Vietnamese patrols, the violent tropical storms, the cruel pirates, the lack of food and water, and the heartless push backs, a large number of boat people perished at sea. It is estimated that the death rate was about 10 to 15 percent of the total number of people arriving at the camps or roughly 200,000[12] to 220,000.[13]

In the camps, host countries adopted the policy of "human deterrence" to prevent new refugees from coming ashore. Conditions in the camps worsened and were kept as grim as possible: food and water were provided at a minimum, housing was almost nonexistent, and sanitation became horrible. Despite this harsh policy, boatloads of refugees kept coming, reflecting an increasingly severe and worsening social and political problem in Vietnam.

Faced with this problem, the United States opened up its arms and allowed 180,000 refugees to seek asylum. Other European countries followed suit, including France, Germany, Canada, and Australia.

In the meantime, France sent its *Ile of Lumiere* ship to the Gulf of Siam to scan and rescue boat refugees before they encountered pirates. Germany did the same with *Cap Anamur*. The Buddhists under the leadership of Chan Khong and Thich Nhat Hanh rented a cargo ship named *Roland* and an oil tanker named *Leapdal*. Both ships were able to save 566 people but were not allowed to come near the shores of Malaysia, Thailand and Singapore. Therefore, a small boat had to ferry food and fuel to the rescue boats. Their private project reached an impasse because they could not unload the refugees in any country.[14]

Orderly Departure Program

An international conference was convened in July 1979 in Geneva to discuss the problem of refugees. Camps in Asia faced a big backlog:

350,000 Indochinese remained in these camps while 200,000 had been resettled. In the first half of 1979, 155,000 new refugees had arrived while only 54,000 had departed. The problem was thought to be unmanageable if the flow of refugees persisted and if the backlog was not dealt with adequately.

UNHCR asked Vietnam to stop dumping its refugees. As France also insisted, Vietnam stopped illegal boat departures and the number of refugees coming ashore on Asian soil dramatically decreased by the end of 1979. Vietnam jailed escapees and even executed a few. Almost overnight the number of arrivals markedly decreased: 56,941 in June, 17,839 in July, 9,734 in August and 2,600 monthly during the last quarter of 1979. Encouraged by the drop in arrivals, ASEAN countries cancelled the push back policy.

To prevent illegal escapes, UNHCR also negotiated an ODP (Orderly Departure Program) to facilitate the departure of qualified people — family reunion and humanitarian cases — to third countries. The first ODP charter flew out of Saigon in June 1979. Over the years, more than 400,000 refugees had been resettled in the U.S. from the ODP program. Vietnamese could enter the U.S. if they had spouses, sons, daughters, parents, grandparents, and unmarried grandchildren. Political prisoners (85,000) who were not eligible under the ODP could emigrate through the HO (Humanitarian Operation) Program. Worldwide resettlement pledges increased from 125,000 to 260,000 for 1979 and 1980. Cash pledges also increased from $120 million to $160 million. The principles of asylum and non–push back were endorsed. The United States became the biggest resettlement country while Japan became the largest financial donor.[15]

From 1975 to 1978, a total of 186 boats carrying 8,674 people were rescued while 110,000 boat refugees escaped from Vietnam. During the first seven months of 1979, while 177,000 escaped only 47 boats were rescued with 4,593 people aboard. Through a program called Disero (Disembarkation Resettlement Offers), a group of countries (United States, Canada, Australia, New Zealand, France, Germany, Sweden, and Switzerland) volunteered to resettle refugees picked up at sea within 90 days. The effect was immediate. During the last five months of 1979, 4,031 people in 81 boats were rescued. But the program eventually failed because Asian countries required that these refugees be screened according to the Comprehensive Plan of Action agreement. As disembarkation difficulties increased, ships would no longer be willing to pick up refugees at sea.

Comprehensive Plan of Action (CPA)

Then in 1986 came a new flood of refugees not from the South but from North Vietnam, which had been under communist control since 1954. Half of them were unaccompanied minors whose role was to set up an "economic anchor" in another country and to later bring their parents to join them. Since they were not persecuted refugees, they were classified as "economic migrants" similar to the illegal South Americans who came to the U.S. seeking a better life. By 1989, about 160,000 refugees remained in the Southeast Asian camps.

The Comprehensive Plan of Action was adopted in 1989 with the following elements:

- Resettlement of refugees arriving prior to a cut-off date would continue while new arrivals would be screened through interviews.
- Persons not deemed to be refugees would be repatriated.
- Vietnam agreed to deter any new clandestine departure.

The focus of the CPA was the 100,000 Vietnamese stranded in various Asian camps. The refugees, however, refused to go home, claiming continuing persecution by the Hanoi government. Despite the fact that Hanoi announced it would not retaliate against returnees, the asylum seekers remained distrustful of their government. They even refused to accept incentives given by UNHCR to those willing to return home ($360 per person, free schooling and job training). After a bitter struggle, UNHCR decided to repatriate the refugees against their will in 1993. Camp officials moved asylum seekers from one camp to another or from one section of the camp to another to create anxiety and instability. Asylum seekers fought back by protesting and later rioting. On April 7, 1994, a force of 1,250 soldiers backed by two armored personnel carriers, a helicopter, over 500 tear gas canisters, a pepper fog machine, and hundreds of mace cans moved against a group of 1,500 refugees at the Whitehead camp in Hong Kong. The refugees had simply refused to move to another camp without warning. Overall, 170 people including children were injured. From that time onward, trust and collaboration between officials and refugees disappeared, to be replaced by hostility or sullen silence. All the camps finally closed down in 2000.

Nothing was more controversial than the concept of screening through interview, which was established in 1989 as part of the CPA (1988 for Hong Kong). Asylum seekers used it as a way to gain resettlement. The first-asylum countries promoted it to get rid of the refugees and third countries promoted it to take the minimum number of people. With screening, UNHCR planned to speed up the process and wrap up the problem of Indochinese refugees. The stakes were therefore high for all the parties involved.

The asylum seekers complained they were not given adequate information to understand the process and no one had prepared them for the interviews. The Hong Kong government was adamant about rejecting as many seekers as possible. Its acceptance rate was 19 percent, much lower than in the Philippines (53 percent) and Indonesia (43 percent). The failure to keep accurate records of the interviews, except for the examiner's notes, made an appeal unlikely, if not impossible.[16] Even though social workers from International Social Service recommended against repatriation of unaccompanied minors, these appeals were overruled by UNHCR.

One former UNHCR official argued against the concept of "economic anchor," suggesting instead that many factors might have led parents to send their children away.[17] Among these were "political factors" such as continuing discrimination and persecution from the Hanoi government, failure to provide free schooling for the children and jobs for the parents, blacklisting those who had served under the Saigon government, and failure to promote democracy. Life was so grim for many defeated southerners that they viewed escape as a means of fighting against political oppression, rather than a search for economic advancement. As far as parents were concerned, they certainly did not want to send their children away without supervision. But they were so desperate that they needed to do something — otherwise these children basically had no future in a climate of oppression and discrimination.

There were also allegations about corruption among immigration officials and police in the Philippines, Indonesia, and Malaysia, and consultants hired by UNHCR. If they did not receive bribes, they would screen out the candidate. The process was sloppy in other situations. Not only were there mistranslations from interpreters, but also hostility of interviewers against former South Vietnamese military personnel (ARVN). One Philippine immigration official screened out a former ARVN major, claiming the major had not been interned in reeducation camps for three years. Actually, he was an amputee who served in a reeducation camp for a few months and was sent to do hard labor in another camp for 20 more months. He was released only because of health problems but remained under house arrest for the next 15 years. He was not allowed to hold any job during that period and finally escaped in 1989. On appeal, the committee reversed the original decision.[18] The same immigration official rejected also 12 other ARVN officers; eight of them had been screened in and accepted for relocation on appeal.

Forced Repatriation

The goal of these asylum seekers, whether they were adults or children, was the same: resettlement in a third country. Many were so desperate that they took whatever country would accept them as refugees, including those they had never heard of like Guyana, Israel, Iran, Ivory Coast, Malawi, Senegal, Argentina, and Iceland. They had worked so hard to get to the camps by buying their way out, avoiding border police, braving sea and storms, surviving dehydration and hunger, escaping from pirate attacks, and suffering from the indignity of living in crowded camps with substandard amenities. Therefore, they were stunned when told they had to repatriate. They had invested everything and suffered a lot in the past and now they had to suffer more. They had nothing to return to. They had lost their homes and belongings. They knew they would be jailed for having escaped once they arrived back in Vietnam.

Although the concept of repatriation sounded good on paper, execution and follow-up was lacking. Officials were adamant about sending home marginal cases, especially after 1995 when they decided to close the camps. There was sub-optimal monitoring of the repatriated unaccompanied children. And if monitoring was done, no long-term follow-up of these cases was performed. Some of them might do well a few months or a year after returning home. Once the allocation money that was given for one single year had disappeared, they might not have money to eat and would be neglected. Occasionally the local UNHCR social workers were not even aware of the presence of repatriated children to be monitored. There was also a lack of follow-up on many children who left home again once they had returned to Vietnam. No one knew what happened to these children. Children who lost their parents to Thai pirates were sent back to elderly grandparents who would not live long enough to fully care for them. On certain occasions, relatives in Vietnam spent all the allocated money on themselves instead of on the children.

It is also a fact that children who escaped abroad were not treated well by the Hanoi government. They were denied identification papers, without which they could not study or apply for work. They would, however, receive these papers if they split the allowance money given to them by UNHCR with local officials. Money allocated for training had to be divided with officials, otherwise the children would not receive any training. Soon the children were left with no money for food or education. Sometimes families did not really want to accept the children back since repatriated children were no longer recognized by the government and thus considered to be economic burdens. The problem got worse if the teenager came back with a child of her own: she would be regarded as no longer pure and would be ostracized by family and friends.[19] She would have a hard time finding a job to make a life for herself and her child. If she did, it would be a low paying job and she would never be able to achieve the dream of her life. The refugee children are "a testimony to the human spirit, to endurance, hope, and dreams in the face of insurmountable odds."[20]

Multiple problems therefore awaited the repatriated children. These problems were made worse by the poverty, greed, lack of understanding and acceptance of their relatives in Vietnam, corruption of the local officials, and lack of adequate monitoring by delegates of the UNCHR. These children therefore were victimized not once, but multiple times throughout this ordeal, especially through their difficult escapes, their incarceration in the camps, and neglect after repatriation. The long-term effects of the escape were profound and never-ending for many former escapees.

As for those who were repatriated, persecution could be a continuing problem. One Westerner remarked that Vietnamese police officials did not regularly follow rules and regulations to the letter and that nothing should be taken for granted.[21]

14

THE LANDS OF FREEDOM

Although more than 50 countries accepted the refugees, the four major resettlement countries included the United States, France, Canada, and Australia. These countries opened their arms and welcomed the refugees like no other places in the world.

United States

The U.S. was the first country to transport and resettle 130,000 refugees back in 1975. The State Department contracted with nine different volags to help these people resettle in an American community. The main agencies were the U.S. Catholic Conference (USCC), Church World Service (CWS), Lutheran Immigration and Refugee Service (LIRS), Hebrew Immigrant Aid Society (HIAS), and International Rescue Committee (IRC). The State Department paid them 500 dollars for each case placed. Some refugees somehow thought the money was intended for their personal use. These volags did not involve themselves directly in the resettlement, but rather relied on the sponsors or sponsoring organizations for that job. It was noted that individual sponsorships have a tendency to break down more easily than congregational ones.

Although the agencies attempted to spread the refugees throughout all the states, secondary migration was rapid. Refugees tended to converge to large cities where they could easily find jobs, friends, and housing. Vietnamese had the tendency to get together, eat, and share their personal experiences with other countrymen. When they came to the States, they were dispersed and sent to small towns where they could not see any countryman for months or even years. Sorely missing these emotional contacts led them to migrate to other states where they could be close to their friends. While only nine percent of Americans moved across state lines, 45 percent of Indochinese refugees relocated to another state during the period 1975–1980.

Chicago and Little Saigon are examples of Vietnamese enclaves in major cities in the U.S. In many cases, these enclaves were the creation of the cities themselves.

Uptown Chicago was a fashionable area between 1900 and 1920. Germans, Swedes, and Irish moved in succession into the area but in the '50s, Uptown gradually declined because its population slowly moved away. Multiple attempts to improve the area structurally and financially failed. Many organizations, including Chinese who wanted to build a second Chinatown, pushed developers to restore the buildings. Despite these restorations, there were no takers. The area remained "a ghost town after dark ... dominated by pimps, prostitutes, and drug pushers who assembled on unlit, crumbling sidewalks."[1] By 1980, 48 percent of the residents lived below the poverty line, compared to 37 percent for the city as a whole. What Uptown needed was an infusion of a large population willing to live and work in a district with a bad reputation and visible signs of decay.

The local government solved the problem by inserting the newly arrived refugees in the low-rent Uptown area. Having no preconceived ideas and nowhere else to go, the newcomers settled in and renovated it. In the beginning, no one dared to venture in the streets after dark, as the area was not deemed safe. Muggings and break-ins occurred frequently. Broken windows, vacant buildings, and unintelligible graffiti were frequently seen. Dirty sidewalks coexisted with potholed streets. The neighborhood exhibited an air of sadness, despair, and resentment. Everything looked grim, poor, and decayed. But slowly one business opened followed by another because of increasing local demands. Refugees had to drive to Chinatown half an hour away through downtown traffic to get their much needed oriental food, spices, seasonings, vegetables, and so on. This was very inconvenient for the newcomers whose wives could not drive in heavy traffic and whose husbands worked one or two jobs to bring home a needed income. Things started to change slowly, as more businesses opened up. The overall mood appeared more optimistic and hopeful, although the refugees remained cloistered in their apartments after

9 P.M. It was like the curfew back home in the early 1970s: they were used to living like hermits. But at least they could go out and eat at the local restaurants and frequent the local grocery stores during daytime.

By the mid–'80s, 10,000 Indochinese refugees lived in Uptown Chicago. Buildings, streets, and sidewalks had been spruced up. A few buildings had been torn down and replaced by a few mini-malls. More than a hundred Asian, mostly Vietnamese, businesses crowded a three-block area along Argyle and adjacent streets. Restaurants, grocery stores, beauty salons, video stores, doctor, dentist, and lawyer's offices, and even a used car dealership could be found. Traffic was so busy that parking places were full all the time, especially during weekends. Asian refugees from neighboring counties and states came to stock up on goods and groceries and to enjoy meals at the various restaurants. Uptown became an entry point, not a permanent place to stay for the majority of refugees who had since moved to surrounding areas to be closer to their workplaces. But they had transformed Uptown Chicago into an Asian business district and at the same time revitalized and improved the area.[2] As a result, the area around the Vietnamese enclave has grown safer and a few American grocery stores have even opened their doors one or two blocks down the road.

The same thing goes for many areas in other cities, like Houston, New Orleans, San Jose, Seven Corners in Arlington, Virginia, and so on. The Vietnamese came in and with their numbers and commercial skills revitalized these areas, turning them into vibrant business districts. In the end numbers matter because without a crowd there would no real buying power and no incentive to open a business or sell anything.

Little Saigon was another success story. The county of Westminster, California, back in the mid–'70s was a farming area southwest of Los Angeles. The area was wide open with large farms, orange groves, and a few scattered communities when the Vietnamese settled in the latter part of 1975. In the beginning, there was no oriental store within an hour drive and the basic ingredients like soy sauce, fish sauce, hot sauce, oriental herbs and noodles, rice, oriental vegetables, and so on were nowhere to be found. There was no French bread or pastries to the liking of the refugees. They had to switch from a basic oriental diet to an American menu and survive as best as they could. This meant not eating the types of food one had grown up with and been used to the last 20, 30, may be 50 years. It was like asking a meat consuming person to turn vegetarian or vice versa. Many refugees were tortured daily by this craving for ethnic food they could not find anywhere. Many salivated when they talked about these ethnic dishes while others turned to dreaming about them. Others would pay a large sum of money to taste a bowl of *pho* or a piece of roast duck.

The other option was to go to Los Angeles Chinatown to buy the required ingredients and bring them back to the area, although Chinese ingredients were not always the same as the Vietnamese. Soon one or two stores opened up to cater to the needs of the Vietnamese. One grocery store popped up here and another there. Housewives would line up at the stores on delivery days to buy and stock up on these ingredients and goods that turned out to be as expensive as gold and disappeared off the shelves as fast as they were displayed. A half-an-hour late arrival at the store could mean no ethnic food until the next delivery date, which could be a few days to a week. Soon a whole block filled with Vietnamese and Chinese stores with Vietnamese signs opened for business. And another block followed, although not right away. A few restaurants serving Vietnamese menus with beef, pork, or seafood dishes opened their doors. They were always crowded and clients had to wait in line to get in. They served, among other things, the typical *pho* soup that came either with seafood, beef, or chicken along with soy sauce, hot sauce, anise, bean sprouts, and oriental herbs. *Pho* soup could be eaten at any time during the day, either at breakfast, lunch, or supper. It is simple, practical, and easy to serve: it is the national Vietnamese food. The Chinese recently began to like *pho* soup for its taste and simplicity. Then there was always rice served a hundred ways — steamed, sauted or fried, with or without meat. One could finish dinner with a glass of Vietnamese *che*, a sweet concoction of different beans and jelly on ice.

Over the years, the Vietnamese section of the city of Westminster has grown to the point it has acquired its own name, "Little Saigon." It was spilled into the neighboring Garden Grove. It has strip malls, stores, pharmacies, doctors' and lawyers' offices, real estate agencies, and gas stations. It has become the refuge for all Vietnamese who fought against and escaped from communist rule. Vibrant and well known, it has been recognized as the capital of the overseas Vietnamese. It is the transplanted replica of the old Saigon, Vietnam, with its feverishness, entrepreneurial spirit, know how, vision, abrasiveness, and excesses.

Little Saigon epitomized the strength, vigor, vitality and hard work of the Vietnamese. Success there was measured in the number of shops opened, the number of transactions or sales made and the amount of money that changed hands. With success came strength and power: the *Viet Kieu* sent home more than two billion dollars yearly to prop up the economy of communist Vietnam, an old adversary. This is a large sum of foreign cash that the Hanoi government could not afford to lose. Little Saigon represented Vietnam abroad for the *Viet Kieu*, a new, free, aggressive, prosperous, and modern community that stood in opposition to the government in Vietnam. For many *Viet Kieu*, it represented the new homeland that replaced the one they had lost 30 years ago. It is the symbol of self-sufficiency, determination, strength, and freedom. It is the phoenix that rose from the ashes of defeat.

It has become staunchly anti-communist like no other city outside Vietnam. When one video storeowner started hanging a picture of uncle Ho in his store, the Vietnamese people reacted by boycotting his store while 15,000 people demonstrated for nearly two months. His business went downhill and he was forced to pull down the picture and go out of business. Since that time, storeowners would fly the American along with the South Vietnamese flag (three red stripes on a golden background). Recently it has earned the right to fly the old Saigon nationalist flag and is designated as an anti-communist city. The Hanoi government appealed, to no avail. The cities of Westminster and Garden Grove passed resolutions banning communists from visiting their communities.

France

While the United States, Canada, and Australia were nations of immigrants, France is a country of immigration. Immigration did not play an important role in the process of building the French nation-state as it did in the U.S., Canada, and Australia, but since 1950, France has opened its borders to asylum seekers at a rate of 100,000 per year and has one of the most generous naturalization policies in Europe. When the Indochinese refugee crisis hit the world during 1975–80, France was embroiled in a major recession and had to declare a halt to immigration.

However, history has its say in the matter. The French felt they had a special duty toward the outcasts of their former colony, although they also maintained consular ties with the Hanoi government throughout the war. In Vietnam the French slowly moved into the vacuum left by the departing Americans. Being known as a haven for the persecuted, France also had to find a way to accept new refugees, especially since these people came from an old colony. The Vietnamese had settled in France as far back as the early days of 1900. By 1920, a rather large Vietnamese colony lived in Paris. The nationalist Phan Chu Trinh and even the communist Ho Chi Minh had set foot in this city. They had both organized meetings and given speeches to advance their fight for the independence of Vietnam. It was unfortunate they stood on opposite ends of the political spectrum.

The large and difficult exodus of people out of Vietnam in the late 1970s caused a worldwide crisis requiring a humanitarian response. Despite having problems with other immigrants at home, France decided on a controversial measure: accept a new group of boat people while expelling a certain number of migrant workers.[3] Although it considered the 1975 diaspora as an American problem, it allowed 1,000 refugees to resettle in France monthly. Responsibility fell on France Terre d'Asile (FTA), a private organization founded in 1971 to provide assistance and services to refugees. The goal was to spread them in reception centers across the country, although half of them would gravitate back toward Paris. This secondary migration was also known in the U.S. The refugees found it easier to find work than housing in Paris while the reverse was true in the provinces. But they preferred to live crowded in the same area than alone in a large apartment.

On the eve of the 1979 Geneva conference on Indochinese refugees, although it had accepted more than 52,000 refugees from 1975 to 1979, second only to the United States, France could not afford not to budge on this humanitarian problem. It offered to resettle an additional 5,000 refugees and persuaded Vietnam to impose a temporary halt to clandestine departures. "The moratorium was better than death at sea," declared the French minister.[4] In late 1979, UNHCR presented its Nansen Medal to President Valery Giscard d'Estaign in recognition of the French open arm policy toward asylum seekers for the last 50 years. The president gave half of the money toward building a school in a refugee camp in Botswana and the other half to finance a rural hospital inside the country for the Cambodian refugees.

Quietly, France continued to accept Indochinese who received automatic refugee status from OFPRA (Office Francais de Protection des

Refugies et Apatrides), a department designed to protect the refugees and those without country. A group of Frenchmen chartered a boat named *Ile de Lumiere* to station off the coast of Malaysia to provide medical assistance to the refugees at the island of Bidong. Politicians jumped into the fray. Jaques Chirac chartered a plane to bring refugees to Roissy. A few days later, Francois Mitterand would welcome his own group of refugees at Roissy.[5]

Overall, France took in more than 120,000 refugees, more than any other European country.

Canada

Canada had admitted 186,000 Eastern European refugees from 1947 to 1952 and 37,000 Hungarian refugees in 1956, 12,000 Czechoslovaks in 1960, 7,000 Ugandan Asians, victims of expulsion in the hands of Idi Amin, and 7,000 Chilean fleeing the Pinochet government.

When the flow of Indochinese refugees increased, Canada opened its arms wider and increased its yearly quota. In July 1979, it again increased its quota from 8,000 to 50,000. The immigration regulations permitted any group of five or more citizens to sponsor a refugee family provided they had the resources and expertise to provide clothing, food, and lodging to the refugees for the first year. In all, more than 7,000 sponsoring organizations volunteered in 1979–80.

Contrary to the U.S. private sponsorships were rather successful compared to government sponsorships in Canada when per capita expenditures were compared: $2,663 versus $3,416. The private sector could provide a cheaper and more adequate sponsorship than the government. However, although the Canadians were in general not supportive of the process, the middle class support and the media's favorable angle made it a success. Canada is noted to be "a nation of immigrants who hate immigrants."[6] UNHCR in 1986 awarded the whole nation its Nansen Medal for having openly welcomed the Indochinese refugees. Canada has become more a nation of asylum than a country of resettlement. Canada took in more than 200,000 refugees, second behind the United States.

A study in Quebec City revealed that the Vietnamese immigrants believed that a specific social order that had been threatened by the communists had to be preserved because it was an expression of Vietnamese culture.[7] The main reason many refugees preferred Canada was because the country was an alternative to those who disagreed with the U.S. involvement in Vietnam.[8] Other Vietnamese who did not like the way the U.S. disengaged from Vietnam also chose to settle in Canada.

Australia

Since 1901, when the Australian Parliament promulgated a "White Australia policy," the country had only received migrants from Britain or the British Empire. The admittance of Indochinese in 1975 constituted a major change in policy that came around slowly.

In 1975, Australia took in fewer than 600 refugees who, having no recognized skills or qualifications would not even be eligible for entry into the country. The quota was increased to 1,000 for years 1976 and 1977. Then in 1978, 51 refugee boats carrying more than 2,000 people bypassed the Southeast Asian countries and landed in Australia. They created a furor in that nation, which suddenly found itself to be a country of asylum. Australia decided to admit an additional 9,000 people in 1978. The quota increased to 15,000 in 1979 and 1980. By 1982, 50,000 refugees lived in the country. Australia in the end took in more than 180,000 refugees, third behind the United States and Canada. The refugees owed a lot to all these countries that welcomed them with open arms in their moments of need. Without them, they would be still lingering in crowded and sub-optimal camps or worse, sent home to be jailed or watched closely by their own government. From these humble beginnings, they have become economically independent and sometimes useful to their host countries.

There is nothing like the ardor, enterprising spirit, and number of immigrants to revitalize poor neighborhoods in large cities. These hungry immigrants would do anything to make a new life for themselves, their families, and their neighborhoods. Examples abounded: Westminster, Califorinia; Uptown Chicago; Houston; San Jose; and Seven Corners in Virginia, to name a few.

15

STRUGGLES AND ACHIEVEMENTS

> We'll spurn no job, however low or mean.
> Hired to clean toilets, we don't wince or flinch....
> Is this all we deserve, this rotten lot?
> — Hau Dien[1]

The refugees did not shun any job, no matter how small or demeaning it was. A general was doing dishwashing in a restaurant while a physician fulfilled the job of a nurse aid in a hospital. A former South Vietnamese senator and ex-cabinet minister sold fried chicken for a grocery store at a corner in the Big Easy before getting a teaching job at a local university. One refugee's son-in-law, who had a law degree, sold vacuum cleaners door to door. People were afraid of Asians at that time and would not let him in. Her two sons worked as mechanics and sold gasoline at night for extra money. Her friend, a former chief justice of the Supreme Court, trained in France, spoke four languages and became a watchman in a Houston hotel. Those who hired him were uneasy with his title, so they called him a telephone operator. But he was really a watchman, for he would open the door to anyone who knocked on it. The refugee sadly commented that while educated people were highly prized in Vietnam, in the industrial American society any skilled worker could be worth more than an educated person.[2] There were thousands and thousands of these overqualified Vietnamese workers who took on menial jobs all over the U.S. at that time.

They had fallen to the bottom of the society and struggled hard to survive and to make ends meet in the new lands. They came home each night crying their hearts out and asking themselves and their families whether they deserved such a "rotten lot." Their prides were wounded and their hearts torn apart. But they quietly moved on because they realized this was the only way out.

They went from having lost their nation to losing their own identities and status. They felt these tragic losses deeply and painfully. There was no worse loss than that of losing a nation, for it not only entailed a loss of identity, but also of heritage and self, especially after they had spent so much energy and effort for two decades to fight to preserve it. They now felt a complete disconnection in their hearts and their souls. Their trials and tribulations seemed endless and revolting and the downhill slide was bottomless. Although it took them a long time to accept these painful events, in the end they got used to them. They knew they could not end lower than that. They had already hit the bottom. Their despair made their lives more meaningful and their search for freedom became more gratifying.

United States

The refugees readjusted to the American society by following one of the three scenarios: the old-line pattern, the assimilation pattern, and the bicultural pattern. In the old-line pattern, the refugees clung on to their old values and refused to learn new ones. They became isolated, friendless, and bitter about life in general by remaining an island in an island and refusing to embrace the new culture. This is frequently seen with the older generation. In general they did not have the flexibility to learn new values, for these values could conflict with the old ones. Adopting the new culture sometimes meant rejecting the old one and rejecting their own selves. That was the dilemma facing these elderly people. That also explained why many people did not want to leave Vietnam despite the fact that they might suffer by remaining under communism. In the assimilation pattern, the refugees completely turned away from their old values and blindly adopted all new customs. This scenario was seen more frequently in women and children who could not value the richness of the old culture. In the bicultural mode, people preserved their old values while continuing to acquire new ideas that were necessary for transition to life in America.³ They were the richer ones emotionally and spiritually, for they were able to assimilate and experience the best of both worlds.

Not all the refugees came to the States at the same time. The migration of refugees to the United States occurred in three phases: the fall of South Vietnam, Cambodia and Laos brought 147,000 refugees between 1975 and 1978; political turmoil and persecution in communist Vietnam brought an additional 453,000 refugees between 1979 and 1982; and 350,000 refugees came for family reunification from 1983 to 1990. Various groups faced different problems. Between 1975 and 1978, refugees sparkled civil protests over their arrivals. In the heels of the military pullout in Vietnam, local people did not feel like opening their arms and hearts to former adversaries; they did not understand that the refugees were not communists, but fought on their side during the war. A local hick once wrote to a refugee: "We don't want one of your kind to live in our town." As large numbers of refugees arrived amidst the 1979–82 recession period, they faced conflicts and opposition over jobs and social services. Local people were upset about the fact that refugees received jobs and benefits, which they were not entitled to, especially in difficult times. Between 1983 and 1990, refugees had to face harassment, property destruction, assaults, and murders as they slowly gained economic status within the communities.⁴

Case 1: Nguyen Dung was a fisherman from Phan Thiet, South Vietnam, before he came to the United States as a refugee. He was given a job of as janitor at a church but did not like it. He was a fisherman in his youth and longed to return to his old job. He soon moved to Seadrift, Texas, where his friend had just bought a boat. The boat — nothing but plywood glued together — cost his friend $6,000. Although his friend felt cheated, he did not know enough to argue back. In Vietnam, that boat was not even good for river travel. They both spent a lot of time and money repairing it.

They finally took the boat out for fishing and worked 16 hours a day. White fishermen became angry with them because of their fishing pattern: the Vietnamese did not follow size and distance rules for fishing and worked too many hours. Troubles started when more Vietnamese fishermen moved into the area and the business became crowded. Vietnamese-caught fish and shrimp were boycotted on the market. A few Vietnamese boats were set on fire following an incident at sea. In the summer of 1979, a white man stabbed a Vietnamese whose friend reacted by shooting and killing the American. A jury later ruled the homicide an act of self-defense. Tempers flared; Vietnamese were beaten and their boats burned. A decline in shrimp harvest was noted one day around the region. The Vietnamese were blamed for excessive fishing, although pollution from oil refineries was also responsible for the decline. By 1980, one third of the 150 boats working in Galveston Bay were owned by Vietnamese. The Ku Klux Klan was called in and crosses were burned on Vietnamese fishermen's yards. Klan members, hooded and armed with high powered rifles, rowed boats in the Gulf of Mexico and acted as vigilantes. Fishermen's children were beaten and harassed in schools. The government stepped in as well as the Southern Poverty Law Center, which filed a lawsuit on behalf of the Vietnamese. A court injunction against the Klan and a state law limiting the number of fishing licenses defused the crisis. Nguyen Dung continued fishing and was happy with his job. He bought his own boat after working for his friend for a year.[5] The KKK never succeeded in chasing the Vietnamese from the gulf coast. Similar incidents also occurred in California, New Orleans, and Mississippi.

Between 1945 and 1965, a historic migration in the U.S. led five million blacks from the rural South to the large cities of the North. By 1980, the black population in cities larger than 200,000 people was 22 percent. In Philadelphia, it was 40 percent. Poverty among blacks was due to economic factors. Central Philadelphia during that same period lost 75,000 blue-collar jobs, the same jobs that natives and refugees with minimal education would like to have had. Unemployment among black men without high school diplomas was 50 percent in 1980.

The resettlement of 20,000 refugees in Philadelphia between 1975 and 1985 sparkled disturbances with the blacks. Blacks and refugees had similar pressing problems. They had large families with only one income earner. They lived in rundown apartments with inadequate heat and in bad need of repair. Tempers flared when refugees as newcomers received social services and help when they needed it while blacks did not. Refugees were not only competing for entry-level jobs, but also for public assistance and social services. A chilly front came in one day and when a Cambodian turned the heat up, the furnace burst. Church groups and volunteering agencies came immediately to the rescue. This action caused resentment among blacks who felt left on the side. Conflicts peaked in 1984 when blacks started assaulting refugees (Hmongs, Cambodians and

Vietnamese) as well as Koreans who opened stores in the neighborhood. Cars were vandalized and rocks thrown into houses. School students were threatened and beaten by other students. An investigation by the FBI pointed to blacks as perpetrators. Some blacks were even shocked by the level of violence. The newcomers became the symbols of and scapegoats for the larger political and economic changes that adversely affected the neighborhood.[6]

Despite hardships, by 1984 the first wave Vietnamese had the same median income as the U.S. population. The press seized the occasion to claim that the refugees had basic values, "work, school, thrift, and family," that made them successful in the U.S.[7] Among a sample of 608 refugees, a comparison of previous and current occupational status revealed that by 1991, the number of white-collar workers had decreased from 35 to 17 percent while blue-collar workers had increased from 18 to 63 percent.[8]

Case 2: Orchid arrived in the States with her husband after a 21-day-long ordeal at sea and a year in a Djakarta refugee camp. They lived with their brother-in-law and his family in a cramped apartment in a mid–Atlantic state. She took on three jobs: babysitting, cleaning bathrooms and working in a restaurant; she also went to college and cooked for her in-laws at home. Besides, she had to care for her baby. She saved as much as possible to send money home to her mother and siblings in Vietnam. The worst job was to clean vegetables in a restaurant during winter. As she dipped her hands in the ice-cold water to wash vegetables, her fingers froze. They became cold and numb after a short while and the pain was unbearable, especially when bean sprouts had to be washed one by one and every single root had to be removed. The other vegetables also had to be dealt with gently, meaning she had to keep her fingers under water longer. Pain could continue until the night and caused her to cry on many occasions; she could not understand the downturn of her life. A few years back, she was pampered and chauffeured to school and her mom had maids to do all the housework and the cooking. Now she had to do the dirty jobs herself. At the same time, she fought with her mother-in-law and her brother-in-law, as they interfered with her private life. Unable to handle family problems, she divorced her husband and moved out of the apartment.

She continued her life as a single mother who also went after a college degree. She worked to pay for her rent while raising her child and at night went to the lab to work on her studies. A teacher assistant helped her and later asked to marry her so that he could stay back in the U.S. Out of compassion she married him and helped him sponsor his Chinese mother and sister to the States. Besides her own duties (work, raise a child, cook, send money to Vietnam), she was assigned the new job of helping her sister-in-law. She drove her to school every day, waited in the hallway until the end of the class, then drove her home. Because she was unable to bear him a child, he divorced her.

Distraught, she went through difficult times before marrying another man many years later. Life was not rosy for Orchid, who struggled to help one husband after the other and her child. Besides working, caring for her husbands and raising a child, she had to handle family problems that turned out to be as big as mountains.

The struggle was long, hard, and tough at times. It was not an uneventful or continuous ascent to success overnight. It went through a lot of ups and downs, many more downward spirals than upward turns, although in the end everything evened out. There were many nights when the refugees cried because they did not know how to break even or move forward. They hit many walls, real or imagined. Despair crept on their faces and doubts poisoned their minds. But they kept going forward, learning the language, cleaning dishes or bathrooms and slowly moving up the ladder one week or year at a time. In the meantime, they studied, learned and acquired the necessary skills and at the same time sent their children to schools so that the next generation would be better placed to deal with problems. Success came on gradually with advancement and better positions and salaries. Many graduated to the middle class while a few made it to the upper class.

The communities around them also changed. Indianapolis is a case in point. When the refugees first landed in that mid-size Midwestern city, they could not find any Vietnamese shop or restaurant catering to their foreign palates. To get the required cooking ingredients, they had to frequent either a Chinese or Korean store that of course did not offer the much-needed Vietnamese ingredients. But it was still better than not having anything familiar to cook with. Thirty years later, the city boasted four grocery stores catering to the needs of Vietnamese and Asian customers; two of the stores even sold eight to 10 different kinds of fish and cooked them on the spot for the customers. The fish stores were soon frequented by both Asians and Americans: the latter had never been able to find in the city enough varieties of fish to satisfy their fish eating palates. There are now five restaurants offering fare from the basic *pho* to various Vietnamese dishes. *Pho* is a noodle soup, a traditional Vietnamese dish that is served steamy hot with either beef or seafood and a few herbs for seasoning. Hoisin and hot sauce could be added to give the soup the right taste and flavor. Nail shops owned by the Vietnamese have also flourished and offer Indianapolis women manicures, pedicures new sets of fanciful nails to be proud of for a few months. Other businesses include a computer store and a furniture store. The impact of Vietnamese refugees has slowly grown in the cities and communities they live in and will no doubt increase with time.

Of course, no Vietnamese community in the U.S. could compare itself to Little Saigon, California, a Vietnamese enclave bordered by Bolsa and Westminster avenues in the middle of Westminster city in Orange County on the southeast side of Los Angeles. This is a community where blocks after blocks of Vietnamese shops, stores, and offices can be encountered and where the language spoken is Vietnamese. A native Vietnamese could live there like in his native country without feeling lost. He could converse in Vietnamese, eat Vietnamese food, have his shirts and pants made by Vietnamese tailors, be treated in a hospital by Vietnamese doctors while being served ethnic food, discuss legal matters with Vietnamese lawyers, deal with Vietnamese customers, and finally be laid to rest on the U.S. soil among his native countrymen if that is his wish. That is in essence a Vietnamese dream fulfilled on American soil.

Politically, in the '70s and '80s the Viet Kieu of Little Saigon (mostly ARVN military personnel) embraced the Republican Party for its strong stance against the communists. Things, however, are changing as generational shifts and misgivings about President George W. Bush's policies have eroded that support. Between 1992 and 2002, "the share of Vietnamese registered Republicans in Orange County fell from about 60 percent to about one third" as more voters declared themselves independents or Democrats.[9] The younger generation of Viet Kieu has become more vocal and has replaced the older warrior generation. They, born and trained in the U.S. worried more about jobs and the economy than the old war that had concluded 30 years ago.

According to the 1992 U.S. Bureau of Census, 70 percent of the refugees lived in 22 urban areas and the majority of them were on the West coast. This reflected the fact that jobs, restaurants and food stores catering the Vietnamese could be easily found in large cities.

Refugee children excelled in their schoolwork. They had higher overall math and science scores than language and reading. Although the refugee community made up less then 20 percent of the school population in 1985, 12 of 14 valedictorians were of Indochinese background.[10] They "brought with them a mixture of Buddhist and Confucian values and traditions, which to steer a successful course for their lives in America. Their values emphasized hard work, education, achievement, self-reliance, steadfast purpose and pride"—virtues similar to American values. However, while the Americans stressed independence and individualism, the Vietnamese system stressed inter-dependence and inter-connectiveness.[11]

They came to this country 30 years ago in crowded on unseaworthy boats, hungry, thirsty, desperate, and defeated. They did not even know what the future had in store for them. It did not matter then because they were nursing the worst pain and sadness on earth: the loss of their beloved country. Now they may drive Lexus, BMW, or Mercedes cars, wear suits, speak on cell phones, and own businesses or offices. They live in large houses and sent their children to top schools in the country. What a difference three decades of peace have made. They are now a part of the American dream, one of the many nationalities that have built up what America is and will be in the future.

France

Being part of the French colonial empire, many Vietnamese in the '50s moved to France to escape the war if they were eligible and had the material means. They either worked for the French in the past or had acquired French citizenship. They knew the language and were exposed to the culture, although culture in colonial Vietnam was different from that of France itself. Although the number of refugees settling in France was smaller than in the U.S., France had seen wave after wave of refugees coming to its shores as early as in the '50s. Refugees were fairly well accepted, partly because they represented only a tiny minority and rarely got involved in French politics.[12]

Back in the 1920s, the Vietnamese in Paris were splintered into two groups: a radical and activist faction led by Ho Chi Minh and a moderate one led by Phan Chu Trinh. Although divided on issues, they did not become polarized until the arrival of Ho (then known as Nguyen Tat Thanh). Both Ho and Phan worked toward a free Vietnam, although the first leaned toward a radical solution while the second proposed a conciliatory approach toward the French.

After the end of the Second World War, most Vietnamese workers and military personnel returned home, except for 3,000 people. They trickled back into France from 1945 to 1954. Some were single students while others included families, usually Catholics who fled Hanoi, went to South Vietnam and then to France.

The post–1954 diaspora lasted about 10 years. Roughly 30,000 to 35,000 Vietnamese moved to France during that period. As they were not familiar with any other country in the world besides France, their main destination was the mother country. When Vietnam was divided between the communist North and the republican South, the Vietnamese population in France was also divided between communists and non-communists. During that period, the communists (UGVF or General Union of the Vietnamese in France) gained the upper hand because the Charles de Gaulle government tilted in their favor. De Gaulle, upset at the American policy in Vietnam, advocated a neutral South Vietnam and pulling the American troops out of that country.[13]

After the fall of Saigon, about 20,000 refugees arrived in France. Having fought against the communists, they swelled the ranks of the anti-communist group, further polarizing the political atmosphere of Paris. French politicians joined the fray as François Mitterand and Jacques Chirac battled for their votes. Mitterand's Socialist party courted the communists while Chirac, then mayor of Paris, supported the anticommunist group. After Mitterand became president in 1981, he offered many social services to the refugees, especially to the communist group. Chirac rose to the occasion by offering city buildings to the non-communist group.[14]

The UGVF headquarters was located on the ground floor of a building in a residential district. It had an automatic security entrance and the visitor had to announce himself before being let in through a second glass door. The system was set up to prevent the organization from being attacked by non-communist groups.[15] It boasted its own Buddhist institute, Chua Truc Lam (Truc Lam Pagoda), located in a small town southwest of Paris. Services were performed twice on Sundays.

When the Vietnamese arrived in the U.S., they pretty much arrived within a few months of each other in 1975. Since there had never been any major Vietnamese settlement in America before that time, they began their lives at the same starting line. Over the years, many pulled ahead because of a combination of preexisting fortune, hard work, luck, and intensive education.

The Vietnamese who had arrived in France in the '50s and '60s had made careers for themselves and had somewhat integrated into the French society. They had realized their "French dream" sometime ago and looked down on the newcomers who had to start at the bottom rung of the society.

The newcomers arrived with great expectations about getting a new life in a new dream country. But Paris was not the old Saigon. Adjustment and integration proved to be difficult for many who were unskilled or did not speak the language fluently. Rules and regulations were completely different. The degrees many had obtained in their native countries were not recognized at the same level as French degrees. Refugees had to take further training or schooling in order to qualify for an equivalency degree. In the meantime, they had to take on menial jobs to survive. Jobs happened to be scarce during that period as France suffered from an economic downturn from 1973 until the mid–1980s. And even expectations from employers were different in France compared those in their native country.

Disillusion soon set in as they were received with hostility and suspicion. Many Frenchmen facing competition for housing and jobs reacted angrily and made life harder for the newcomers. The refugees were easily suspected of being thieves because of ignorance of the laws or inability to understand the signs. One lady was suspected of shoplifting because she left the store through the wrong door. She was grabbed by security guards and deeply embarrassed for being searched in front of everyone.[16]

The Hanoi government on one hand supported the UGVF, but on the other hand looked suspiciously at anyone having been trained in the Western world. Although the Hanoi leaders received minimal education, they were awarded important positions in the government according to their military successes and allegiance to the party. They thus viewed the French-educated professionals who returned to Vietnam hoping to contribute something to the country a serious threat to their own positions.

Professionals returning to Vietnam could not find jobs similar to those they had in France. They were shunned and regarded with suspicion by leaders as well as lay people. A French-educated engineer, for example, offered his service to Hanoi but was given a job in the rice field. Frustrated and feeling mistreated, he returned to France. Since Hanoi's rejection of the French-Vietnamese in 1975, the latter, although sympathetic to the communist cause, were resigned to stay in France.[17] With time they became bitter toward the Hanoi regime, although they refrained from being too vocal, otherwise they would not be able to return to Vietnam for a visit. A few rebellious members openly blamed Hanoi leadership for the country's failing economy.[18]

The anti-communist groups remained splintered into 100 smaller organizations, although they always tried to present a unified front. Their goal was to compete for power within the Vietnamese community. Not being backed up by the Hanoi government as the UGVF was, their resources were pretty scarce. Their Buddhist temple, Khanh An, in a southwest suburb of Paris is reputed to be very political. It is discreet and looks like any other house in the neighborhood while the communist Truc Lam Pagoda is grandiose and conspicuous.

The presence of anticommunist groups was obvious as they competed for recognition among the newly arrived refugees. Years ago they used to set up demonstrations against any social or cultural event organized by the UGVF. With time their activities slowed down somewhat, although they still organize a demonstration commemorating the fall of Saigon every year on April 30.

The UGVF organized Tet at the beginning of the New Year with French as the primary language. The non-communists had their Tet celebration one week later with a less sophisticated crowd, which usually conversed in Vietnamese. Booths set up in the hallways promoted the various non-communist organizations. Yellow- and red-striped flags of the former South Vietnamese government decorated the walls and gave the meeting a subtle political overtone.[19]

Nowhere was the political atmosphere among refugees more polarized than in France. It started back in the '20s with the arrival of Ho in Paris and was fueled by the struggle for freedom in Vietnam in the '50s and the second Vietnam War in the '60s and '70s. The fall of Saigon reignited the fight that kept on smoldering. The French political climate that alternated between socialist and rightist governments only added further fuel to the debate.

Although the Viet Kieu (overseas Vietnamese) had become economically and socially successful in the host countries, on the political front they mirrored the political leanings of the countries they lived in. In France, they were equally divided between communists and anti-communists, because of the French's tolerance of the socialists and because of the presence of the two factions in the Vietnamese community in France since 1920. They had fought the Vietnam war on Vietnamese soil and they will continue to fight against each other in France the rest of their lives. With the U.S. being firmly anti-communist, the anti-communist faction in this country has been fairly active and has dominated the political scenery. Only once had a *Viet Kieu* flown a communist flag in his shop in Little Saigon, California. This action caused a major uproar in the community and the other *Viet Kieu* boycotted and protested in front of his shop until he went bankrupt. Little Saigon has since remained the city of the transplanted Vietnamese, an oasis and the refuge for those who had lost their country to the war. Little Saigon is for the Vietnamese what Little Havana in Miami represents for the Cubans.

In the span of three decades, Vietnamese have succeeded economically beyond their wildest dreams. This is exemplified by the number of strip malls, nail shops, restaurants and other businesses that bear Vietnamese names and by the two billion dollars that have been sent home to prop up the native country's economy. Vietnamese culture and cuisine stand out as something original and different from the Chinese. Viet Kieu's children have also succeeded on the educational arena and have shown their originality.

16

Epilogue

The 1954 exodus and the 1975–92 diaspora dealt with movements of people from North to South and from Vietnam to other countries. Although the similarity of the two events was obvious, major differences could also be noted. On both occasions, the deep and uncontrollable fear the Vietnamese nationalists had for communists led them to leave their homeland to search for freedom elsewhere. Between these two events and for almost two decades, they fought against the invaders, trying to keep them at bay. Their failure to defend South Vietnam led them to escape this time to foreign shores.

The first exodus was fairly simple and short as the escapees moved from North to South, a trip of less than a thousand miles. The environment remained the same despite a change in climate and weather. They still lived in a distinct Vietnamese environment with its culture and traditions. The post–1975 journey was longer, more complicated and much more dangerous, as the refugees had to cross open seas to reach foreign shores. After a period of screening, they moved to a third country for the final resettlement stage. The new country of residence is usually an American or European state that has a different flavor, culture and tradition: there would be no more Vietnam and its tropical environment. Adaptation and retraining were required unless they were happy with personal isolation and disconnection.

The first exodus involved close to one million people, mostly northerners, while the second one moved more than 1.3 million southerners. The first group was mostly Catholics while Buddhists seemed to be more prevalent in the second group. The first exodus was limited in time and scope: it lasted from August 1954 to May 1955 and involved movements between North and South Vietnam, while the second spread out over a

15 year-period from 1975 to 1992 and consisted of multiple waves of migrations to foreign soils. In the first case, foreign cargo ships provided safe transportation under the leadership of the United Nations. In the second case, the refugees bought their own way out on rickety boats: they faced violent pirates and dangerous storms during their trip. They had to cross open seas to reach the Philippines, Thailand, or Malaysia. And this was just the first leg of their multi-nation trip. The post–1975 journey was therefore riskier, more unpredictable than the first one and resulted in many casualties from pirates, storms, or engine failure. If the first exodus was local in nature, the second one had an international flavor; the first one was just a rehearsal for the second and more complicated journey. The first trip was coordinated by foreign countries while the second exodus was unplanned and unscheduled; no one knew which country they would land in. The first exodus had a visible end to it: people knew they would be relocated to South Vietnam. The second one was an open-end process. The refugees did not know whether they would survive the trip or not; whether they would be relocated, be repatriated, or remain forever in the camps; they did not know which country would accept them. If Vietnam was known to be a country of warriors, it was also known as a seafarer state — its citizens had to migrate twice in one century. No other country had experienced such a traumatic and agonizing ordeal in recent history.

This is the story of oppressed people who decided against all odds to leave their country, some twice, to search for freedom elsewhere in the world. They left their homeland not because they did not like it; as a matter of fact, many wept heavily when they saw the Vietnamese shoreline for the last time. A few, knowing they would never be able to come back and visit their fatherland, jumped overboard and drowned themselves. Other people escaped because they could not tolerate an oppressive regime that had become insensitive to their need for freedom.

No one could doubt their patriotism, for they had fought against communism and for their own freedom for 21 long years. No one could doubt their boundless sacrifice and their deep love for peace. By bearing arms and by sacrificing for their country, they defended peace not only for themselves, but also for their children and the world. Alas, despite their willingness, bravery and passion for their cause, they were overwhelmed by their clever enemies.

Unwilling to live under the communists' totalitarian regime, they decided to escape abroad no matter where it would lead them. Frightened and confused, they jumped onboard unseaworthy boats and departed from their country letting, like good Confucians would, *thuong de* (the Almighty) take care of their future. They did not know where they were heading, what they would do, and how they would survive in a new and foreign place. Was there a new country for them? Who would accept them, a bunch of ragtag and defeated people? They did not even know whether they could survive their ordeal through rough seas, let alone in a new country.

And defeated they were. Badly defeated. They just remembered the people who fought to get onto helicopters to fly out of the I and II corps, the northern regions of South Vietnam in March and April 1975. They glanced at the people trying to get onto the helipad on top of the U.S. Embassy in Saigon on April 29, 1975. They noticed all the guns, boots, and uniforms the soldiers abandoned on April 30 on the roads back to Saigon. All these images of failure and retreat reminded them of a massive breakdown of a war-machinery that somehow failed to defend the country against its enemy. And then they had to flee the country with defeated minds and sore bodies. They did not know what to think. They felt a deep sadness and an unshakable torpor taking hold of them. They just lay on the floor of the boat stricken by a grim sadness, the sadness of those who were defeated and did not know when they would be able to get back and fight again. That torpor would paralyze them for a while. Their will broken, their pride lost, and their homeland conquered, they did not want to eat, move or even talk. They did not even want to live. They remained in that state of torpor for quite some time before waking up and unsteadily walking away. They would feel the pain of defeat lingering in them for a long time.

The total number of Indochinese refugees willing to lose everything to search for an elusive freedom in the end numbered one million in 1954 and close to three million after 1975. This number spoke about their unanimous intolerance toward oppression and their love for freedom. Three factors affected the diaspora: an oppressive state, people's yearning for freedom, and the welcoming spirit of the United Nations and the people of the world. Without any one of these factors, the diaspora would not have ended.

Socialist Vietnam

Socialist Vietnam was the reason behind these diasporic movements, not only the 1954 exodus, but also the 1975 and post–'75 waves. Leaders had the power and ability to cause and control any exodus from their countries by promoting justice, freedom, and prosperity. It was imperative that leaders lived by the rules of international law and provided enough nurturing for their people to grow materially, emotionally and spiritually.

The Ho Chi Minh regime and subsequent ones had failed by any civilized standard to uphold civil rights in the country and to give their people basic freedoms. They failed to give them prosperity, for freedom and economic prosperity came hand in hand. Without freedom and transparency, no citizen dared to buy, invest, or trade anything of value. Without trade and commerce, people would get nowhere and would remain forever poor.

Socialist Vietnam failed to enhance people's pride: pride in working and believing in their country. By stealing power by force in 1945 and 1975, it was illegitimate. By failing to give the people it claimed to serve the basic freedoms, it is despotic. By forcing people to escape, it is autocratic. By silencing its citizens to reeducation camps and by sending them to the new economic zones, it is cruel. That was the past. It is time now for the country to guarantee freedom, equality, and equal rights to all citizens in its constitution so that they can heal, move forward, and enjoy the joys of life and democracy.

Rajaratnam, Singapore's foreign minister, once remarked that socialist Vietnam was so callous and inhumane in its refugee policy that "a poor man's alternative to the gas chamber is the open sea."[1] Therefore, it drove all its opponents to take to the sea and to risk death at the hands of nature or pirates. No other country would treat its people that poorly.

The People

The Vietnamese bore witness to the mistreatment by the socialist regime. Unable to survive under such a regime, they bided their time until they could escape out of the country, either legally or illegally. They tried and tried until they succeeded or died. Some had tried a few times, others more than 10 times. By escaping they knew they would put their own lives on the line. But this was the only way they could hope to find freedom somewhere else. They did not know, however, how hard and difficult their journey would be, but only hoped for the best. A few in fact later regretted having taken the leap of faith, although the majority viewed the experience with pride and joy despite all its horrors and difficulties.

The willingness to risk their lives in order to live freely was a unique feature of these boat people. The risks, which included not only imprisonment when caught escaping, but also death, were numerous and grave in nature. Although they worried about seasickness, inclement weather, and death by starvation, from storms, and in the hands of pirates, they decided the risk was worth the freedom they were seeking. For them freedom has no price and they were willing to die for it. They were not deterred by the thought of death, for many had seen death closely enough during the war that it had become familiar to them. Many simply thought since they had not died during the war, they would probably not die during peace.

They had to be desperate to think about trading their lives for freedom. The other alternative for them was to live forever under a ruthless and authoritative regime without being able to be themselves, to express their own feelings, and to speak the truth. This way of living was felt to be worse than the loss of life. In the end they were glad they had taken the leap of faith and jumped into the unknown. The effort had freed them and made their lives richer and more meaningful.

UNHCR

Despite a substandard performance, the United Nations High Commission on Refugees at least tried to solve the issue of refugees and work with Vietnam and other foreign nations and organizations to help deal with the biggest problem in the late part of the 20th century. It was not always easy because Vietnam disregarded basic human rights and did not worry about sending people to their deaths.

The other organizations and countries did their best to handle the problem. Southeast Asian nations bore the brunt of the exodus and felt cheated, as no other nation would open its arms wide enough to help relocate the refugees. They had also been harsh on the refugees by refusing them asylum and by pulling them out to the seas to their deaths. As the crisis worsened, all nations came to terms with the diasporic problem. They opened up their purses and arms and began admitting more and more refugees.

A total of 1.2 million settled in the U.S. An additional half a million went to Canada, Australia and France, and a quarter of a million to China. Therefore, 78 percent of the refugees settled in four Western countries and 12 percent in China. The remaining 10 percent went to the rest of the world and gave the program a global reach.

The tragedy of the Indochinese in general, and of the Vietnamese in particular, has opened the eyes of the world on communism and its threat to its people and other nearby nations. There is no other country in the world like communist Vietnam that had chased away its own people twice, mistreated them badly for four decades, and still remained in power. The world reacted wisely by advising the Hanoi government in 1979 to be more compassionate toward its people and to slow down the waves of refugees.

First, this tragedy should not have happened to any nation or group of people. The pain, suffering, and trauma inflicted were too much to bear and the consequences are unimaginable. The effects are lingering to this day in the minds and hearts of these victims and probably will for the rest of their lives. Second, whatever the United Nations and the countries of the world could do to prevent these tragedies from happening and to solve the crisis would be in the long range better for everyone— the principal agent, the victims, and the world.

During the same period, the refugees slowly recovered and began their gradual return to civilization by learning the necessary language and skills. Coming from the backwaters of Vietnam and the camps in Southeast Asia, America was to these refugees a heavenly land of culture and civilization. There was a lot of catch up and work to be done. With time, they mastered these skills and became economically and socially independent and successful. Success and independence, however, were slow and gradual. At home the economy turned sour and soon the *Viet Kieu* had to send money home to prop up the economy of their old nemesis, communist Vietnam. Still regarded as outsiders although financially sound, the *Viet Kieu* returned home to provide technological and financial support and know-how to their native country, although it was not always freely or well accepted. We can only hope that Hanoi will do its best to open the society up and to allow the *Viet Kieu* to help bring the country up to par with the rest of the world.

Chapter Notes

Introduction
1. Freeman 2003: 3.

Chapter 1
1. Karnow 1983: 124. The two Phan were unrelated nationalists and both fought for independence. While Phan Boi Chau suggested violent methods, Phan Chu Trinh advised cooperation with the French. In November 1925, Chau was tried and sentenced to death; the sentence was later commuted to home confinement due to his popularity. After 14-year exile in France, Trinh returned to Vietnam only to die of tuberculosis in March of 1926.
  Quoc ngu is the romanized version of the Vietnamese language. Invented in the seventeenth century by a French priest Alexandre de Rhodes, it was suggested by literati by the end of the 19th century, but did not become the national language until 1930.
  VNQDD or Viet Nam Quoc Dan Dang, the Vietnamese version of the Chinese Kuomingtan political party.
2. *Ibid.*: 107.
3. *Ibid.*: 138.
4. *Ibid.*: 149–150. Binh Xuyen was a gang group similar to the Mafia that plied its trade in Saigon in 1940–1950 and whose services were frequently utilized by the French. Viet Minh: communist resistance front against the French formed by Ho Chi Minh in 1941. In South Vietnam, the movement switched its name to Viet Cong.
5. *Ibid.*: 153.
6. *Ibid.*: 155.
7. Bui, Diem 1987: 46.
8. Summers 1995: 50.
9. Dommen 2001: 251–253.

Chapter 2
1. Wiesner 1988: 1.
2. Dommen 2001: 247.
3. Duong Thu Huong 1988: 25–29.
4. Thu Lam 1989: 65–66.
5. Khue, L.M. The merriment was short-lived. In Appy, C.G., ed., pp. 508–509.
6. Turner 1975: 140–141.
7. Duiker 2000: 477–479.
8. Courtois 1999: 568–570.
9. Duiker 2000: 465–466.
10. Wiesner 1988: 299–301; Duiker 2000: 486–488.
11. Ngo, Vinh Long 1991: 131–132.
12. *Ibid.*: 245.
13. *Ibid.*: 249–250.
14. Larsen 1986: 156–157.
15. Thu, Lam 1989: 47.
16. Wiesner 1988: 1.
17. Thu, Lam 1989: 45.
18. Do 2004: 5–6.
19. Bui, Diem 1987: 56–57.
20. Wiesner 1988: 7.
21. Appy 2003: 47.
22. Thu, Lam 1989: 90.
23. *Ibid.*: 24.
24. *Ibid.*: 33–35.
25. *Ibid.*: 65.
26. Tenhula 1991: 45.
27. Wiesner 1988: 4. Bao Dai was the last emperor of Vietnam. He abdicated in favor of Ho Chi Minh in 1945 and left for the French Riveria where he lived until his death in 1997. Bao Dai became head of the State of Vietnam in 1954 and named Ngo Dinh Diem prime minister. In 1955, Diem in a referendum deposed Bao Dai and became president of the Republic of Vietnam.
28. Dooley 1956: 11.
29. *Ibid.*: 150–153.
30. *Ibid.:* 175.
31. *Ibid.*: 134–138.

Chapter 3

1. Redmond, D. The doctor who won the war in Indochina. In Appy, C.G., ed., pp. 47–49.
2. Larsen 1986: 184–185, 189, 243.
3. Dooley 1956: 34.
4. Redmond in Appy, pp. 48–49.
5. Fisher 1997: 37–38.
6. Karnow 1983: 222. Landsdale was a U.S. Air Force officer who worked for the CIA. Known as a counterinsurgency expert, he was sent to Vietnam in 1954 to help Ngo Dinh Diem establish his political base.
7. Larsen 1986: 188.
8. Wiesner 1988: 8–10.
9. Larsen 1986: 186–187.
10. Wiesner 1988: 13.
11. *Ibid.*: 10–11.
12. *Ibid.*: 7–9, 17.

Chapter 4

1. Dommen 2001: 666–667.
2. *Ibid.*: 669–670.
3. *Ibid.*: 754.
4. *Ibid.*: 759.
5. *Ibid.*: 764.
6. Snepp 1977: 14.
7. Dommen 2001: 786.
8. Summers 1995: 174–180.
9. Isaacs 1983: 44–47.
10. Summers 95: 182.
11. *Ibid.*: 190.

Chapter 5

1. Wiesner 1988: 315–316.
2. Isaacs 1983: 354–355.
3. Vo 2004: 13–15, Wiesner 1988: 317–319, Isaacs 1983: 343–344.
4. Isaacs 1983: 360–361.
5. *Ibid.*: 374.
6. Wiesner 1988: 333.
7. *Ibid.*: 387–390.
8. Wiesner 1988: 325.
9. Isaacs 1983: 344.
10. Vo 2004: 16–21.
11. Isaacs 1983: 396.

Chapter 6

1. Luu, Van Vong in Huynh, Sanh Thong 1996: 190.
2. Rutledge 1992: 2–3. Operation Frequent Wind began on April 9, 1975, as the central cities started falling one by one to the advancing North Vietnamese army. It was designed to evacuate Americans. Options I and II were step by step airlifts; option III was a combined air and sea lift while option IV was a helicopter lift from Saigon itself. It had been estimated that although 7,000 Americans needed to be evacuated, the true figure was 35,000. There was also a vague plan to evacuate 200,000 South Vietnamese who would be in danger in case of a North Vietnamese takeover. Henry Kissinger and U.S. Ambassador Graham Martin had decided to hold the evacuation until the last minute, preventing many people from being evacuated. General Homer Smith circumvented the policy by organizing illegal "black flights." Overall 8,000 people were evacuated from the rooftop and courtyard of the U.S. Embassy on 29 and 30 April thanks to the hard work and sacrifice of the chopper cavalry. Many "high risk" South Vietnamese were unfortunately left behind.
3. Snepp, F. There was classified confetti all over the trees. In Appy, C.G., ed., p. 498.
4. *Ibid.*: 502.
5. Isaacs 1983: 469–70.
6. Tenhula 1991: 75–76.
7. Isaacs 1983: 474–476.
8. Snepp in Appy, C.G., ed., p. 503.
9. *Ibid.*: 565–566.
10. Isaacs 1983: 461–463.
11. Isaacs 1997: 150–151.
12. Robinson 1998: 18–19.
13. Isaacs 1983: 487.
14. Do 2004: 58.
15. Vo 2004: 19–21.
16. McKelvey 2002: 23.
17. Larsen 1986: 242–243.
18. Mackie 1997: 26–30.
19. Robinson 1998: 128.
20. Le, Linda 1993: 65.
21. Larsen 1986: 249–252.
22. Strand 1985: 33.
23. *Ibid.*: 41.
24. Strand 1985: 47.
25. Rutledge 1992: 4.

Chapter 7

1. Grant 1979: 54–55.
2. Dorais 1987: 75–76. The NEZ (new economic zones) are virgin forested areas people are forced to clear and transform into farming zones.
UNHCR: United Nations High Commission on Refugees.
ARVN: Armed Forces of the Republic of Vietnam (Saigon).
3. Vo 2004: 135–140.
4. Wain 1981: 44. A tael: Chinese unit of weight equal to 1.21 ounces or 37.79 grams.
5. Do 2004: 40.
6. Isaacs 1997: 154.
7. Grant 1979: 85–86.

8. *Ibid.*: 94–95. PSB: Public Security Bureau, a branch of the Interior Ministry whose plain-clothed policemen spy on people. They wield considerable power from the fear they sow among people.
9. *Ibid.*: 110–111.
10. Wain 1991: 18.
11. Grant 1979: 118–120.
12. *Ibid.*: 122–123.
13. *Ibid.*: 124–126.
14. McKelvey 2002: 41.
15. Hiebert 1996: 11–13.
16. Grant 1979: 28–29.
17. McKelvey 2002: 4.
18. Do 2004: 67–68.
19. McKelvey 2002: xiii.
20. *Ibid.*: xvii.
21. Vo 2004: 32, 55–56. Conex is a metallic container used to transport goods and left over by the Americans; the communists used it as a jail cell after 1975.
22. McKelvey 2002: 65–67.
23. Hawthorne 1982: 35; Vo 2004: 191–195.
24. Dorais 1987: 85.
25. McKelvey 2002: 97. HO or Humanitarian Operation was designed to bring ARVN soldiers who had spent more than three years in reeducation camps to the U.S.
26. Le, Tri 2001: 270–271.
27. Robinson 1998: 176.
28. Takaki 1998: 451.
29. Grant 1979: 162.

Chapter 8

1. Borton 1984: 71–78.
2. Huynh, J. 1994: 71.
3. *Ibid.*: 208.
4. Nguyen, Kien 2001: 227–240.
5. Wain 1991: 88–89.
6. Lan, Nguyen 2000: 37–38.
7. Wain 1991: 86–92.
8. *Ibid.*: 103–106.
9. Nguyen, Long 1991: 146–150.
10. Englemann 1990: 344–348.
11. Taylor 1989: 303.
12. McKelvey 2002: 26.
13. Grant 1979: 16.
14. Huynh, J. 1994: 252–253.

Chapter 9

1. Page 1988: 560–563.
2. McNamara 1997: 11–12. LCM is 50 by 14 foot mechanized boat with a 450 horsepower engine.
3. *Ibid.*: 155–156.
4. Lu, Thanh 1997: 172.
5. Taylor 1989: 348.
6. Vo 2004: 182

7. Bousquet 1991: 85–86.
8. Grant 1979: 61–62.
9. *Ibid.*: 107.
10. Rutledge 1992: 28–29.
11. Isaacs 1997: 152–153.
12. Grant 1979: 63.
13. Truong, Tang 1986: 282.
14. *Ibid.*: 289.
15. Englemann 1990: 333–335.
16. Taylor 1989: 358.
17. Grant 1979: 59.
18. Robinson 1998: 19–20.
19. McKelvey 2002: 87.
20. Hein 1995: 46–47.

Chapter 10

1. Huynh, Sanh Thong 1996: 192–193.
2. Lan, Nguyen 2000: 38–40.
3. Kim, Ha 131–133. The Para soldiers came from the defunct Cambodian nationalist army. The Khmer Rouge were the communist Cambodians.
4. *Ibid.*: 153–156.
5. Engelmann 1990: 248–249.
6. *Ibid.*: 245–246.
7. Wain 1981: 100.
8. Engelmann 1990: 251–252.
9. Tran, Vu 1999: 2–3.
10. Grant 1979: 51–53.
11. Engelmann 1990: 328–329.
12. *Ibid.*: 340–341.
13. McKelvey 2002: 160–161.
14. Grant 1979: 7–8.
15. *Ibid.*: 18–19.
16. Wain 1991: 44.

Chapter 11

1. Rutledge 1992: 17–18.
2. Engelmann 1990: 346–352.
3. Borton 1984: 110.
4. Das: December 22, 1979.
5. Nhat, Tien 1981: 13, 22–23.
6. *Ibid.*: 8–9.
7. Engelmann 1990: 323–324.
8. Nhat, Tien 1981: 79–88.
9. *Ibid.*: 16–17.
10. Grant 1979: 83.
11. Borton 1984: 83–84.
12. Robinson 1998: 170.
13. Grant 1979: 63–64.
14. Takaki 1998: 453.

Chapter 12

1. Huynh, Sanh Thong 1996: 197.
2. Borton 1984: 7.
3. Engelmann 1990: 353.
4. Grant 1979: 75.

5. *Ibid.*: 77–79.
6. Kim, Ha 1997: 171–175.
7. *Ibid.*: 197–201.
8. Freeman 2003: 35.
9. Huynh, J. 1994: 276.
10. Lan, Nguyen 2000: 43–44.
11. Freeman 2003: 35–36; Robinson 98: 94–98.
12. Freeman 2003; 20–21.
13. Chau Nguyen 2000: 104–105.
14. Freeman 2003: 25.
15. *Ibid.*: 22.
16. Ha, Nguyen 2000: 59–60.
17. Freeman 2003: 26.
18. *Ibid.*: 32.
19. *Ibid.*: 04.

Chapter 13

1. Isaacs 1997: 153–155.
2. Grant 1979: 30.
3. *Ibid.*: 71.
4. Chan, Khong 1993: 190–191.
5. *Ibid.*: 187.
6. Robinson 1998: 60; Wain 91: 204–205.
7. Wain 1991: 199.
8. Nguyen, Long 1981: 160–161.
9. Robinson 1998: 42.
10. Grant 1979: 73.
11. Robinson 1998: 43.
12. Grant 1979: 81.
13. Hein 1995: 48.
14. Chan, Khong 1993: 190–191.
15. Robinson 1998: 53–56.
16. Freeman 2003: 88–89.
17. *Ibid.*: 91.
18. *Ibid.*: 96–97.
19. *Ibid.*: 133–137.
20. *Ibid.*: xiii.
21. Robinson 1998: 267.

Chapter 14

1. *New York Times* December 1985.
2. Hein 1995: 54–58. Viet Kieu denotes the overseas Vietnamese, those born in Vietnam or abroad and linked to the diaspora.
3. Cooper 2001: 195.
4. Robinson 1998: 144–145.
5. Cooper 2001: 197.
6. Robinson 1998: 141–143.
7. Dorais 1987: 44.
8. *Ibid.*: 106.

Chapter 15

1. Hau, Dien in Huynh, Sanh Thong 1996: 199.
2. Larsen 1986: 262–263.
3. Tenhula 1991: 85.
4. Hein 1995: 72.
5. Tenhula 1991: 99–101, Rutledge 1992: 43–44, Hein 1995: 75–80.
6. Hein 1995: 83–90.
7. *Ibid.*: 135.
8. *Ibid.*: 139.
9. Chea: Associated Press, October 20, 2004.
10. Nathaan 1991: 9–13.
11. *Ibid.*: 139.
12. Bousquet 1991: 79–81.
13. *Ibid.*: 51–53.
14. *Ibid.*: 59.
15. *Ibid.*: 109.
16. *Ibid.*: 89.
17. *Ibid.*: 117–118.
18. *Ibid.*: 135.
19. *Ibid.*: 159.

Epilogue

1. Wain 1991: 156.

BIBLIOGRAPHY

Appy, C.G. *Patriots: The Vietnam War Remembered from All Sides.* New York: Viking, 2003.
Borton, L. *Sensing the Enemy: An American Woman Among the Boat People of Vietnam.* Garden City, NY: Doubleday, 1984.
Bousquet, G.L. *Behind the Bamboo Hedge: The Impact of Homeland Politics in the Parisian Vietnamese Community.* Ann Arbor: University of Michigan Press, 1991.
Bui, Diem. *In the Jaws of History.* Boston, MA: Houghton Mifflin, 1987.
Butler, D. *The Fall of Saigon.* New York: Simon and Schuster, 1985.
Caplan, N., M.C. Choy, and J.K. Whitmore. *Children of the Boat People: A Study of Educational Success.* Ann Arbor: University of Michigan Press, 1991.
Cargill, M.T., and J.Q. Huynh. *Voices of the Boat People: Nineteen Narratives of Escape and Survival.* Jefferson, NC: McFarland, 2000.
Chan Khong. *Learning True Love: How I Learned and Practiced Social Change in Vietnam.* Berkeley, CA: Parallax, 1993.
Chau Nguyen. "Hainan, Hong Kong, and Tuen Mun Camp." In Cargill, M.T., and J.Q. Huynh, eds., *Voices of the Boat People: Nineteen Narratives of Escape and Survival.* Jefferson, NC: McFarland, 2000.
Chea, T. "Little Saigon voters aren't rushing to embrace John Kerry." October 20, 2004. http://kcal9.com/california/CA-Kerry-VietnameseA-kn/resources_news_html.
Cooper, N. *France in Indochina: Colonial Encounters.* New York: Oxford, 2001.
Courtois, S., N. Werth, and J.L. Panne, et al. *The Black Book of Communism: Crimes, Terror, Repression.* Cambridge, MA: Harvard, 1999.
Das, K. "The Tragedy of the *KG 0729.*" *Far Eastern Economic Review,* December 22, 1979.
Do, T. *Saigon to San Diego: Memoir of a Boy Who Escaped from Communist Vietnam.* Jefferson, NC: McFarland, 2004.
Do, Xuan Long. "Dinh Viet: A Legal Trailblazer." *New Horizons,* 2000.
Dommen, A.J. *The Indochinese Experience of the French and the Americans.* Bloomington: Indiana University Press, 2001.
Dooley, T.A. *Deliver Us from Evil.* New York: Farrar, Straus, 1956.
Dorais, L.J., L. Pilon-Le, and Nguyen Huy. *Exile in a Cold Land: A Vietnamese Community in Canada.* New Haven, CT: Yale Southeast Asia Studies, 1987.
Duiker, W.J. *Ho Chi Minh: A Life.* New York: Hyperion, 2000.
Duong, Thu Huong. *Paradise of the Blind.* New York: Perennial, 1988.
Engelmann, L. *Tears Before the Rain: An Oral History of the Fall of Saigon.* New York: Oxford, 1990.
Fisher, J.T. *Dr. America: The Life of Thomas A. Dooley, 1927–1961.* Amherst: University of Massachusetts Press, 1997.

Freeman, J.M. Private communication, 2004.
Freeman, J.M., and N.D. Huu. *Voices from the Camps: Vietnamese Children Seeking Asylum*. Seattle: University of Washington Press, 2003.
Grant, B. *The Boat People: An Age Investigation*. New York: Penguin, 1979.
Ha, Kim. *Stormy Escape: A Vietnamese Woman's Account of Her 1980 Flight*. Jefferson, NC: McFarland, 1997.
Ha, Nguyen. "Our Lady of the Boat." In Cargill, M.T., and J.Q. Huynh, eds., *Voices of the Boat People: Nineteen Narratives of Escape and Survival*. Jefferson, NC: McFarland, 2000.
Hawthorne, L. *Refugee: The Vietnamese Experience*. Melbourne, Australia: Oxford, 1982.
Hein, J. *From Vietnam, Laos, and Cambodia: A Refugee Experience in the United States*. New York: Twayne, 1995.
Hiebert, M. *Chasing the Tigers: A Portrait of the New Vietnam*. New York: Kodansha, 1996.
Huynh, J.N.Q. *South Wind Changing*. Saint Paul, MN: Graywolf, 1994.
Huynh, Sanh Thong. *An Anthology of Vietnamese Poems*. New Haven, CT: Yale University Press, 1996.
Isaacs, A.R. *Vietnam Shadows: The War, Its Ghosts, and Its Legacy*. Baltimore, MD: Johns Hopkins University Press, 1997.
_____. *Without Honor: Defeat in Vietnam and Cambodia*. Baltimore, MD: Johns Hopkins University Press, 1983.
Karnow, S. *Vietnam: A History*. New York: Viking, 1983.
Lan, Nguyen. "Gold Rings and Jeans." In Cargill, M.T., and J.Q. Huynh, eds., *Voices of the Boat People: Nineteen Narratives of Escape and Survival*. Jefferson, NC: McFarland, 2000.
Larsen, W.W., and T.T. Nga. *Shallow Graves: Two Women and Vietnam*. New York: Random House, 1986.
Le, Huu Tri. *Prisoner of the Word: A Memoir of the Vietnamese Reeducation Camps*. Seattle, WA: Black Heron, 2001.
Le, L. *Slander*. Lincoln: University of Nebraska Press, 1993.
Lu, Van Thanh. *The Inviting Call of Wandering Souls: Memoir of an ARVN Liaison Officer to United States Forces in Vietnam*. Jefferson, NC: McFarland, 1997.
Mackie, R. *Operation New Life: The Untold Story*. Concord, CA: Solution, 1997.
McKelvey, R.S. *A Gift of Barbed Wire: America's Allies Abandoned in South Vietnam*. Seattle: University of Washington Press, 2002.
McNamara, F.T. *Escape with Honor: My Last Hours in Vietnam*. Dulles, VA: Brassey's, 1999.
Ngo, Vinh Long. *Before the Revolution: The Vietnamese Peasants Under the French*. New York: Columbia, 1991.
Nguyen, Kien. *The Unwanted*. Boston, MA: Little, Brown, 2001.
Nguyen, Long. *After Saigon Fell: Daily Life Under the Vietnamese Communists*. Berkeley: University of California Press, 1981.
Nguyen, Thi Thu Lam. *Fallen Leaves: A Memoir of a Vietnamese Woman from 1940 to 1975*. New Haven, CT: Yale Southeast Asia Studies, 1989.
Nhat, Tien, Phuc Duong, and Thuy Vu. *Pirates on the Gulf of Siam*. San Diego, CA: Boat People S.O.S. Committee, 1981.
Page, T., and J. Pimlott. *Nam: The Vietnam Experience 1965–75*. New York: Mallard, 1988.
Robinson, W.C. *Terms of Refuge: The Indochinese Exodus and the International Response*. London: Zed, 1998.
Rutledge, P.J. *The Vietnamese Experience in America*. Bloomington: Indiana University Press, 1992.

Snepp, F. *Decent Interval: An Insider's Account of Saigon's Indecent End Told by the CIA's Chief Strategy Analyst in Vietnam.* New York: Random House, 1977.
Strand, P.J., and W. Jones. *Indochinese Refugees in America: Problems of Adaptation and Assimilation.* Durham, NC: Duke University Press, 1985.
Summers, H.G. *Historical Atlas of the Vietnam War.* New York: Houghton Mifflin, 1995.
Takaki, R. *A History of Asian Americans: Strangers from a Different Shore.* Boston, MA: Little, Brown, 1998.
Taylor, T. *Where the Orange Blooms: One Man's War and Escape from Vietnam.* New York: McGraw-Hill, 1989.
Tenhula, J. *Voices from Southeast Asia: The Refugee Experience in the United States.* New York: Holmes & Meier, 1991.
Tran, Vu. *The Dragon Hunt.* New York: Hyperion East, 1999.
Truong, Nhu Tang. *A Viet Cong Memoir: An Inside Account of the Vietnam War and Its Aftermath.* New York: Vintage, 1985.
Turner, R.F. *Vietnamese Communism: Its Origin and Development.* Stanford, CA: Hoover Institution Press, 1975.
"Vietnamese Reviving a Chicago Slum." *New York Times,* 26 December 1995.
Vo, N.M. *The Bamboo Gulag: Political Imprisonment in Communist Vietnam.* Jefferson, NC: McFarland, 2004.
Wain, B. *The Refused: The Agony of the Indochina Refugees.* New York: Simon and Schuster, 1981.
Wiesner, L.A. *Victims and Survivors: Displaced Persons and Other War Victims in Vietnam, 1954–1975.* New York: Greenwood, 1988.

INDEX

An Loc 48–50
Ao Dai 9, 129
Atrocities 22, 28–29
Australia 124, 138–140, 180, 198

Bao Dai 12, 15–16
Bao Loc 28
Ben Cai 118–119
Bich 95
Binh Xuyen 13, 41
Boat people 84, 115–129, 164, 167
Buddhist 25, 40, 43, 122–123
Bui Chu 17, 24, 29

California 82, 167, 198
Cambodia 49, 50, 130–132, 159
Canada 179–180, 198
Cap Anamur 150, 167
Catholic 17, 21, 24, 28, 40, 46, 122–123
Cham 42, 43
Chan Khong 167
Chicago 174–175
China 84, 89, 97, 130, 159, 163, 198
Chirac 179, 189
Communist 17–19, 22–23, 26, 28–30, 96, 109, 117, 159, 177
Compassion fatigue 163
Conex 83, 95
Convoy of Tears 56, 59
Corruption 90, 96, 159
CPA 160, 169–170
Cruelty 60–61
Cua Lo 29
Cung 119, 149

Dai Viet 12, 13
De Gaulle 189
Diaspora 32, 102, 115, 128, 163
Dien Bien Phu 14, 27, 44
Dinh, Captain 135
Disero 168
Dong 27

Doumer, Paul 10
Duong Thu Huong 18

Eastern Offensive 48
England 16
Exodus 17, 25, 35, 39, 40, 84, 178, 193

Family syndrome 60
Florida 82
France 12–14, 42, 78, 120, 164, 177–178, 188–191
Frequent Wind 65, 116

Galang 160
Gallieni 11
Geneva Accords 15–16, 44, 48
Giap, Vo Nguyen 14, 48–49
Guam 70, 75–77, 127

Hai Hong 91, 124
Hai Phong 13, 21, 29, 31–33, 126
Ho (Humanitarian Organization) 168
Ho Chi Minh 12, 13, 16, 21, 36, 78, 94, 178, 188, 196
Hoa 89–90
Hoang Cuong 93
Hong Kong 158
Hue (city) 12, 38, 43, 45, 57, 61

Indonesia 160–161
Isle de Lumiere 150, 154, 167

Japan 12, 22, 163

Khmer 43, 89, 120
Khmer Rouge 102, 131–132, 140, 156
Kien 104
Kim Ha 131
Kim Vinh 137
Kissinger, Henry 47–49, 64, 116
KoKra 147–148

208 INDEX

Lam Binh 139
Lan Nguyen 131
Land reform 18–19
Laos 16, 49, 183
Le Duc Tho 20
Le Minh Dao 62
Le Minh Khue 19
Le Nguyen Vy 62
Le Van Hung 62
Little Saigon 82, 100, 121, 175–177, 187, 192
Lu Van Thanh 117
Ly Tong Ba 49, 62

Mai 158
Malaysia 138, 148, 152–155, 165, 167
Manh 120
Mao Zedong 20
Marginalization 92
Martin 64, 68, 116
McNamara, Terry 116
Mekong 19, 36, 43, 84, 102, 105, 118, 131
Mersing 90, 138, 139, 152, 166
Minnesota 82
Mitterand 179, 189

Nam Tien 36, 43
Navarre, General 14
New York 82
NEZ 83–84, 95–96, 120
Ngo Dinh Diem 14, 36, 39
Ngo Quang Truong 48, 57
Nguyen Dung 183, 184
Nguyen Gia Tho 101
Nguyen Khoa Nam 62
Nguyen Van Thieu 47–50, 64, 122
Nhat Tien 148
Norway 78, 126

ODP 119, 167
Oppression 23, 84, 95, 170

Paris Accords 15, 50, 55
Pennsylvania 78, 82
Pham Van Xinh 133
Phan Boi Chau 9, 11
Phan Chu Trinh 9, 11, 178, 188
Phat Diem 14, 17, 24
Philippines 32, 39, 70, 117, 134, 152, 159, 170, 194
Phong 85
Phu Quoc 58–59, 63, 74
Phu Xuan 43
Pirate 113, 119, 125, 140, 145, 165

PSB 89–90, 105–108, 124, 134
Pulau Bidong 118, 123, 126, 146, 152–154
Push back 84, 137, 165, 167

Quang Tri 48, 57
Quoc ngu 9
Quyet 138
Quynh Luu 21

Rach Gia 105, 123, 139, 147
Refugee 98, 148–149, 164, 166
Repatriation 158–159, 162, 171–172
Resettlement 31, 34, 39, 41, 65, 119, 157–160
RMP 144

Saigon 28, 35, 45–47, 55, 65–68, 87
Schweitzer, Ted 149–150
Sealift 33, 57
Sibonga 164
Singapore 133, 140, 152, 161–162, 164, 196
Southern Cross 90–91
Switzerland 168

Tael 90, 106–109, 143
Tet Offensive 45, 61
Texas 82
Thailand 89, 130, 137, 140, 152, 155–156
Thieu *see* Nguyen Van Thieu
Thuy Ngoc 148–151
Tran Vu 135–136
Truong Chinh 21
Truong Nhu Tang 124
Tuan 120

UNHCR 127, 138, 150, 168, 179, 197
United States 173–177, 182–188, 198

Van Tran 66
Viet Cong 18, 102–103
Viet Minh 12–13, 18, 26
Vietnam, North 20, 22, 89, 131
Vietnam, South 47, 49, 134
VNQDD 11, 12
Volag 78, 81, 173
Vung Tau 7, 36, 59, 133

Washington, DC 55
Washington (state) 82

Xuan Loc 62, 116

Yen Bai 9, 11
Yuvali 163

www.ingramcontent.com/pod-product-compliance
Ingram Content Group UK Ltd.
Pitfield, Milton Keynes, MK11 3LW, UK
UKHW042001140426
5217IPUK00015B/921